Everyday Environmentalism

Law, Nature & Individual Behavior

by Jason J. Czarnezki

ELI Press

ENVIRONMENTAL LAW INSTITUTE

Washington, D.C.

Contents

About the Author

Jason J. Czarnezki is a Professor of Law in the Environmental Law Center at Vermont Law School, home to one of the nation's leading environmental and natural resources law and policy programs. He has held academic appointments at Marquette University Law School, DePaul University College of Law, and Sun Yat-sen (Zhongshan) University in Guangzhou, China, as a J. William Fulbright Scholar. Previously, Professor Czarnezki served as a law clerk to the Honorable D. Brock Hornby of the U.S. District Court for the District of Maine and as a law clerk for the Bureau of Legal Services at the Wisconsin Department of Natural Resources. Professor Czarnezki, who received his undergraduate and law degrees from The University of Chicago, was born and raised in Milwaukee, Wisconsin, and currently lives in Montpelier, Vermont.

How to Use This Book & Acknowledgements

My goal in writing this book is to raise awareness of core environmental policy concerns that are implicated in individual daily decision-making and that to this point, in my view, have gone unnoticed and underappreciated. This book is for any person interested in the environment and conservation, the impacts of modern consumption and consumerism, and the relationship between humanity and nature. The book raises awareness about the environmental effects of everyday life and the roles that government and law can play in shaping consumer decision-making. It also provides individuals with ideas on how to change their choices and influence policy within their communities.

The book's contents will also prove useful to undergraduate and graduate students studying in fields such as environmental studies, ecology, environmental law, natural resources, public policy, economics, agriculture, and political science, as well as government officials and policy-makers interested in influencing the environmental effects of everyday decision-making.

I would encourage the adoption of this book in university and college classrooms and graduate school seminars. Professors and teachers may chose to assign individual chapters as well, perhaps as supplemental reading in traditional law school courses, especially introductory courses on regulatory policy, environmental law, and natural resources law. However, when assigning singular chapters, I strongly recommend including the Introduction and Conclusion in the required reading.

For introductory students, this book is designed to provide both solid grounding in environmental literacy and a set of comprehensible and actionable solutions. Often instructors of standard university "Introduction to Environmental Studies" courses hear students lament that the environmental field is "hopeless," "sad," "full of problems," or simply "depressing." While the substantive chapters do outline serious consequences of consumption and pollution, the thrust of the book is positive and action oriented. Instructors can use the text to reassure college students that there are, indeed, individual actions that can make a difference, both in their everyday actions and as a way to influence policy within their communities. Each chapter provides opportunities to discuss specific and immediate steps, as well as the impact of individual choices on regional and global events.

For use of individual chapters, Chapter One, on the history and consequences of consumption, may be a useful supplement to courses on environmental history, economics, and natural resources law; Chapter Two (on climate change), to courses on international environmental law, climate change, and air pollution; Chapter Three (carbon and waste footprints), to courses on regulation of toxic substances, waste generation, the Resource Conservation and Recovery Act, transportation policy, the Clean Air Act, climate change, energy policy, development, and informational labeling; Chapter Four (food), to courses on agriculture, pesticides law, food systems and food labeling, growth management, and eco-labeling; Chapter Five (sprawl), to courses on zoning, land use planning, property law, natural resources law, the Clean Water Act and wetlands and water resources; and Chapter Six (unforeseen destruction of small organisms), to courses on wildlife policy, endangered species, and biodiversity.

This book would not have been possible without the support of my loving and brilliant partner, Andrea Voyer, whose comments on my manuscript proved extremely insightful and helpful. And I appreciate the great understanding and patience of our daughters Lauretta and Hazel, as well as our dogs Jupi and Rodman. I owe my commitment to environmental protection to my conservationist grandfather Gerald Czarnezki.

My academic career would not have been jumpstarted without the help of Douglas Baird, Lisa Bernstein, Michael Cain, Judge D. Brock Hornby, Gerry Rosenberg, and Cass Sunstein. This book could not have been completed without the helpful advice of J.B. Ruhl and Michael McChrystal; the editorial support of Scott Schang, Janet Weller, and the Environmental Law Institute Press; the assistance of Ginny Burnham, Sharon Hill, Cynthia Lewis, and Wendy Smith; and the wonderful feedback from Holly Doremus, Timothy Duane, Rebecca Purdom, Michael Vandenbergh, and my faculty colleagues at the Vermont Law School.

I wish to thank my many research assistants at Marquette University Law School and Vermont Law School, including Stephen Boyett, Dustin Brucher, Katelyn Bush, Ashley Campbell, Robert Scharf, and Amy Landis. I also benefited from the financial support of Marquette University Law School and Vermont Law School.

Finally, I especially wish to thank Melissa McCord, whose dedication and hard work in research and editing proved far more valuable than I might have ever imagined.

Introduction

> [A]nd God said unto them, Be fruitful, and multiply, and replenish the earth, and subdue it: and have dominion over the fish of the sea, and over the fowl of the air, and over every living thing that moveth upon the earth.
>
> *Genesis* 1:28 (King James)

Whether by divine right or via modern progress, humanity has seen fit to consume nature and expand its dominion over the earth. With this consumption and expansion, our nation and the world face many major environmental and public health problems including fresh water scarcity, species loss, land degradation, global climate change, and overreliance on fossil fuels. More than 800 million people, around 13% of the world's population, already do not have enough water to lead healthy lives.[1] Due to global climate change, ocean water may submerge entire regions. Around 80% of the world's energy supply comes from the non-renewable resources of oil, gas, and coal, while renewable solar, wind, and tidal resources are often ignored.[2] And many countries, especially the United States, use energy and natural resources at an insatiable rate.

Focusing on actions within the United States, this book addresses personal and individual, seemingly insignificant, choices that, taken in the aggregate, can have potentially enormous effects on the natural environment. Environmental policy, thus far, has not adequately addressed the relationship between individual action and large-scale environmental problems, a determination of what tools can effectively change ecologically problematic everyday choices, and what roles, if any, environmental regulation and law should play in changing individual behavior. Thus, this book provides information and suggests avenues to promote "everyday environmentalism," i.e., environmentally conscious decision-making in daily life that can limit the negative ecological footprint of individual behavior.

To begin, Chapter One describes the historical and present-day forces in the United States that have helped lead to today's culture of convenience, consumerism, development, and consumption, which in turn contribute to the serious environmental problems addressed in this book. Chapter Two uses the now well-known climate change crisis as an example to show the potentially exceptional scope of

---

1. United Nations World Water Assessment Programme, Water: A Shared Responsibility, The United Nations World Water Development Report 2, Executive Summary 43 (2006), *available at* http://unesdoc.unesco.org/images/0014/001444/144409E.pdf.

2. Int'l Energy Agency, Renewables in Global Energy Supply: An IEA Fact Sheet 3 (2007), *available at* http://www.iea.org/textbase/papers/2006/renewable_factsheet.pdf.

ecological destruction caused by man, the difficulty of raising awareness about climate change, and the challenges facing law and policy in regulating greenhouse gases. As discussed in subsequent chapters, the consequences of individual behavior face similar obstacles: large environmental impacts in the aggregate, the need to raise awareness of the consequences of everyday choice, and determining the best regulatory tools for achieving everyday environmentalism.

The three chapters following Chapter Two deal with three areas of individual behavior that impact the environment. Chapter Three explores a set of individual decisions that may have the greatest environmental impacts, those influencing household carbon and waste footprints. Chapter Four discusses the ecological costs of our food choices, and Chapter Five describes the environmental costs of sprawl, using wetlands loss as an example. Each of these chapters describes the ecological harms of everyday choice, reviews current environmental policy efforts to change individual behavior in these areas, and considers what measures might most effectively promote everyday environmentalism. Chapter Six proceeds to discuss a serious but largely unknown concern—the destruction of small organisms that play critical roles in various ecosystems—and explores how these unforeseen losses result in part from individual choice.

Each of these chapters demonstrates key themes of this book: (1) that historical and current individual consumption patterns significantly contribute to most major environmental problems; (2) that the power of aggregate individual impacts on the environment remains both unknown and underappreciated; and (3) that the mere process of seeking out rarely considered environmental concerns in our daily lives may begin to promote structural changes in social and cultural norms that can have immediate environmental benefits, as well as facilitate long-term systemic change in public policies.

But what legal and public tools will effectively change individual behavior? The final chapter, Chapter Seven, sets out the key premise: that gaining knowledge about the consequences of daily consumption and effective individual behavioral modifications can mitigate negative environmental impacts and trigger everyday environmentalism. In other words, education works. Individuals need to know the consequences of their behavior and know what they can do to change their behavior. Knowledge and understanding of the *aggregate* impacts of individual behavior can not only teach individuals what to do differently from a practical standpoint but trigger personal changes.

However, perhaps the greatest challenge in changing individual behavior is recognizing that the proper law, regulatory tool, or public policy initiative must be matched to the appropriate behavior to effectively facilitate change. Imagine that a person does something harmful to the environment such as driving too much, eating a food that is produced unsustainably, or choosing to live in a suburban development far from work and built upon a filled-in wetland. How might that person make a different choice? First, and most basically, he or she should know there might be problems with his or her choice. But, second, the goal is to change not only that one person's behavior but also many other people's behavior, too, since it is the aggregate harm that is a problem—too many people drive too much, or too many people make similar food choices, or too many people live in sprawling communities. How can individual behavior be changed to limit its aggregate ecological impacts? Should law play a role by instituting bans or market incentives or taxes? Should community organizers use peer pressure or simply educate their neighbors? Should products have eco-labels that inform consumers about the environmental costs of their production?

This book recommends that legal regimes and policy initiatives focus on six "decision-making tools" when considering how to best influence the environmental effects of individual behavior:

(1) Identify and support concerted efforts to raise awareness of the environmental costs and power of individual behavior;

(2) Evaluate what level of government or private action, if any, is best suited to change specific individual behaviors, recognizing that often much more can be done at the local and community level;

(3) Create more ambitious informational labeling regimes such as "eco-labeling," so that purchasers can evaluate the ecological and carbon footprints of products and services;

(4) Develop regulatory tools that use market incentives to change individual behavior, and economically value "ecosystem services," those services risked by development and provided by nature without which we have to pay for man-made products that replace those services;

(5) Tailor policy to particular individual decision-making points, and target specific audiences and products, as some individuals, populations, purchases, and activities are more ecologically detrimental than others; and

(6) Design and continue to adjust community programs based on empirical findings about which efforts effectively shift social and cultural norms.

In addition, there needs to be recognition that a reciprocal relationship exists between individuals and governance. Individual knowledge and cultural norms shape new progressive policies, and law often simply displays existing social rules. In other words, law not only shapes people, but people shape law.

In each of Chapters Two through Six, in addition to raising public awareness and discussing existing public policy, this book identifies regulatory tools that could be used to respond to specific environmental problems caused by individual behaviors. The chapters provide only a few examples—energy consumption and waste, food choices, sprawl, a recognition of unforeseen impacts—but whenever policymakers seek to influence individual behaviors resulting in ecological harm, they should consider to what extent and how each of the above six "decision-making tools" should play a role. Or, put more boldly, modifying individual behavior toward everyday environmentalism should be one of the goals of any public planning process or legislative action.

In the future, the cutting edge of environmental law will focus on public awareness, informational mechanisms, economic and market incentives, and empirical inquiry into the appropriate target audience and product, the correct government level for action, and how to best influence social norms and support community initiatives. Ideally, the nature of the specific environmental problem and the relevant individual behavior pattern, in turn, will influence how each of these options is used to achieve everyday environmentalism.

John Gast, "American Progress" (1872)

CHAPTER ONE

Concerning Consumption

In today's culture, perhaps it is far too easy to throw away recyclable waste, grab a bottle of water, or print that e-mail message on paper made from a felled tree. Taken individually, these actions seem harmless, and their environmental impacts typically are not recognized. "The increased cognitive severance for consumers between environmental cause and effect exacerbates the potential environmental impact of such increased consumption."[1] This distance is evidenced in energy consumption, food choices, and home preferences. Televisions magically turn on, fast-food restaurants permeate our cities, and large homes overrun the suburban landscape. Many who engage in these activities remain happily ignorant of the environmental costs of common behavior and activity patterns.

Environmental ignorance couples dangerously with regulatory reluctance. Short-term economic gains drive modern public policy,[2] and this public policy ignores individual behavior.

> The dominance of economistic reasoning and the pragmatism of growth politics conspire to insulate from policy scrutiny the individual black boxes in which consuming is understood to occur. As a result, an entire realm of questions cannot be asked. No

---

1. RICHARD J. LAZARUS, THE MAKING OF ENVIRONMENTAL LAW 220 (2004).
2. THOMAS PRINCEN, MICHAEL F. MANIATES, AND KEN CONCA, CONFRONTING CONSUMPTION 5 (2002). ("Economic growth, facilitated at every turn by public policy, becomes the lubricant for civic processes of democratic planning and compromise.")

one in public life dares—or needs—to ask why people consume, let alone question whether people or societies are better off with their accustomed consumption patterns.[3]

Thus, modern culture and politics inhibit public discussion of the very questions this book chooses to address: Why do we use so much electricity in the home? Should we change our diets? Why do we live where we do? And an empirical query: why do people consume what they do?

This chapter traces the links between historical consumption and economic development patterns in the United States, the resulting ecological harms, and the societal reluctance to deal with a new era of environmental concerns driven by the consequences of individual behavior. Part A describes the early American historical forces that helped lead to today's culture of convenience, development, and consumption in the United States. Part B discusses the more recent phenomenon of American consumption defined by consumerism, overconsumption, and commoditization. While modern discussions of environmentalism and sustainable development fail to address "escalating consumption levels and, especially, the roots of such escalation,"[4] this chapter focuses on this historical perspective to demonstrate the deep roots of modern consumption patterns and their environmental consequences. As discussed in this book, efforts to change these embedded patterns and moderate their environmental impacts necessarily will demand use of a wide range of legal and policy tools.

A. Manifest Destiny

Modern consumption patterns in the United States are rooted in a tradition both of depending upon natural resources for survival and of taking pride in defeating nature. The rise of a market- and consumer-driven economy has shaped current individual preferences and developmental decisions, leading to a lack of balance between market forces and natural resources.

While Native American Indians managed the landscape and consumed the land's natural resources, the rate and scope of consumption increased when European settlers landed in the New World. Expansion followed, fueling a movement later called "manifest destiny" in the 1840s when the United States embarked on efforts to enlarge its territory.[5] Manifest destiny meant that this expansion, perceived as

---

3. *Id.* at 5.

4. *Id.* at 2.

5. This discussion of manifest destiny, expansionism, and American history's relationship to natural resources and the environment draws upon the following sources: ANDREW C. ISENBERG, THE DESTRUCTION OF THE BISON: AN ENVIRONMENTAL HISTORY, 1750-1920 (2000); CAROLYN MERCHANT, THE COLUMBIA GUIDE TO AMERICAN ENVIRONMENTAL HISTORY (2002); FREDERICK MERK, MANIFEST DESTINY AND MISSION IN AMERICAN HISTORY: A REINTERPRETATION (1963); RODERICK NASH, WILDERNESS AND THE AMERICAN MIND (1982); ANDERS STEPHANSON, MANIFEST DESTINY: AMERICAN EXPANSIONISM AND THE EMPIRE OF RIGHT (1995); Donald Worster, *The Vulnerable Earth: Toward a Planetary History*, *in* THE ENDS OF THE EARTH (Donald Worster ed., 1988); DONALD WORSTER, THE WEALTH OF NATURE: ENVIRONMENTAL HISTORY AND THE ECOLOGICAL IMAGINATION (1993).

being arranged by God to create a vast democratic republic, fulfilled a duty to take possession of the land from those races that were perceived to waste it.

Manifest destiny "sanctioned the spatial motion that encouraged control over natural resources as Europeans swept westward bearing the torch of 'civilization.'"[6] John Quincy Adams, in exhorting the case for acquiring the Oregon territory in the northwest United States, said:

> We claim that country – for what? To make the wilderness blossom as the rose, to establish laws, to increase, multiply, and subdue the earth, which we are commanded to do by the first behest of God Almighty.[7]

Setting the Stage for a New Nation

The European colonists came to the New World viewing the natural world as something to control. Western thought and Judeo-Christian tradition "generated a powerful bias against the wilderness," associating undeveloped land with the super-natural and realm of evil.[8] More pragmatically, settlers took pride in defeating their surroundings, which they felt threatened their survival. Soon after arrival, settlers identified commodities they could extract from or grow in their new environment for trade: furs, fish, and forest products in the North, and tobacco and later cotton in the South.

The settlement and formation of the United States occurred as modern capitalism emerged, illustrated by Adam Smith's *The Wealth of Nations*, an early treatise on capitalist economic organization, published in 1776. Capitalism was thought to deliver a better life to people "through the technological domination of the earth."[9] Capitalists urged people to produce not only to sustain themselves and their families but also to develop surplus in order to make money in the marketplace. This view precipitated a more expansive view and use of resources, permitting society to "regard everything around them—the land, its natural resources, their own labor—as potential commodities that might fetch a profit in the market."[10]

The rise of individualist capitalism in the United States was perceived to protect early American values. Yet, the form this took in both early and modern American society and law oscillated between the values of conservation and planned development on the one hand and resource consumption and unchecked economic growth on the other. The founding fathers feared strong centralized power and corruption from the Old World, where they perceived that too few people had held too much power and land. Consequently, to avoid this situation, they argued that citizens should sustain themselves on their own land, a historical model for sustainability.

---

6. CAROLYN MERCHANT, ECOLOGICAL REVOLUTIONS: NATURE, GENDER, AND SCIENCE IN NEW ENGLAND 201 (1989).

7. MERK, *supra* note 5, at 31.

8. NASH, *supra* note 5, at 10-17, 22.

9. Worster, *supra* note 5, at 11.

10. *Id.* Labeling the environment as a market commodity becomes increasingly problematic when natural resources are undervalued or *not* valued in the market, not because it is immoral or improper.

Thomas Jefferson and J. Hector St. John de Crevecoeur, in *Letters from an American Farmer*, suggested that private land ownership gave people independence and freedom, and they and others believed that turning the land into private property could help avoid Old World corruption. Jefferson thought the nation's citizens should consist of the yeoman farmer, dependent on no one. To realize this, each generation must have "the material means to stake out its own future, provided it would always be an agrarian and pastoral one."[11]

This promotion of the agrarian lifestyle faced a Hamiltonian capitalist movement that successfully built the nation's infrastructure and banking system and helped yield a more advanced state of land use. Commentators urged people to turn the wilderness into fields and farms "with such frequency ... as to become commonplace."[12] Andrew Jackson, in his inaugural address in 1830, asked, "what good man would prefer a country covered with forests and ranged by a few thousand savages to our extensive Republic, studded with cities, towns, and prosperous farms, embellished with all the improvements which art can devise or industry execute."[13]

Over time, American law and public policy facilitated industrialization, as well as corporate growth and the modern market economy, resulting in development far more centralized and imposing than imagined during the late 18th and early 19th centuries. While these changes simultaneously paved the way for technological progress and increased living standards, yet another trend emerged. The criticism: "[s]ince 1790, power . . . flowed increasingly into the hands of persons concerting their purposes in corporate entities that by their nature are quite unsentimental about the earth."[14] The movement from agrarian roots to commercial industrialization stimulated by a market economy increasingly fostered major ecological problems due to corporate manufacturing and the otherwise beneficial rising standard of living.

Promoting the Market Economy & Achieving Manifest Destiny

The emergence of modern capitalism also shaped land policy in the United States, promoting both land acquisition and private development on a much larger scale. From the 1780s through the mid-1860s, the government acquired hundreds of millions of acres through state cessions, Indian treaties, and purchases from states and foreign nations. Following these mass land acquisitions, the U.S. government, well-intentioned and for the public benefit, sold or disposed of about a billion acres in the 150 years after the drafting of the Constitution. For example, the government subsidized railroad construction by granting nearly 100 million acres to railroads. The market economy fostered the development of canals, bridges, and roads that carried goods to and from the market. These transportation networks, while necessary, "brought sudden sweeping change to the landscapes and communities through which

---

11. STEPHANSON, *supra* note 5, at 22.
12. MERCHANT, ECOLOGICAL REVOLUTIONS, *supra* note 5, at 204.
13. NASH, *supra* note 5, at 41.
14. ROGER G. KENNEDY, MR. JEFFERSON'S LOST CAUSE: LAND, FARMERS, SLAVERY, AND THE LOUISIANA PURCHASE 60 (2003).

they passed."[15] Similarly, farmers and homesteaders, in search of more abundant and fertile land than was available in the East, acquired, by cheap price or occupation, nearly 300 million acres of public lands mostly in the West. Soon, fueled by a commercial boom and increased demand for food in America and Europe, inland subsistence farmers shifted to market farming. Technologies, according to historian Walter Prescott Webb, like the Colt six-shooter (1835), barbed wire (1874), the John Deere plow (1846), mechanized harvesters, and other agricultural implements, helped farmers control the Plains and increase production. All of this promoted the nation's growth and prosperity and raised American standards of living.

Over time, the government's promotion of manifest destiny and resource consumption expanded to the point that it overwhelmed the government's parallel role as a resource steward. The responsibility of the government as a resource steward had been championed by conservationists, such as Henry David Thoreau, George Perkins Marsh, and John Muir, who are credited with starting the environmental movement through their writings on ecology and natural history, founding conservation groups like the Sierra Club, and protecting park lands. According to the harsh conclusion of sociologist and economist Thorstein Veblen, as Americans settled the frontier, they worked to convert "all public wealth to private gain on a plan of legalised seizure."[16] "There was a kind of order to the taking: what was most easily available for quick riches went first"—fur-bearing animals, gold and other minerals, timber, iron, other metals, oil, natural gas, water power, irrigation rights, and transportation rights-of-ways.[17] The resource-rich frontier became an "ongoing extension of market relations,"[18] reflecting little balance between responsible consumption and unlimited growth. Take, for example, the near extermination of the American bison. Fur traders, employed by trading companies, started exploring the West and capturing the animals in the 1820s. Steamboats, which began to travel the Missouri River in the early 1820s, attracted traders to the northern plains to hunt bison. The railroads, arriving later, contributed to the collapse of the bison population by helping hunters easily reach the herds. Even more people journeyed West to kill bison after hide tanning technologies improved. By the 1870s, commercial hunting had decimated the bison population. The size of the North American bison herd was an estimated 30 million in 1800. By 1889, people had slaughtered millions of bison, taking them to the brink of extinction with a population of just 1,000. Wrote Carolyn Merchant, "Living nature disappeared from the everyday experience for most Americans by the mid-twentieth century."[19]

Industrialization and urbanization continued at a rapid pace in the United States. "There were 140,000 industrial establishments in the United States in 1859; many

15. WILLIAM CRONON, NATURE'S METROPOLIS: CHICAGO AND THE GREAT WEST 72 (1991).

16. THORSTEIN VEBLEN, ABSENTEE OWNERSHIP AND BUSINESS ENTERPRISE IN RECENT TIMES: THE CASE OF AMERICA 168 (1923).

17. Wilbur R. Jacobs, *The Great Despoliation: Environmental Themes in American Frontier History*, 47 PAC. HIST. REV. 1, 18 (1978).

18. CRONON, *supra* note 15, at 53.

19. CAROLYN MERCHANT, AMERICAN ENVIRONMENTAL HISTORY: AN INTRODUCTION 110 (2007).

were hand or neighborhood industries. Just forty years later, there were 207,000, excluding hand and neighborhood industries. By 1900, the United States was the world's leading manufacturing nation."[20] The growth of cities and factories fostered air, water, and noise pollution, as well as garbage production and disease. With the advent of motor vehicles, urbanization gave way to suburbanization. With Henry Ford's creation of the automobile assembly line in 1914, more than 100,000 autos could come off assembly lines each day, and soon more than 100 million passenger cars were driven in the United States.[21] The trends of commoditization, industrialization, and urbanization (and then suburbanization) continued from the 19th into the 21st century, accompanied by ever more extensive impacts on land use, natural ecosystems, and food systems.[22] Thus, the historical tradition of using resources with little acknowledgment of environmental factors was firmly established as the underlying platform on which modern U.S. industrial and consumer activity were built.

B.   Modern American Consumption

Modern America is a post-World War II construct. Modern American consumption patterns are rooted in the pre-War past but are more immediately driven by American economic changes after World War II. World War II stimulated technological innovation and provided Americans with exciting new consumer products. These products soon became broadly available on a much larger scale to meet the consumer demand fostered by a growing population, increased wealth, and more leisure time.[23] Air conditioners, televisions, processed and packaged foods, and automobiles dramatically changed the American lifestyle.

> The war had ushered in a technological revolution that generated plastics and pesticides, atomic weapons and energy, revolutionary new drugs, and a whole universe of domestic consumer goods aimed at eliminating the drudgery of everyday life. The growth of these industries, and others that would inevitably follow in their wake, promised an unprecedented period of productivity, prosperity, and affluence. Proud of their technological achievements, most Americans celebrated the apparent victory of human technology and science over nature.[24]

This supposed "victory" over nature continued through the new millennium with increased consumer spending for manufactured goods, growing and continued

---

20. MARTIN MELOSI, EFFLUENT AMERICA: CITIES, INDUSTRY, ENERGY, AND THE ENVIRONMENT 50 (2001).

21. DONALD WORSTER, THE WEALTH OF NATURE: ENVIRONMENTAL HISTORY AND THE ECOLOGICAL IMAGINATION 7 (1994).

22. See, e.g., WILLIAM CRONON, NATURE'S METROPOLIS: CHICAGO AND THE GREAT WEST (1992); THEODORE STEINBERG, NATURE INCORPORATED: INDUSTRIALIZATION AND THE WATERS OF NEW ENGLAND (2004).

23. See HAROLD G. VATTER & JOHN F. WALKER, HISTORY OF THE U.S. ECONOMY SINCE WORLD WAR II (1996); JOSEPH PETULLA, AMERICAN ENVIRONMENTAL HISTORY: THE EXPLOITATION AND CONSERVATION OF NATURAL RESOURCES (1997).

24. MARK CHRISTOPHER CARNES, THE COLUMBIA HISTORY OF POST-WORLD WAR II AMERICA 341 (2007).

demand for fossil fuels for energy production and transportation, and the com-moditization of agricultural goods. Increasingly, social status was defined through acquisition of large homes, fancy cars, and state-of-the-art electronics and appliances.

These expanding American consumption trends, while discussed in various history and economics books, generally have not been examined in environmental history texts. Yet, it is apparent that the continued increase in available consumer goods led to the grand scale of consumption that characterizes modern America and contributed to the resulting environmental degradation. Perhaps these modern consumption trends are not surprising, given the nature of the "progress" following World War II. Even *The Cambridge History of American Theatre* states,

> The end of World War II brought unprecedented wealth and power to the United States and historical precedents suggest that such hegemony might have presaged a vigorous and energetic theatre.... But this was not to be. A certain confidence, sense of well-being, and exuberance, of course, did manifest itself in American culture, but more often in consumer goods than in arts. Cars, for example, began to sprout tailfins—futuristic icons of useless excess—with the 1948 Cadillac; homes began to fill with gleaming white appliances; sleek "entertainment centers" disguised as furniture became the centerpieces of living rooms, and movies increasingly abandoned the "noir" tones of black and white for the saturated colors of Technicolor.[25]

By 1960, nearly 90% of American homes had a television. By the 1970s, $40 billion had been spent on road construction to accommodate as many cars as half the U.S. population. The nation had reached a point where "the maintenance of America's comfort and convenience level requires enormous quantities of energy and a bottomless pit of natural resources."[26]

This rapid consumption stripped domestic natural resources and fostered envi-ronmental pollution. The tragedy of modern American consumption is that it has lacked the influence of sustainability, conservation, basic necessity, artistic and educational endeavors, or any other broader social goals.[27] Instead, American consumption is driven by individualism and consumerism, "the crass elevation of material acquisition to the status of a dominant social paradigm"; commoditization, "the substitution of marketable goods and services for personal relationships, self-provisioning, culture, artistic expression, and other sources of human well-being"; and overconsumption, "using more than is necessary."[28]

---

25. DON B. WILMETH & C. W. E. BIGSBY, THE CAMBRIDGE HISTORY OF AMERICAN THEATRE: POST-WORLD WAR II TO THE 1990S 89 (2000).

26. PETULLA, *supra* note 23, at 333.

27. PRINCEN ET AL., *supra* note 2, at 1 (stating "Consumption and consumerism have long been consigned to the edges of polite talk among North Americans concerned about environmental degrada-tion and the prospects of sustainability. How much, and what, do we consume? Why? Are we happier in the process? How much is enough? How much is too much for the social fabric and health of the planet?" and suggesting that society does not want to address these questions because people want the "good life," and do not want to challenge "consumer sovereignty" and our modern economic system).

28. PRINCEN ET AL., *supra* note 2, at 3.

Americans simply have adopted a culture of spending more money and absorbing more resources in order to accumulate more. Consumerism has emerged as a "cultural orientation maintaining that the possession and use of an increasing number and variety of goods and services is the principal cultural aspiration and the surest perceived route to personal happiness, social status, and national success."[29] It is useful to put this qualitative trend into quantitative terms. Worldwide per capita growth in consumption for many resources is expanding 8 to 12 times faster than population growth.[30] Worldwide consumption expenditures reached $24 trillion in 1998, doubling in just over two decades.[31] In the United States alone, aggregate personal consumption expenditures rose by 74% between 1990 and 2000,[32] and, as seen in Figure A, per capita consumption continues to increase.

Figure A: U.S. Per Capita Personal Consumption Expenditures in Real Dollars, 1960-2005

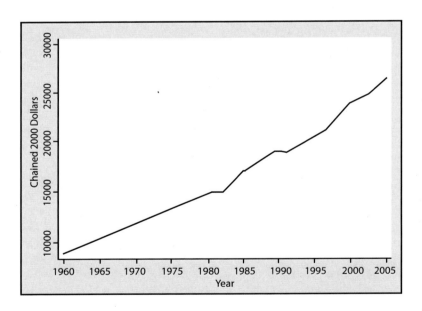

Data Source: U.S. Census Bureau, *Statistical Abstract of the United States: 2007* 434, Table 655 (2007), http://www.census.gov/prod/2006pubs/07statab/income.pdf. The "chained dollars" measure is meant to reflect real prices over time.

---

29. RITA ERICKSON, "PAPER OR PLASTIC?" ENERGY, ENVIRONMENT AND CONSUMERISM IN SWEDEN AND AMERICA (1997) (citing Paul Elkins, *The Sustainable Consumer Society: A Contradiction in Terms?*, 3 INT'L ENVTL. AFF. 243 (1991)).
30. PRINCEN ET AL., *supra* note 2, at 4.
31. *Id.* at 219.
32. *Id.*

Consumption has not only depleted natural resources and thinned the wallet; it has also fattened the waistline, as nearly two-thirds of Americans are overweight and nearly one-third are obese.[33] Individuals throughout the world, and Americans in particular, seem destined to test the bounds of resource consumption. And, unfortunately, consumers "dislocate the patterns and choices of daily life from larger problems and trends,"[34] including, notably, the aggregate environmental impacts of those choices.

Land use and development are no exceptions. U.S. land consumption churned at a rate of about 2.2 million acres per year during the 1990s, up more than 30% from the 1980s.[35] Of the nearly 9 million acres developed between 1997 and 2001, most projects used previously undeveloped land, otherwise known as "greenfields."[36]

There are other costs to expanding our dominion over natural resources and relying on the convenience generated by technological progress. Consider the following statistics. In 2005, Americans generated 4.54 pounds of solid waste per person per day.[37] Estimated U.S. water usage was 408 billion gallons per day in 2000.[38] The average American household uses 101 gallons of water each day,[39] and people are drinking more and more bottled water, leaving piles of plastic waste in need of recycling. To meet the demand for paper used by the copy centers on every corner and the low-cost printers available at any electronics superstore, combined with the acreage used for increased development, the United States will lose at least 23 million acres of forest by 2050.[40] Changes in consumer activity have also resulted in increased energy use, as "energy demand is shifting away from manufacturers and towards consumers."[41]

These modern consumption patterns are a product of the historical development and industrialization of the United States, including increased consumer spending and demand for energy intensive goods. These historical and social trends provide the foundation for understanding contemporary patterns of consumption of natural resources, undoubtedly a cause of global climate change and other serious adverse environmental effects.[42] The bottom line is that significant environmental problems

---

33. U.S. CENSUS BUREAU, STATISTICAL ABSTRACT OF THE UNITED STATES: 2007, at 131 tbl. 198, *available at* http://www.census.gov/prod/2006pubs/07statab/health.pdf.

34. ERICKSON, *supra* note 29, at 3.

35. NATURAL RES. CONSERVATION SERV., U.S. DEP'T OF AGRIC., NATURAL RESOURCES INVENTORY, 2001 ANNUAL NRI (2003), *available at* http://www.nrcs.usda.gov/technical/NRI/2001/urban.pdf.

36. *Id.* ("Between 1997 and 2001, almost 9 million acres were developed, of which 46 percent came from forest land, 20 percent from cropland, and 16 percent from pasture land.").

37. U.S. EPA, MUNICIPAL SOLID WASTE IN THE UNITED STATES: 2005 FACTS AND FIGURES, at 4 tbl. 3, *available at* http://www.epa.gov/osw//nonhaz/municipal/pubs/mswchar05.pdf.

38. SUSAN S. HUTSON ET AL., ESTIMATED USE OF WATER IN THE UNITED STATES IN 2000 (2004), *available at* http://pubs.usgs.gov/circ/2004/circ1268/.

39. AMY VICKERS, HANDBOOK OF WATER USE AND CONSERVATION 12 (2001).

40. LAZARUS, *supra* note 1, at 219; SUSAN M. STEIN ET AL., FORESTS ON THE EDGE 2 (2005), *available at* http://www.fs.fed.us/projects/fote/reports/fote-6-9-05.pdf.

41. ERICKSON, *supra* note 29, at 113.

42. *See, e.g.,* ALAN DUNING, HOW MUCH IS ENOUGH? THE CONSUMER SOCIETY AND THE FUTURE OF THE EARTH (1992).

have occurred due to the continued depletion and degradation of public resources, with little consideration as to the ultimate costs, whether known and ignored or simply unforeseen.

Judge J. Skelly Wright, in a famous environmental law case interpreting the National Environmental Policy Act, recognized that we must be concerned with the "destructive engine of material 'progress,'" putting "progress" in quotations to question the long-term value of so much economic development.[43] And environmental historians have noted that the origins of environmental degradation are alive in the present and that their histories are "to be useful not just in helping us understand the past but in helping us change the future."[44] Accordingly, Chapter Two looks at the history of the climate change crisis and examines how "progress" and the massive use of fossil-fuel energy, which inputs greenhouse gases into the air, has resulted in global climate change. To date, the climate change crisis provides a unique window for understanding why environmental regulation of cutting-edge problems remains difficult and can serve as a baseline for understanding why regulating individual behavior may even prove more troublesome. Further, as Chapter Two illustrates, the key question is how in the future additional focus can be brought to bear on ways to shift current social and cultural norms and modify individual behavior to help mitigate this crisis through everyday environmentalism.

---

43. Calvert Cliffs Coordinating Committee v. U.S. Atomic Energy Commission, 449 F.2d 1109 (D.C. Cir. 1971).

44. William Cronon, *The Use of Environmental History*, 17 ENVTL. HIST. REV. 1, 3 (1993).

CHAPTER TWO

Learning From the Climate Change Crisis

According to the Nobel Prize-winning Intergovernmental Panel on Climate Change (IPCC), "[w]arming of the climate system is unequivocal," and "most of the observed increase in global average temperatures since the mid-20th century is very likely due to the observed increase in anthropogenic [greenhouse gas] concentrations."[1] The climate change crisis exemplifies the resulting severity of gross human consumption on environmental health, the difficulties in raising awareness for environmental problems, and the challenges of drafting effective environmental policy and legal regimes. Both climate change and the ecological costs of daily choice derive from diffuse causes, a democratization of pollution,[2] whether from many individual sources or many countries. As discussed in subsequent chapters, the same obstacles facing climate change mitigation face any movement towards everyday environmentalism: (1) the need for awareness and education about the significance and cause of the ecological problem, and (2) the challenge of determining how best to regulate and legislate against the causes of these problems.

Part A of this chapter reviews the basic causes and widespread impacts of the global climate change crisis and discusses the difficulty of raising and maintaining public awareness of the climate change crisis, as well as the challenge of educating policymakers about effective legal and policy responses. Part B then turns to the steps that have been considered and taken thus far to address climate change, ranging from action at the national and international levels down to the regional and local levels. Part C, in turn, assesses the promise and limitations of law in addressing mitigation of climate change. Overall, the chapter argues that we must find ways to mitigate climate change and encourage more responsible consumption through increased knowledge and public awareness, by targeting the appropriate regulatory tools and level of government action, as well as incorporating scientific information into decision-making processes and learning from successes and failures of past and existing public policy and legislation.

Ultimately, the challenges facing law and policy in regulating greenhouse gases and in regulating individual behavior prove to be the same: significant environmen-

---

1. IPCC, CLIMATE CHANGE 2007: SYNTHESIS REPORT, *Summary for Policymakers, available at* http://www.ipcc.ch/pdf/assessment-report/ar4/syr/ar4_syr_spm.pdf.

2. *See generally* Timothy P. Duane, *Environmental Planning and Policy in a Post-Rio World*, 7 BERKELEY PLANNING J. 27 (1992).

tal impacts in the aggregate arising from multiple diffuse sources, the need to raise and maintain broad awareness of the consequences, and identification and use of the best regulatory tools for promoting environmentally conscious decision-making.

A. Understanding the Climate Change Crisis

Concerns about global climate change emerged in the 1970s, though as early as 1896 Swedish chemist Svante Arrhenius first advanced the theory that carbon dioxide emissions from coal combustion could lead to global warming. Considering this time-frame and the potentially disastrous consequences of climate change, the current state of public awareness and political action remain disheartening. Perhaps this can be attributed in part to the complexity of the science that struggles to mesh with the rigidity and formalism of legal rules, as well as the incremental and seemingly remote nature of many of the environmental impacts of climate change. At least in the United States, many in the public and political realms still seem to have difficulty grasping and reacting to the significance of climate change.

The Climate Change Problem

The greenhouse effect is a natural process in which greenhouse gases allow sunlight to enter and prevent heat from leaving the earth's atmosphere—the process is essential to keeping the planet's surface warm. However, the earth now is warming rapidly due to human activities, especially the burning of fossil fuels, which emit greenhouse gases. In fact, the concern expressed by the international scientific community has grown more forceful over the years, as experts have finally concluded that humanity caused most of the global warming over the last 50 years.

Greenhouse gases include water vapor, carbon dioxide, methane, and nitrous oxide, among others. Water vapor naturally forms in the earth's atmosphere. Other greenhouse gases, though, are increasing in the atmosphere due to the burning of coal, oil and gasoline, and natural gas, as well as deforestation, livestock farming, wetlands destruction, and fertilization. Since pre-industrial times, greenhouse gas emissions have grown significantly, increasing 70% from 1970 to 2004.[3] In the United States alone, total greenhouse gas emissions rose by 16.3% from 1990 to 2005.[4] As a result, the earth's surface temperature is 1.4°F warmer now than a century ago, with most of that increase occurring since 1978.[5] As seen in Figure B, through the year 2009, the warmest years of the past century are 1998, 2002, 2003, 2004, 2005, 2006, 2007, and 2009.

---

3. IPCC, *Fourth Assessment Report, Climate Change 2007: Mitigation of Climate Change, Summary for Policymakers,* provides statistics not otherwise cited in this section.
4. U.S. EPA, INVENTORY OF U.S. GREENHOUSE GAS EMISSIONS AND SINKS: 1990-2005 § 2.1 (April 2007), *available at* http://www.epa.gov/climatechange/emissions/downloads06/07Trends.pdf.
5. NAT'L ACADEMY OF SCIENCES, UNDERSTANDING AND RESPONDING TO CLIMATE CHANGE 2 (2006).

Figure B: Global Annual Mean Surface Air Temperature Change

Global annual surface air temperature relative to 1951-1980 mean temperatures. Source: Goddard Institute for Space Studies, NASA, http://www.giss.nasa.gov/research/news/20100121/.

Global temperatures are projected to increase with continued demand for fossil fuels and destruction of natural "carbon sinks" like forests that consume carbon dioxide. The U.S. Energy Information Administration predicts that total carbon dioxide emissions will more than double from 1990 to 2030.[6] Though it has less than 5% of the world's population, the United States accounts for more than 25% of the world's carbon dioxide emissions, and its emissions show no signs of slowing. Furthermore, China has overtaken the United States in overall carbon dioxide emissions, and its emissions are projected to continue to increase at a significant rate, thus worsening greenhouse gas projections.

The consequences of the seemingly small temperature increases from climate change are potentially huge. Yet, many citizens in the United States view these consequences as remote and of little relevance to their daily lives. However, these subtle changes are beginning to affect various aspects of daily life and already are felt in one of society's less serious, though much beloved, activities: sports. Football practice schedules have changed, World Cup and Olympic skiing events face extreme snow patterns, and Alaska's Iditarod sled dog race has not begun at its traditional start in Wasilla since 2002 because of too little snow. These shifts were

---

6. U.S. ENERGY INFO. ADMIN., INTERNATIONAL ENERGY OUTLOOK 2006, at 73 tbl. 12, *available at* http://www.fypower.org/pdf/EIA_IntlEnergyOutlook(2006).pdf. This prediction does not take into account the Kyoto Protocol, a 1997 international agreement to limit greenhouse gas emissions discussed later in Part D.

all the result of climate change. A warmer climate may even worsen the quality of baseball bats for Major Leaguers because ash trees require a cool climate, while their insect enemy, the emerald ash borer, thrives in warmer temperatures.[7] As discussed below, though, the public in the United States generally has not appreciated these changes as potentially resulting from climate change.

Appropriately, scientists generally have focused on consequences of far greater global concern. To date, global warming has changed weather patterns, increased El Niño events, shifted animal and plant ranges, and changed growing, flowering, breeding, and migration seasons. Ocean temperatures are rising, and mountain glaciers are shrinking.

> Glacier National Park in Montana is a fitting emblem for the great change sweeping the world's cold places. Dan Fagre has studied the glaciers in the park for 15 years. A scientist for the U.S. Geological Survey, he has the numbers at his fingertips: 27 glaciers left in the park out of the 150 a century ago, 90 percent of the ice volume gone. He gives the remainder another 25 years. "It will be the first time in at least 7,000 years that this landscape has not had glaciers."[8]

Looking toward the future, climate change likely will significantly increase water temperature and decrease water levels in the Great Lakes, harming ecosystems and limiting fresh water availability.[9] More significantly, rising ocean levels could submerge entire regions and whole countries.[10]

"If vulnerable parts of the ice that blanket Greenland and Antarctica succumb, rising seas could flood hundreds of thousands of square miles—much of Florida, Bangladesh, the Netherlands—and displace tens of millions of people."[11] Arctic sea ice, in certain seasons, has already thinned by 40% and decreased in its extent by 10% to 15%. As seen in Figure C, Arctic sea ice has shrunk to its lowest level since satellite measurements began, opening up the historically impassable Northwest Passage.

---

7. Alexander Wolff, *Going, Going Green*, SPORTS ILLUSTRATED, Mar. 12, 2007, at 38, 41-42.

8. Tim Appenzeller, *The Big Thaw*, NAT'L GEOGRAPHIC, June 2007, at 71. A subsequent report from the spring of 2010 indicated that only 25 glaciers were left in Glacier National Park, *available at* http://www.nrmsc.usgs.gov/research/glacier_retreat.htm.

9. UNION OF CONCERNED SCIENTISTS, CONFRONTING CLIMATE CHANGE IN THE GREAT LAKES REGION (2003) 21, 26, 36, *available at* http://www.ucsusa.org/assets/documents/global_warming/chapter3.pdf.

10. United Nations Framework Convention on Climate Change, May 9, 1992, S. Treaty Doc. No. 102-38 (1992), 31 I.L.M. 849 (1992), *available at* http://unfccc.int/essential_background/feeling_the_heat/items/2917txt.php.

11. Appenzeller, *supra* note 8.

**Figure C: Opening of the Northwest Passage
Mosaic Image of the Arctic Ocean, September 2007
European Space Agency's Envisat Satellite Advanced Synthetic
Aperture Radar**

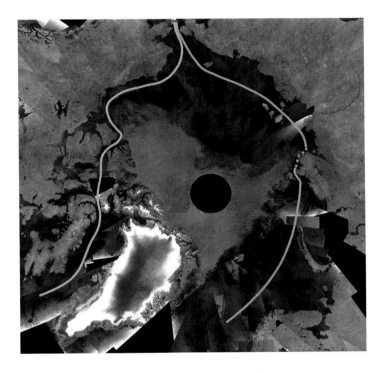

The dark grey color represents the ice-free areas. The most direct route of the Northwest Passage (high-lighted by the line on the left) across northern Canada is shown fully navigable, while the Northeast Passage (line on the right) along the Siberian coast remains only partially blocked. Source: European Space Agency, http://www.esa.int/esaCP/SEMYTC13J6F_index_1.html.

NASA predicts that "[a]t this rate, the Arctic Ocean could be nearly ice-free at the end of summer by 2012, much faster than previous predictions."[12]

While the problem of global climate change and its basic consequences are certainly no longer unknown, a great many of its indirect impacts and costs, especially those affecting public health and welfare, remain underappreciated. These harms include increased incidence and distribution of medical disorders and health concerns, which likely will cause economic losses and higher healthcare costs.[13]

---

12. Seth Borenstein, *Ominous Arctic melt worries experts*, AP, Dec. 12, 2007.

13. For information on how global climate change will impact human health, see Paul R. Epstein, *Is Global Warming Harmful to Health?*, SCI. AM., Aug. 20, 2000; Joanne Silberner, *Theories Tying Human*

According to Dr. Paul Epstein, Director of the Center for Health and the Global Environment at the Harvard Medical School, while more obvious direct effects include increased deaths due to heat waves and drowning, global climate change will also spark the resurgence and spread of infectious disease, especially in lesser developed countries with sub-standard medical care. A major reason why—mosquitoes. These insects pose an immense threat due to the disease-causing microorganisms that female mosquitoes acquire when sucking blood from infected animals or humans. Viruses and parasites, causing malaria, dengue fever, yellow fever, and encephalitis, reproduce inside the insect and can jump to the next mosquito victim. In the warmer air temperatures on earth, mosquitoes will multiply faster, bite more, and carry pathogens reproducing at a greater rate. The zone of disease transmission has increased already and is expected to continue to expand.

Insects are not the only ones that will take advantage of climate change. The increased carbon dioxide in the atmosphere will cause plants to reproduce more quickly and increase their toxicity, resulting in increased exposures to allergens such as ragweed, pollen, and poison ivy. Thus, the consequences of global climate change are both far-reaching and significant for public health and the environment. Yet, as the ongoing climate change debate shows, generating public awareness and understanding in the United States of the significance of climate change remains a challenge.

Public Awareness

A real challenge then for the climate crisis is finding a successful means to rally people to the cause and properly frame the issue to invoke broad public recognition and support for policy change.[14] For climate change, at least in the United States, it took the 1997 Kyoto Protocol (which ultimately was not signed), an Oscar-winning documentary, a former U.S. Vice President, and decades of debate for global warming truly to enter the public conscience. The documentary *An Inconvenient Truth*, narrated by Al Gore, in the role of climate change ambassador, propelled the problem into the public's consciousness. The movie, based on Gore's best-selling book, made $50 million worldwide at the box office, sold millions of DVDs, and won the 2006 Academy Award for documentary feature. For his efforts in promoting awareness of the dangers of climate change, Gore, along with the IPCC, won the Nobel Peace Prize.

Yet, this new awareness has by no means led to a landslide of ambitious attempts, socially, politically, legally, or otherwise, to avert the crisis, and this failure rings especially true in the United States. According to *Newsweek* magazine polling data, in 2006 only one-third of Americans thought planetary warming was "mainly

---

Health, Climate Gain Ground, NAT'L PUB. RADIO, *available at* http://www.npr.org/templates/story/story.php?storyId=12178339&sc=emaf; *Links Between Illness and Global Warming?*, NAT'L PUB. RADIO, *available at* http://www.npr.org/templates/story/story.php?storyId=5511686&sc=emaf.

14. *Cf.* GEORGE LAKOFF, DON'T THINK OF AN ELEPHANT! KNOW YOUR VALUES AND FRAME THE DEBATE (2004).

caused by things people do." In 2007 nearly half of those polled believed a lot of disagreement existed about whether human activities are a major cause of global warming and also felt scientists disagreed as to whether the planet is warming at all.[15] Despite Gore's campaign, the "Live Earth" concerts, and many calling for a reduction in greenhouse gases, the science is often poorly understood by the public. Even when understood, scientific data does not mesh well with the political landscape,[16] and scientific evidence is often undermined, sometimes through deliberate misinformation by industry groups.[17] Raising awareness becomes a major challenge, and any public relations campaign has limitations, especially when, despite scientific consensus, those with divergent economic and political interests have access to their own public relations machine.[18] Similarly, there has always been a troubled relationship between law and science.[19] Simply put, law seeks certainty and rules that can be practically implemented, while science deals with nuanced and complex data that is far from absolute.

In addition, the sources of greenhouse gases are increasingly diffuse, geographically dispersed and pervasive, making it difficult to identify primary sources as the "target" to be fixed. Thus, no single, universal impact or symbol has been identified that reaches broad sectors of the public. A logo of a rising thermometer will not do the trick. Perhaps the cause should adopt the polar bear as the face for preventing the climate crisis.[20] Polar bears already are fighting for their survival, facing habitat loss due to increased ice melt that limits their ability to feed on seal pups living on the ice. The U.S. Geological Survey predicts that shrinking sea ice may eliminate two-thirds of the world's polar bears in the next 50 years.[21]

But ultimately, the environmental impacts of climate change are subtle and slow-moving, demonstrated only over a long time frame. These remote impacts and subtle changes do not grab the public's attention, particularly where impacts on an immediate population or area are not clear. As a result unfortunately, it may be events like the next Hurricane Katrina or the flooding of parts of the eastern seaboard or the loss of the entire country of Kiribati in the Pacific Ocean that may best remind us of climate change's potential costs.[22] "[A]lthough it is impossible to

15. Sharon Begley, *The Truth About Denial*, NEWSWEEK, Aug. 13, 2007, at 22.
16. Peter Borah, *Karl Popper and Antarctic Ice: The Climate Debate and Its Problems*, The Core (2010), *available at* http://thecore.uchicago.edu/Summer2010/feature-karl-popper.shtml.
17. Begley, *supra* note 15.
18. *See* Patrick A. Parenteau, *Anything Industry Wants: Environmental Policy Under Bush II*, 14 DUKE ENVTL. L. & POL'Y FORUM 392 (2004).
19. Oliver Houck, *Tales from a Troubled Marriage: Science and Law in Environmental Policy*, 302 SCI. 1926 (2003).
20. Gore's documentary *An Inconvenient Truth* does contain an animated short of a polar bear swimming in the Arctic Ocean and trying in vain to climb onto the last piece of floating ice.
21. U.S. GEOLOGICAL SURVEY, USGS SCIENCE TO INFORM U.S. FISH & WILDLIFE DECISION MAKING ON POLAR BEARS: EXECUTIVE SUMMARY, *available at* http://www.usgs.gov/newsroom/special/polar_bears/docs/.
22. AL GORE, AN INCONVENIENT TRUTH 92-93 (2006); Robert L. Glicksman, *Global Climate Change and the Risks to Coastal Areas from Hurricanes and Rising Sea Levels: The Costs of Doing Nothing*, 52 LOY. L. REV. 1127, 1129, 1142-43 (2007); *Climate: CAP Panel Analyzes Link Between Powerful Storms,*

demonstrate a cause-and-effect relationship between global climate change and the occurrence or strength of any particular storm, there is a respectable and growing body of scientific opinion to support the proposition that human-induced climate change has created an environment conducive to more intense tropical cyclones such as hurricanes."[23] Pending the occurrence of such catastrophes, given the general lack of public awareness on other fronts, many consequences of climate change seem geographically remote or unlikely to occur. This public mindset, in turn, makes political action even more unlikely. Without greater resources allotted for creating public awareness and understanding, the real concern is that only such catastrophes will serve as the catalysts for more immediate policy initiatives, which then may arise too late.

The Policy Challenge

In addition to the challenge of creating awareness of climate change through educational initiatives and public outreach campaigns, a second challenge is developing and implementing effective environmental policy and programs to limit adverse human impacts on the earth and our own health. This proves no easy task in environmental legislation since it requires the codification of rules based on scientific information, both hard science and social science. For example, how much should one be able to pollute or what technology or incentive is the best to lessen pollution? What programs will effectively modify corporate, commercial, or individual behavior?

According to Professor Oliver Houck, law and science have had a "troubled marriage."[24] Good science can generate general consensus in a discipline (e.g., greenhouse gas emissions are too high resulting in climate change), but science is rarely dispositive as to detailed specifics (e.g., what reductions in greenhouse gases are needed and how can these reductions be achieved?). Thus, even in the face of scientific consensus, law, in its search for certainty and strict regimes, has had difficulty dealing with the complex details of many environmental and ecosystem cycles, resulting in regulatory inefficiencies and problems with jurisdictional coordination. Put more simply, in the environmental field, the disciplines of law and science can have difficulty seeing eye to eye.

The challenge is in determining what creative public, social, and private initiatives can overcome this difficulty. As discussed in Part B below, the climate change crisis has been the focus of considerable international concern and a range of policy initiatives. Yet, the goal of reaching consensus on how to move forward to mitigate climate change has been elusive at both the international and national

---

Human-Caused Global Warming (Environment & Energy TV broadcast, Sept. 14, 2007) (transcript available at http://www.eenews.net/tv/transcript/660).

23. Robert L. Glicksman, *Global Climate Change and the Risks to Coastal Areas from Hurricanes and Rising Sea Levels: The Costs of Doing Nothing*, 52 LOY. L. REV. 1127, 1129, 1142-43 (2007).

24. Oliver Houck, *Tales from a Troubled Marriage: Science and Law in Environmental Policy*, 302 SCI. 1926 (2003).

levels. The key regulatory policy issues that complicate reaching agreement on mitigating climate change include standard-setting (e.g., what emissions reductions and technology to require) and intergovernmental coordination (e.g., a lack of international consensus and national action, often leading to sub-national and local initiatives). The position of each country on these issues is influenced by a broad range of factors, such as level of economic development, level of energy consumption, technological capabilities, and the country's own natural resources and vulnerability to climate change impacts. The relative costs and benefits of any particular policy approach differ for differently situated countries, as do the abilities of individual countries to design and implement legally binding programs to achieve any commitments to reduce emissions. Thus, international and national policies addressing climate change face the significant hurdle of either finding a common approach that effectively motivates a broad range of participants, or, alternatively, generating acceptance and consensus in support of a mixture of approaches that reflects tailoring to different goals for differently situated participants.

At their base, these climate change policy challenges present the same basic questions posed by policy initiatives to influence individual behavior that impacts the environment: (1) What regulatory techniques or incentives will be most effective, and (2) what level of institution is best suited to implement the resulting program? For climate change policy initiatives, the answers include greenhouse emissions targets and creating market mechanisms through tradable emissions permits, perhaps administered by international, national, or regional cooperative agreements.

B.   The Response of Law

The unsustainable current rate of natural resource consumption, and resulting greenhouse gas emissions, have sparked a range of environmental problems and some intriguing attempts to solve them. Efforts to curb climate change illustrate various traditional and alternative responses to environmental harm and serve as an excellent backdrop for considering the challenges posed by other emerging environmental problems, such as the relationship between individual behavior and the environment. Climate change and the environmental effects of everyday actions face the same challenges of determining what level of government action is appropriate. In both contexts, local and regional initiatives often arise where international law and national legislation have failed to materialize. Meeting these challenges will require consideration of the full range of legal tools and options available, as well as consideration of how and when to complement these legal mechanisms with other policy approaches and voluntary initiatives.

Legal Mechanisms

Tools to abate environmental problems can be codified in law through, for example, emission standards, information dissemination, and market incentives. Although greenhouse gas emissions must be cut drastically and immediately, relatively little has been done in terms of establishing laws that will help ensure these cuts.

> Barely a month passes without a new finding on the dangers posed by rising CO2 levels—to the polar ice cap, to the survival of the world's coral reefs, to the continued existence of low lying nations. Yet the world has barely even begun to take action. This is particularly true of the United States, which is the largest emitter of carbon dioxide by far.[25]

The international community has made many strides, particularly in the European Union. By comparison, only over the past few years have American climate change law and policy begun to take form, mainly through domestic climate initiatives such as regional and municipal programs and state laws. Action at the federal level has not kept pace. However, following the Supreme Court's conclusion that the U.S. Environmental Protection Agency (EPA) may regulate greenhouse gases,[26] both EPA and some members of U.S. Congress have been focused on the issue, with climate change legislation perhaps making the legislative agenda in 2011. In the meantime, EPA has taken initial steps to regulate greenhouse gases under the Clean Air Act by determining that greenhouse gases are "air pollutants" under the Act, thus mandating the creation of national air quality standards for greenhouse gases.[27]

Legal mechanisms aimed at mitigating the climate crisis include international and foreign law, U.S. law and policy, domestic state and regional initiatives, and local and municipal efforts.[28] Litigation has played a role in nearly all of these forums, as relevant actors often seek enforcement of existing regimes and permission to engage in additional mitigation efforts.

International and Federal Law

The international community formally recognized the potential dangers of climate change in 1988 when the World Meteorological Organization and the United Nations Environment Programme established the IPCC, whose working groups assess the impacts of climate change. The IPCC's first report proved to be a catalyst for the 1992 adoption of the United Nations Framework Convention on Climate Change (UNFCCC), providing a loose framework and stating nonbinding goals for stabilizing greenhouse gas concentrations. It soon became apparent that binding targets and timetables were needed to achieve the UNFCCC's goals,

---

25. Elizabeth Kolbert, *The Climate of Man-III: What Can Be Done?*, THE NEW YORKER, May 9, 2005, at 54. Though, at this point, China has passed the United States in total greenhouse gas emissions.

26. Massachusetts v. EPA, 127 S. Ct. 1438, 1459, 1462-63 (2007).

27. Endangerment and Cause or Contribute Findings for Greenhouse Gases under Section 202(a) of the Clean Air Act, *available at* http://epa.gov/climatechange/endangerment.html.

28. For a comprehensive climate change law text, see MICHAEL B. GERRARD, ED., GLOBAL CLIMATE CHANGE AND U.S. LAW (2007).

especially once the framework's reduction goal to 1990 greenhouse gas levels by 2000 became regarded as inadequate. The Kyoto Protocol, negotiated in 1997 and entered into force in 2005 when ratified by Russia, features binding "quantified emissions limitation and reduction commitments" keyed to 1990 emissions, calling for an average reduction in developed countries of about 5% below 1990 levels in 2008-2012.[29] The Protocol permits lesser-developed countries to use a base period other than 1990 and approves additional flexible mechanisms, such as emissions trading and the European Union's "bubble" allowing for emission commitment reallocation among its member states.[30]

The United States participated in the Kyoto conference, sending an envoy led by then-Vice President Al Gore; it, however, failed to ratify the treaty after President George W. Bush repudiated the Protocol. In fact, even *prior* to the completion of the Kyoto Protocol, a near unanimous Senate passed a resolution objecting to the United States becoming a signatory.[31] The Senate objected to the Kyoto plan due to differing standards for developing countries and concerns about harm to the U.S. economy, including job loss, trade disadvantages, and increased energy and consumer costs.[32]

As evidenced in the Copenhagen Accord of 2009, the continued lack of support from the United States, as well as China and India, for binding emissions limits has hindered international efforts to mitigate greenhouse gases. The Copenhagen Accord sets no binding emissions limits on countries. The Accord is a non-binding agreement that recognizes decision-making "according to science," creates a monetary fund to help the transition away from fossil fuels in developing countries, and formally lists the climate change mitigation measures that signing countries have agreed to take on. However, in the absence of a coherent federal policy based either on an international treaty or federal legislation, U.S. climate change action consists of a hodgepodge of domestic initiatives at all levels of government.

To date, the U.S. government has not enacted a single law explicitly requiring any public or private entity to mitigate its greenhouse gas impact on the global climate. The Clean Air Act, originally passed in 1963 with major amendments in 1970, 1977, and 1990, does state that EPA must regulate air pollutants that "may reasonably be anticipated to endanger public health or welfare," where air pollutants include "substance or matter which is emitted into or otherwise enters the ambient air."[33] Despite the statute's plain language, EPA historically waffled on whether the agency had the jurisdiction to regulate greenhouse gases and, even if it did, whether it was sensible to do so. Finally, in 2007 litigation forced the U.S. Supreme Court to lament the dangers of climate change, to find with "little trouble"

29. Kyoto Protocol to the United Nations Framework Convention on Climate Change, Dec. 10, 1997, U.N. Doc. FCCC/CP/197/L. 7/Add. 1, art. 3.1 & Annex B, *reprinted in* 37 I.L.M. 22 (1998).

30. *Id.* at art. 3, 6, 17.

31. Byrd-Hagel Resolution, S. Res. 98 (1st Session, 105th Congress) (1997).

32. *Id.*

33. Clean Air Act (CAA) § 108(a)(1)(A), 42 U.S.C. § 7408(a)(1)(A); CAA § 109(b)(1), 42 U.S.C. § 7409(b)(1); CAA § 302(a)(1), 42 U.S.C. § 7602(a)(1); CAA § 302(g), 42 U.S.C. § 7602(g).

that EPA is authorized to regulate greenhouse gases, and to conclude that EPA had "refused to comply with this clear statutory command" by not regulating greenhouse gases if these gases cause or contribute to climate change.[34] Consequently, in the absence of Congressional action on federal climate change legislation,[35] EPA moved to assess options to regulate greenhouse gases under the Clean Air Act, and, in December 2009, made an "endangerment finding" concluding that carbon dioxide is a criteria air pollutant subject to regulation under the Clean Air Act. This determination paved the way for the development of regulatory greenhouse gas emission standards in the United States, meaning that EPA would need to address in subsequent regulations the policy challenges inherent in determining which sources to regulate, how to do so, and at what level.

State and Local Efforts

In the absence of effective federal climate change policy, a number of state governments have pursued individual as well as cooperative initiatives to lessen the U.S. carbon footprint. For example, the Western Climate Initiative (WCI), launched in 2007 and comprised of the governors of Arizona, California, New Mexico, Oregon, and Washington as well as the premier of British Columbia, successfully brokered a regional greenhouse gas emission goal—an aggregate of 15% below 2005 levels by 2020.[36] The WCI cooperative effort needs state legislatures to implement the group's proposed market-based reduction plan. Similarly, under the Regional Greenhouse Gas Initiative (RGGI), comprising states in New England and the Mid-Atlantic, participants are developing a "cap-and-trade" program based upon individual state statutory and regulatory authority. The states hope to significantly reduce carbon dioxide emissions from power plants by utilizing emissions allowances that can be bought and sold and by providing for the ability to offset plant emissions using emission reductions from low-cost alternatives.[37]

Individual states have aggressively implemented their own greenhouse gas reduction plans.[38] For example, California passed the Global Warming Solutions Act, limiting state global warming emissions to 1990 levels by 2020 and mandating an emissions reporting system.[39] In 2004 California adopted a comprehensive set of greenhouse gas emissions regulations for new motor vehicles and later applied to

---

34. Massachusetts v. EPA, 127 S. Ct. 1438, 1459, 1462-63 (2007).

35. The Pew Center on Global Climate Change (http://www.pewclimate.org/) tracks congressional legislation. For an evaluation of federal legislative proposals as of late 2007, see Victor B. Flatt, *Taking the Legislative Temperature: Which Federal Climate Change Legislative Proposal is "Best"?* (Parts I & II), http://colloquy.law.northwestern.edu/main/2007/12/taking-the-legi.html & http://www.law.northwestern.edu/lawreview/colloquy/2007/32/.

36. WESTERN CLIMATE INITIATIVE STATEMENT OF REGIONAL GOAL 1 (2007), *available at* www.azclimatechange.gov/download/082207_statement.pdf.

37. See the RGGI website at http://www.rggi.org/.

38. For a survey of the responses of all American states, see Pace Law School Center for Environmental Legal Studies, *The State Response to Climate Change: 50-State Survey* in GERRARD, *supra* note 28, at Chapter 11.

39. CAL. HEALTH & SAF. CODE §§ 38530, 38550 (2007).

EPA for a waiver from less rigorous, federal Clean Air Act standards. Eleven states have adopted California's greenhouse gas regulations pursuant to the Clean Air Act, which allows any state to adopt California standards for new motor vehicles.[40]

American and foreign municipalities have also pursued emissions policies and pragmatic greenhouse gas mitigation programs. A number of cities have endeavored to cut greenhouse gas emissions levels by a specific level, including Växjö, Sweden, which cut its emissions by 30% since 1993, and Portland, Oregon, which set a goal of reducing emissions by 10% below 1990 levels by 2010.[41] Other cities have sought out focused, practical reduction methods, using a variety of approaches. For example, Denver, Colorado, replaced traditional incandescent bulbs in traffic signals with more energy efficient Light-Emitting Diode signals. Honolulu, Hawaii; Berkeley, California; Seattle, Washington; and Barcelona, Spain, have developed building energy efficiency codes that foster the installation of solar panels, low-flow toilets, and water pipe insulation, as well as promote implementation of Leadership in Energy and Environmental Design (LEED) standards.[42] Stockholm, Sweden, provides incentives for the use of clean vehicles and boasts the highest percentage of clean vehicles in Europe. More systematically, the International Council for Local Environmental Initiatives has developed the "Cities for Climate Protection Campaign," an international effort in which cities commit to a climate change action program, including establishing emissions targets and developing policies to reach these goals.[43]

As illustrated, efforts to mitigate greenhouse gas emissions are diverse in nature. In addition to governmental programs, scholars and policymakers have suggested more information disclosure, reliance on ancient conceptions of the public trust doctrine (a principle holding that the state should hold and preserve in trust our natural resources for the common good), and economic programs such as cap-and-trade (where emission levels are set or "capped" and emissions allocations are

---

40. CAA § 177, 42 U.S.C. § 7507. Despite early court decisions upholding a state's authority to set its own greenhouse gas regulations, EPA initially denied California's waiver in 2007. Green Mountain Chrysler Plymouth Dodge Jeep v. Crombie, No. 2:05-cv-302, 2007 U.S. Dist. LEXIS 67617 (D. Vt. Sept. 12, 2007), *available at* http://www.vtd.uscourts.gov/Cases/05cv302.html; Press Release, EPA, America Receives a National Solution for Vehicle Greenhouse Gas Emissions (Dec. 19, 2007), *available at* http://yosemite.epa.gov/opa/admpress.nsf/6424ac1caa800aab85257359003f5337/41b4663d8d3807c5852573b6008141e5!OpenDocument; *Notice of Decision Denying Waiver of Clean Air Act Preemption for California's 2009 and Subsequent Model Year Greenhouse Gas Emission Standards for New Motor Vehicles as of Feb. 29, 2008*, 73 Fed. Reg. 12156 (Mar. 6, 2008). Under the Obama Administration, however, EPA reviewed the earlier denial and granted the waiver in June 2009. 74 Fed. Reg. 32744 (July 8, 2009).

41. Robert B. McKinstry, Jr., *Laboratories for Local Solutions for Global Problems: State, Local and Private Leadership in Developing Strategies to Mitigate the Causes and Effects of Climate Change*, 12 PENN ST. ENVTL. L. REV. 15, 57 (2006); Hari M. Osofsky & Janet Koven Levit, *The Scale of Networks? Local Climate Change Coalitions*, 8 CHI. J. INT'L L. 408, 409 (2008); Karl Ritter, *Cities Take the Lead on Climate Change*, ASSOCIATED PRESS, Oct. 13, 2007.

42. For information on municipal efforts, see U.S. EPA, State and Local Greenhouse Gas Mitigation Case Studies, http://yosemite.epa.gov/OAR/globalwarming.nsf/content/ActionsStateCaseStudies.html; C40 Large Cities Climate Summit, *Case Studies*, *available at* http://www.nycclimatesummit.com/casestudies.html; J. Kevin Healy, *Local Initiatives*, in GERRARD, *supra* note 28, at Chapter 12.

43. ICLEI, http://www.iclei.org/index.php?id=800.

bought and sold in the market) or carbon taxes (taxes on greenhouse gases emitted from the burning of fossil fuels). Legal scholars and lawyers have advocated and pursued litigation to stop greenhouse gas production and raise climate change awareness, including the assertion of traditional common law tort and nuisance principles. In addition, whether legally mandated or a product of the free market, renewable technologies such as wind and solar power and alternative fuels will play a role in mitigating climate change.

In summary, many legal options and technological opportunities exist, in terms of science and governmental action to mitigate environmental harm. Various levels of government, international, federal, state and local, and regulatory tools and economic incentives are being used to regulate and moderate commercial and government actions that have an impact on the environment. Less developed are efforts to address everyday, individual behaviors that contribute to climate change or cause other environmental impacts. Yet, given the diffuse sources of greenhouse gases, the challenges of addressing the impacts of individual behaviors will need to be addressed. As discussed below, climate change policy can usefully serve as a backdrop to foreshadow the challenges to regulating environmental concerns caused by individual behavior in the aggregate. Unfortunately, at all levels, while law and policy can work to mitigate environmental harm such as greenhouse gas emissions, a lack of public awareness, difficulties in inter-governmental coordination, and scientific uncertainty and complexity often frustrate potentially successful initiatives.

C. The Limitations and Promise of Law

To address the climate change problem, as with the problem of individual behavior, decision-makers must determine what solutions will be most effective and who should implement them. In doing so, law and policy addressing greenhouse gas emissions and individual behavior face similar obstacles in determining how to increase knowledge and public awareness and target the appropriate regulatory tools, behaviors, and level of government action. In addition, policymakers must incorporate scientific information into decision-making processes, and understand the successes and failures of past and existing public policy and legislation.

Modern environmental concerns often are not localized; instead, as climate change illustrates, they cross any number of jurisdictions, requiring international, national, or regional solutions. Unfortunately, such coordination and cooperative efforts across multiple jurisdictions often fail to materialize because of competing social and economic interests of nations and localities.[44] Even where multi-jurisdictional agreements are reached, their implementation often falls short, failing to achieve the desired environmental gains. At times, that leaves mitigation efforts in

---

44. RICHARD J. LAZARUS, THE MAKING OF ENVIRONMENTAL LAW, 32-38 (2004) (discussing the fragmentation of law-making authority, federalism, and decentralization in environmental law).

the hands of local government and voluntary action, where policies and outreach can be better tailored both in terms of public outreach and effective solutions. Thus, while national and state legislation, combined with international collaboration, remain the current model of environmental law, the appropriate role of local efforts must be considered. Although local efforts may fail to reach important pollutant sources and may encounter inefficiencies and increased costs in a smaller market, they also might stimulate technological innovation, permit experimentation of alternative policy designs, and raise awareness of environmental dangers and the need for federal regulation in place of a regulatory patchwork.[45] These pros and cons are doubly true for voluntary actions that carry significant costs for small gains. But local and extra-local efforts (e.g., community-based and municipal programs at institutional levels smaller than formal local government, such as schools, libraries, local planning commissions, stakeholder groups, and non-profits) take on symbolic value and promote sound environmental management. Said the environmental controller in Växjö, Sweden:

> People used to ask: Isn't it better to do this at a national or international level? We want to show everyone else that you can accomplish a lot at the local level.[46]

To effectively address environmental problems related to everyday behavior, law and policy must harness the unappreciated power of local and community initiatives that encourage more intentionality in the daily lives of individuals that too often spurn eco-friendly choices in favor of short-term convenience.[47] Improving cultural norms and everyday environmentalism will raise awareness, change daily decision-making, and make broader and larger public policy goals easier to achieve. That said, the international community, and national and state legislation, will need to consider how to target individual behavior by providing individuals with the proper resources and infrastructure to influence choice. For example, these larger jurisdictions can provide uniform and reliable informational labeling to enable informed choice, and fund and coordinate public education campaigns.

Any environmental policy regime, even a larger jurisdictional effort, is far from a guaranteed success. Perhaps a reason for this challenge is scientific complexity and uncertainty.[48] As a formal rules-based regime, law often struggles to incorpo-

---

45. Kirsten H. Engel & Barak Y. Orbach, *Micro-motives for State and Local Climate Change Initiatives*, 2 HARV. L. & POL'Y REV. 119, 121 (2007); Jonathan B. Wiener, *Think Globally, Act Globally: The Limits of Local Climate Policies*, 155 U. PA. L. REV. 1961, 1963 (2007).

46. Ritter, *supra* note 41.

47. *Cf.* Michael P. Vandenbergh, *Order Without Social Norms: How Personal Norm Activation Can Protect the Environment*, 99 NW. U. L. REV. 1101, 1165-66 (2005); Michael P. Vandenbergh, *The Private Life of Public Law*, 105 COLUM. L. REV. 2029, 2037-41 (2005).

48. LAZARUS, *supra* note 44, at 17, 19-21 ("The amount of complex scientific information—from physics, chemistry, geology, and biology—underlying any effective pollution control standard is simply extraordinary."); Holly Doremus & A. Dan Tarlock, *Science, Judgment, and Controversy in Natural Resource Regulation*, 26 PUB. LAND & RESOURCES L. REV. 1, 36-37 (2005), *reprinted in* 37 LAND USE & ENVTL. L. REV. 335 (2006); Holly Doremus, *Science Plays Defense: Natural Resource Management in the Bush Administration*, 32 ECOLOGY L. Q. 249, 297-99 (2005); Hari M. Osofsky, *The Intersection*

rate the complex and uncertain details of any environmental system. For example, if a decision is made to mandate use of the best available emission technologies in cars and power plants and build infrastructure for clean cars, clean energy, and mass transportation, then the assessment must turn to what technologies merit development and investment. If picking "best available" technologies is simply too difficult, or flexibility is desired in options for achieving emissions reductions, then the focus turns to what are the optimal emissions levels and what products will effect the most change if regulated. These broad policy questions persist regardless of whether the concern is climate change, industrial pollution, municipal waste, or individual impacts, such as the household carbon footprint.

Initiatives to influence the effects of individual behavior present similar issues. What behaviors to target, among what populations, and through what means? Individual activities, in the aggregate, have tremendous effects on the environment, including contributing to the climate crisis. Changing the difficult dynamics of individual action requires nuanced decisions about what actions will prove most effective. Individual behavior can be influenced via information generation, social and cultural norms, economic incentives, and regulatory requirements. Implementation can occur through government action, community efforts, and private action. To choose the appropriate means to promote everyday environmentalism, decision-makers should, first, identify areas of environmental concern and endeavor to understand the underlying science; second, learn from the past, understanding former and current law and policy to avoid past mistakes, and accept creative, even if small, solutions; and third, recognize the intrinsic challenges facing law and policy in terms of coordination and complexity, especially when attempting to change personal choices and household decisions.

Educated decision-making and efforts to understand the influence of individual actions on environmental and human health will be needed to answer the key questions—namely, what public initiatives and private efforts, especially at the local and community levels, will effectively meet the challenges of consumer behavior and infrastructure, influencing how we live, what we eat, where we live, and the costs of these choices?

The following three chapters deal with three areas of individual behavior that impact the environment: household energy and consumption patterns, food choices, and sprawl. These chapters describe the ecological harms of everyday choice, evaluate existing policy efforts to change individual behavior in these areas, and address what measures might most effectively promote "everyday environmentalism." In each of these cases, the aggregate costs of individual action are quite high, and existing public policy efforts have had only limited success. As discussed in these and subsequent chapters, the achievement of greater success will require that legal regimes and policy initiatives support a concerted and basic effort to raise

---

of Scale, Science, and Law in Massachusetts v. EPA, 9 OR. REV. INT'L L. 223 (2007), *available at* http://ssrn.com/abstract=1014905.

awareness of the environmental costs and power of individual behavior; create more ambitious informational eco-labeling; develop regulatory tools that economically value nature; effectively use local decision-making and community initiatives to change existing norms; and be tailored to particular individual decision-making points and target audiences as some individuals, populations, products, and activities are more detrimental than others.

CHAPTER THREE

The Carbon and Waste Footprints

By turning on the lights, filling the kettle, taking the children to school, driving to the shops, we are condemning other people to death.

George Monbiot, *Heat: How to Stop the Planet Burning* 22 (2006)

With historical consumption increases, the average individual environmental footprint in the United States has grown significantly. This chapter evaluates the significance of the aggregate ecological footprint of individual activities and choices that occur in the home and explores options for mitigating the environmental costs of these choices. Unfortunately, current social and cultural norms for individual behavior generally do not consider, let alone seek to mitigate, the carbon and waste footprints arising from individual behavior in the home.

Part A reviews the environmental costs and impacts of household energy consumption, transportation choices, and waste production. Prior to determining what environmental policy should do to instill behavioral changes in household behavior, Part B discusses the existing policies and laws that currently influence these everyday behaviors. Thus, these sections underscore the aggregate ecological costs of household behavior and provide greater understanding of government's current roles in both lessening and contributing to the individual carbon and waste footprint. In light of the six decision-making tools identified in the Introduction, Part C considers the array of policy and regulatory tools that could be used to reduce the carbon and waste footprint of everyday behaviors in the home. In particular, Part C asserts that policymakers should focus (1) on the use of both traditional government action and market incentives to improve infrastructure and products in order to provide consumers with a broader range of eco-friendly choices and (2) on activating eco-friendly social and cultural norms through information dissemination and eco-labeling devices that promote greater awareness and understanding of the consequences of these everyday activities on the environment.

A. A Day in the Life

Consider the daily activities of the average American homeowner. He or she takes out the trash, flushes the toilet, turns on the lights and the television, mows and waters the lawn, runs the dishwasher, and drives to work. While sustainable living remains a broad concern, it is, for many, a discretely located topic. Most daily individual choices happen in the home, yet the consequences of garbage and energy waste from the home, as well as transportation choices, are not well known.

Household Energy Use & Carbon Footprints

Energy usage and the carbon footprints of individuals and the households in which they live are responsible for a significant portion of overall greenhouse gas emissions in the United States. While some ecological impacts arising from the home cannot easily be modified due to the existing infrastructure, many behaviors could be effectively changed if individuals had greater information about the tradeoffs between environmental costs and convenience. As noted later in Chapter Seven, awareness on the part of both policymakers and consumers of tradeoffs that are low-cost to consumers and high-value to the environment is essential to environmentally conscious decision-making. Understanding these tradeoffs and second-best solutions is particularly important when consumers balk and existing infrastructure precludes the most eco-friendly option.

Homes require a lot of energy, primarily for heating, cooling, and running appliances. In terms of electricity consumption alone, the average American household uses about 11,000 kilowatt-hours per year.[1] A ton of coal consumed at a power plant creates 2,000 kilowatt-hours of electricity.[2] Put another way, imagine household energy consumption as more than five tons of coal delivered to your doorstep each year. The main energy hogs are heating systems, refrigerators, central air conditioning, water heaters, lighting and other appliances. The household carbon footprint becomes far larger after adding motor vehicle usage.

Can individual behavior really harm the environment, especially compared with large-scale industry? Without a doubt, individuals have a significant, and to this point understated, impact on the environment. Individuals in the United States contribute 30% to 40% of greenhouse gas emissions nationwide, which accounts for 8% of the *world's* total.[3] As seen in Table 1, the total amount of emissions from U.S. individuals is larger than every foreign country in the world except China.

---

1. U.S. Energy Info. Admin., Dep't of Energy, Electricity Consumption by End Use in U.S. Households, 2001, *available at* http://www.eia.doe.gov/emeu/recs/recs2001/enduse2001/enduse2001. html#table2 (stating average electricity consumption total equals 10,656 kWh).

2. U.S. Energy Information Administration, *Coal Demand*, http://www.eia.doe.gov/neic/infosheets/coaldemand.html.

3. *The Forum, Creating the Carbon-Neutral Citizen*, 24 ENVTL. L. FORUM 46 (2007); Michael P. Vandenbergh & Anne Steinemann, *The Carbon-Neutral Individual*, 82 N.Y.U. L. REV. 1673 (2007). In defining individual behavior, Vandenbergh and Steinemann include emissions from personal motor vehicle use, personal air travel, mass transport, and emissions attributable to household electricity use.

Table 1: Top Ten Nations by 2000 Carbon Dioxide Emissions

Country	Emissions (in billions of lbs.)
United States	11,582
China	6938
U.S. Individual Share	*4090*
Russian Federation	3074
Japan	2478
India	2108
Germany	1716
United Kingdom	1112
Canada	1058
South Korea	932

Source: Michael P. Vandenbergh & Anne K. Steinemann, *The Carbon-Neutral Individual*, 82 N.Y.U. L. REV. 1673, 1695 (2007). Vandenbergh and Steinemann use year 2000 data, and China's emissions are now greater than any other nation. *Gas Exchange: CO2 Emissions* 1990-2006, 447 NATURE 1038, 1038 (2007).

"The average American individual's share of total emissions in 2000 was more than 14,000 pounds of carbon dioxide, for a total of 4.1 trillion pounds for all Americans. By comparison, all of American industry emitted 3.9 trillion pounds in 2000."[4] And per capita energy use in the United States far exceeds per capita energy use in Europe.[5]

Household infrastructure, such as heating choices, can have real environmental consequences. Unfortunately, most people have few heating options, and most individuals do not choose their own heating systems. Homes and apartments already have in place their main heating option when residents move in, whether it is an oil burner to produce hot forced air, a natural gas boiler for hydronic heat, or electric baseboards. Similarly, the fuel type used for generating electricity, and the accompanying carbon footprint, is often dictated by geographic location. Changing heating systems is expensive, and the necessary infrastructure for a fuel change may not be available. About one-half of the electricity in the United States comes from burning coal, and one-fifth each from natural gas and nuclear power. Burning coal emits nearly twice as much carbon dioxide as natural gas, while using wind or solar power produces zero carbon emissions.

The key is for the individual to "control energy use."[6] Individuals might update to more energy efficient equipment, or they may simply change behavior. Admittedly, energy use choices contain difficult tradeoffs, from the standpoint of money,

4. Vandenbergh & Steinemann, *supra* note 3, at 1677.
5. WORLD BANK, THE LITTLE GREEN DATA BOOK 2007, at 25, 225 (2007), *available at* http://siteresources.worldbank.org/INTDATASTA/64199955-1178226923002/21322619/LGDB2007.pdf.
6. ED BEGLEY, JR., LIVING LIKE ED: A GUIDE TO THE ECO-FRIENDLY LIFE 20 (2008) ("The key to saving energy in your home is *controlling* energy use.").

convenience, culture, and social status. These tradeoffs can be particularly difficult when seeking to preserve our cultural environment. Historical preservation of older homes has real value, but old homes often are energy inefficient and costly to upgrade without destroying the historical character of the home. Further, many cannot afford major changes in their home's infrastructure, such as new heating systems, solar panels, or urban wind turbines. However, the smaller an individual's home and car, the better the savings on energy costs. And even those who are not ecologically minded should be able to appreciate the economic benefits of preserving natural resources and limited financial resources in a challenging economy, both at the individual level and the national level.

Happily, simpler options to control energy use also exist, i.e., ones that do not present such complicated tradeoffs. Putting aside the alarm clock, why are electrical appliances always on or in standby mode? Why not wear a sweater and turn down the thermostat a couple degrees? Why don't more people buy compact fluorescent light bulbs (CFLs)? Why isn't better information available to help people install energy efficient appliances such as furnaces, refrigerators, washing machines, and water heaters, as well as insulation and windows? Social scientists and market researchers provide answers to some of these questions. For example, CFLs would become more popular with better marketing, consumer education, and programmatic initiatives. Specific recommendations include having manufacturers back up long-life claims with guarantees, permitting consumers to see and use new technology through in-store light-bulb displays, focusing product marketing on specific important attributes (e.g., energy savings and long-life for CFLs), developing incentive structures that focus on retailers and manufacturers, and making sure that consumer discount programs do not obscure the retail price so much that repeat purchasing becomes unlikely.[7] These options and examples reveal ways in which educational, social, and economic decision-making tools can be used to influence individual behavior.

While medical concerns, disabilities, and some types of projects require the use of fossil-fueled equipment, in the aggregate, significant amounts of energy are used by individuals for the sake of convenience and saving time, when a little elbow grease would suffice. In these instances, the tools' costs in terms of dollars and environmental consequences can offset the efficiency and convenience benefits. In other words, the costs of the products should be high enough or the knowledge about their impacts understood well enough so that consumers can determine whether the time saved is worth the cost. It is in these instances, when cost-benefit analysis for product use is a close call, that public awareness and economic tools can play a greater role. Consider computers left on, phone chargers always plugged in, riding lawn mowers, electric hedge trimmers, hand blenders, and chainsaws. These modern conveniences may fail simple cost-benefit analysis if it becomes

---

7. LJ SANDAHL ET AL., COMPACT FLUORESCENT LIGHTING IN AMERICA: LESSONS LEARNED ON THE WAY TO MARKET (2006).

clear that hand-powered tools actually perform better and cost less for the pocket book and environment, even if they take a bit longer to do the job. Or if the current cost-benefit analysis counsels to continue the activity, government can consider whether to increase the cost of purchase or use through economic regulation.

Transportation

Given the connection between transportation and individual pollution, society needs to examine transportation choices more closely. The average car consumes around 600 gallons of gasoline and emits 77.1 pounds of hydrocarbons, 575 pounds of carbon monoxide, 38.2 pounds of oxides of nitrogen, and 11,470 pounds of carbon dioxide per year.[8] In the aggregate, these numbers add up. The number of households with vehicles, as of 2001, totaled 98.9 million, with an average of 1.9 vehicles per household.[9] That means that, as of 2001, nearly 190 million household vehicles were using more than 112 billion gallons and emitting more than 2 *trillion* pounds of carbon dioxide each year. These figures represent *just* U.S. household motor vehicle use, not industrial or commercial transportation.

Americans drive a lot (a behavioral problem), have a lot of fossil-fuel-burning motor vehicles (an infrastructure problem), and live in sprawling areas where residents have to drive to get anywhere (a land use development problem as discussed in Chapter Five). Behavior, infrastructure, and development have an interdependent relationship as any one can trigger the other. Americans enjoy the individual freedom of the open road, which is not surprising given the massive publicly funded interstate highway system and the absence of walkable communities, good mass transit options, and bike lanes. On average, Americans drive more than 30 miles each day, spending more than 20 minutes to commute more than 12 miles to work each day, a function of residential development removed from business districts.[10] While the United States has only 5% of the world's population, it contains 30% of the world's automobiles and contributes 45% of the world's automotive carbon dioxide emissions, equivalent to the amount of carbon in a coal train 50,000 miles long annually.[11] The fuel economy of the majority of the most popular U.S. manu-

8. U.S. EPA, *Greenhouse Gas Emissions from a Typical Passenger Vehicle*, (2005); U.S. EPA, UNIT CONVERSIONS, EMISSIONS FACTORS, AND OTHER REFERENCE DATA (Nov. 2004), *available at* http://www. epa.gov/climatechange/emissions/downloads/emissionsfactorsbrochure2004.pdf.; U.S. EPA, Emission Facts: Average Annual Emissions and Fuel Consumption for Passenger Cars and Light Trucks (2000), *available at* http://www.epa.gov/otaq/consumer/f00013.htm.

9. U.S. Energy Info. Admin., Dep't of Energy, U.S. Per Household Vehicle-Miles Traveled, Vehicle Fuel Consumption and Expenditures, 2001, *available at* http://www.eia.doe.gov/emeu/rtecs/nhts_survey/2001/tablefiles/page_a02.html.

10. PATRICIA S. HU & TIMOTHY R. REUSCHER, U.S. DEP'T OF TRANSPORTATION, SUMMARY OF TRAVEL TRENDS, 2001 NATIONAL HOUSEHOLD TRAVEL SURVEY, at 12, 45 (2004), *available at* http://nhts.ornl. gov/2001/pub/STT.pdf; Press Release, U.S. Census Bureau, *New York has Longest Commute to Work in Nation, American Community Survey Finds* (2004), *available at* http://www.census.gov/Press-Release/ www/releases/archives/american_community_survey_acs/001695.html.

11. JOHN DECICCO & FREDA FUNG, ENVIRONMENTAL DEFENSE, GLOBAL WARMING ON THE ROAD: THE CLIMATE IMPACT OF AMERICA'S AUTOMOBILES, iv (2006), http://www.edf.org/documents/5301_Global-warmingontheroad.pdf.

facturer models in 2005 actually declined two years later, while most of the popular Asian cars improved fuel economy during the same timeframe.[12]

Transportation choices have varying, though not surprising, environmental consequences. The eco-hierarchy is easy to explain, as can be seen in Figure D. Foot and pedal power, as well as mass transit, have a far smaller carbon footprint than motor vehicle use.

Figure D: Transportation Emissions

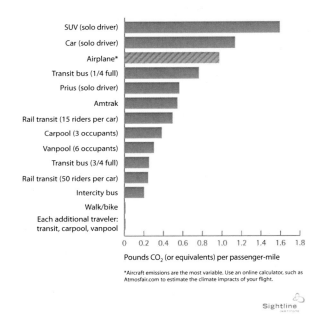

Pounds CO$_2$ (or equivalents) per passenger-mile

*Aircraft emissions are the most variable. Use an online calculator, such as Atmosfair.com to estimate the climate impacts of your flight.

Sightline

Source: Sightline Institute, *How Low-Carbon Can You Go: The Green Travel Ranking*, http://www. sightline.org/maps/charts/climate-CO2byMode.

Meanwhile, Americans are reluctant to give up driving. Unfortunately, the American car fleet is filled with older cars and gas guzzling larger vehicles. Programs to encourage a more eco-friendly fleet lag despite technological advances in hybrid and electric cars and various government incentive programs. Even when and where possible, people typically do not consider carpooling or walking to take care of errands. Overall, the increased carbon footprint at home results

---

12. JACK GILLIS & MARK COOPER, CONSUMER FEDERATION OF AMERICA, STILL STUCK IN NEUTRAL: AMERICA'S CONTINUED FAILURE TO IMPROVE MOTOR VEHICLE FUEL ECONOMY 6 (2007), *available at* http://www.consumerfed.org/pdfs/Still_Stuck.pdf.

from a pattern of individual choices, often made without adequate information or consideration for the resulting environmental impacts.

Individual choice, however, is not the sole cause of the individual aggregate transportation carbon footprint. The dominant American residential landscape is now suburban (see Chapter Five), requiring driving as part of daily life. The available path to work, the local grocery store or a favorite restaurant, for many Americans, is not a subway or a sidewalk, but instead a divided highway and a large parking lot. Furthermore, as reflected in the 2009 federal stimulus package, governments continue to spend far more resources on roads and highways than railroads and mass transit.

Waste & Recycling

"[M]y house is an ecological disaster."[13] Many Americans can make this claim when it comes to trash. Households in the United States throw away lots of trash. Americans in their homes and businesses generate nearly 2,000 pounds of solid waste each year, almost 5 pounds each day.[14] By contrast, only about one and one-half pounds of material per person per day are sent to a recycling facility. While recycling rates have increased, so have the volumes of garbage generated, especially in the United States, the number one producer of trash worldwide.

The majority of household solid waste ends up in landfills. A full two-thirds of the 250 million tons of municipal garbage is trucked to landfills each year, while just one-third is recovered in recycling or composting programs. Now, due to increased costs and municipal budget cuts, homeowners often have even less access to curbside recycling programs than they had a decade earlier.

Residential waste accounts for 55% to 65% of total municipal solid waste generation, with the remainder coming from schools, hospitals, and businesses.[15] Nearly 60% of this waste is easily recyclable and compostable, specifically paper products (34%) and yard trimmings and food scraps (25%). These materials should never get pitched in the first place; yet, only about 50% of paper products are recycled, and local composting programs are in their infancy. Although plastics account for 12% of municipal waste, less than 10% of plastics are recovered for future use. Even municipalities that have recycling programs often collect only No. 1 and No. 2 plastics (and not plastics with other "resin identification code" numbers).[16] Recycling for many types of plastics simply is not available in many places. Consumers are burdened by figuring out what plastics they can recycle

---

13. GEORGE MONBIOT, HEAT: HOW TO STOP THE PLANET BURNING 63 (2006).

14. Aggregate solid waste data available are from the U.S. EPA, Wastes, Non-Hazardous Waste, Municipal Solid Waste, *available at* www.epa.gov/epawaste/nonhaz/municipal/index.htm.

15. U.S. EPA, MUNICIPAL SOLID WASTE GENERATION, RECYCLING AND DISPOSAL IN THE UNITED STATES: FACTS AND FIGURES FOR 2006, *available at* http://www.epa.gov/epawaste/nonhaz/municipal/pubs/msw06.pdf.

16. *See* SPI Material Container Coding System, http://www.plasticsindustry.org/AboutPlastics/content.cfm?ItemNumber=825&navItemNumber=1124.

through their local programs and by the need to drive certain materials to specified recycling facilities.

Americans may be even less aware of the amount of hazardous waste lying around their homes: Americans generate 1.6 million tons of household hazardous waste per year.[17] These products include paints, cleaners, oils, batteries, and pesticides, which can contain corrosive, toxic, and ignitable ingredients. Amazingly, the average home can accumulate nearly 100 pounds of household hazardous waste in its various nooks and crannies, most often in the basement and the garage, under the sink and in the broom closet. Not surprisingly, most manufacturers do not emphasize the hazardous attributes of their products or the need for care in their disposal. For example, most people do not know that spent batteries of all types (including AA) do *not* belong in the kitchen trash can. The environmental benefits of rechargeable batteries are either not recognized or are considered secondary due to the fact that single use batteries are seen as relatively inexpensive. Even efforts to recycle single use batteries can be frustrated because many potential recycling companies in the United States, unlike in Europe, landfill batteries because no law requires them to do otherwise.

Another worrisome trend is the proliferation of so-called e-waste, the mountains of unwanted or obsolete electronics like computers, televisions, and video game systems. Americans discard about 2 to 3 million tons of electronic waste (most of which ends up in landfills) annually, and the problem grew in 2009 when millions of American analog televisions became outdated in the age of digital broadcasting. Even more e-waste remains holed up in storage facilities, attics, and basements across the country. Electronic waste often contains hazardous materials such as heavy metals that can leach through landfills polluting soil and water.

Despite growing acknowledgement of the hazards of e-waste disposal, relatively little e-waste is recycled. Due to the hazardous and complex nature of these products, recycling e-waste can be a time-consuming and expensive process, though some companies still find it quite profitable. Proper management of e-waste has also become of great concern on the environmental justice front, since e-waste from sovereigns like the European Union that ban its exportation ends up illegally in developing countries with weak environmental protection.[18] The poor burn plastic off wires and break parts to obtain metal for sale, releasing harmful toxins and carcinogens into their lungs and the environment. Thus, policy decisions about which behaviors and audiences to target for e-waste management must take into account complex environmental and social justice concerns, as well as seek to establish incentives to modify individual behavior.

The aggregate environmental consequences of home heating infrastructure, fossil-fuel-powered home and garden tools, personal motor vehicles, and solid

---

17. U.S. EPA, Pollution Prevention, *available at* http://www.epa.gov/superfund/students/clas_act/haz-ed/ff_07.htm.

18. Chris Carroll, *High-Tech Trash: Will your Discarded TV or Computer End Up in a Ditch in Ghana?*, NAT'L GEOGRAPHIC, Jan. 2008.

waste are only now becoming fully understood both in terms of impacts and the challenges they present for environmental regulation. As discussed in Part C, the future may bring about additional efforts and approaches to regulate individual behaviors and to create infrastructure that enables behavioral change. In the meantime, as discussed in Part B below, some existing economic realities and legal initiatives may have some effect in moderating the patterns and consequences of these daily activities.

B. Modern Economics and Regulation of Household Behavior

Individuals, households, and consumer products can be subject to direct or indirect environmental regulation. Direct regulation includes "command-and-control" regulation of individual action, setting standards for what individuals may or may not do, or requiring or banning the use of certain products and technologies. Direct regulation might also mandate industrial change for consumer products. Individual behavior can also be indirectly influenced by subsidizing consumer purchasing of certain products or by providing consumers with additional product information.

While individual behavior and its environmental impact go largely unregulated and unnoticed, there are some existing programs advocating everyday environmentalism in the home that have various levels of effectiveness and costs. On the whole, however, public policy does little to promote practices that produce short- or long-term economic *and* environmental gains. Similarly, private individuals, absent public mandates, often fail to change their own behaviors in light of environmental benefits, understandably focusing on their pocketbooks instead.

Before asking what environmental policy should do to instill behavioral changes in the household, one must discuss existing legal regimes and policy, as well as emerging programs, that make consumer and household environmental concerns part of modern day environmental law.

Making the Energy Efficient Home

What does it mean to reduce the household energy footprint? In essence, lowering your individual carbon footprint by reducing fuel use, finding renewable and green sources of energy, and buying products that use less energy. Achieving this goal may mean using the push mower and rake rather than their fossil-fuel-burning counterparts (the riding lawnmower and the leaf blower), possibly installing better windows, insulation or solar panels, or simply purchasing a more energy-efficient small appliance. While behavioral changes may prove reasonably inexpensive (e.g., raking leaves or lowering the thermostat), changes in infrastructure can cost far more (e.g., installing new windows, solar panels, or an urban wind turbine). The following discussion focuses on how government programs already play some role in fostering behavioral changes and installing better infrastructure by (1) supplying information to consumers, (2) setting energy standards for products, and (3) creating economic incentives to encourage households to engage in energy-efficient behavior. Thus, a review of current practices shows how government institutions already influence individual behavior through the tools of information and economic market mechanisms and by targeting appropriate products.

First, governments can and do provide information to promote behavioral change. Begun as a voluntary product-labeling program, the Energy Star program is now a joint effort of EPA and the U.S. Department of Energy to promote the consumer purchase of energy efficient products for the home.[19]

The program helps consumers by allowing the Energy Star label, displayed here, to be placed on energy-efficient products ranging from computer printers to dehumidifiers and by providing tools for assessing the energy efficiency of existing homes and new home designs. The program claims to have prevented 40 million metric tons of greenhouse gases and saved more than $16 billion in utility bills in 2007 alone,[20] with much of this reduction and savings coming from the labeling of consumer products.[21] While the Energy Star program could do a better job of overseeing the label's integrity,[22] by focusing consumer buying power, these labels can increase the market for certain products and product characteristics. Governmental procurement has the same power, with the added ability to influence individual buying behavior through direct mandate or indirectly through increasing market availability.

However, the Energy Star program is designed to cover more than consumer products like appliances and computers. In fact, entire newly built single-family

19. *See* Energy Star, http://www.energystar.gov/.

20. ENERGY STAR, ENERGY STAR OVERVIEW OF 2007 ACHIEVEMENTS, *available at* http://www.energystar.gov/ia/partners/publications/pubdocs/2007%20CPPD%204pg.pdf.

21. Jay P. Kesan & Rajiv C. Shah, *Shaping Code,* 18 HARV. J.L. & TECH 319, 371 (2005) (citing EPA Climate Protection Div., The Power To Make a Difference: ENERGY STAR and Other Partnership Programs, EPA 430-R-00-006 (July 2000)) ("Moreover, the entire Energy Star program for labeling consumer products has prevented emissions of 5.7 million metric tons of carbon equivalent and saved over two billion dollars on energy bills in 1999 alone.").

22. U.S. EPA OFFICE OF INSPECTOR GENERAL, ENERGY STAR PROGRAM CAN STRENGTHEN ITS CONTROLS PROTECTING THE INTEGRITY OF THE LABEL (2007), *available at* http://www.epa.gov/oig/reports/2007/20070801-2007-P-00028.pdf.

homes and multi-family units can become Energy Star qualified. Homes can be built far more efficiently than in the past, and consumers can buy an Energy Star certified home. However, in light of the many homes already in existence, as a policy matter there is concern that too great a focus exists on new construction instead of promoting and improving the efficiency of older homes. Indeed, as of 2008, less than 4% of U.S. housing stock was built within the last four years as the average home dated to 1973.[23]

Information about home energy usage in existing homes can be delivered at multiple points. Existing homes need energy audits to recommend energy saving changes. Energy Star recommends contractors to do audits through its Home Performance program, though many non-affiliated contractors can do energy audits in most local areas. Buyers also can gain information about home energy use upon purchase.[24] Ideally, existing and prospective homeowners would know the potential upgrades needed to help efficiency, as well as fully appreciate their initial costs and their long-term economic and environmental payback. Ironically, as early as 1977, through President Carter's Residential Conservation Service, utility companies and fuel companies were tasked with providing customers highly discounted home energy audits to increase energy conservation.[25] However, just five years later, during the Reagan Administration, the program lapsed and went unfunded.

Armed with information about energy efficiency in appliances and homes, individuals can select more environmentally sound products, look for new homes that better conserve energy, and weatherize existing homes. These informational labeling and information dissemination programs are only the beginning. Public labeling efforts can include carbon footprint labeling for all consumer products (including food as discussed in Chapter Four), and government resources can be used to raise citizen awareness about the aggregate ecological costs of energy inefficiency and the need for greater conservation efforts.

Second, in addition to generating and providing information, governments can create standards, whether voluntary or mandatory, to reduce the household carbon footprint. With more than 80 million residential buildings and with continued population growth, the United States must create "greener" buildings.[26] The U.S. Green Building Council, established in 1993, has created Leadership in Energy Efficient Design standards, commonly known as LEED standards, which have become the standard bearer for environmentally conscious building design in the United States. LEED standards exist not only for new homes but also for commercial developments, healthcare centers, and schools. But, again, LEED finds more influence in the application of standards for designing new homes, and its "LEED for Existing

---

23. U.S. CENSUS BUREAU, AMERICAN HOUSING SURVEY FOR THE UNITED STATES: 2007 at 1 tbl. 1A-1 (2008), *available at* http://www.census.gov/prod/2008pubs/h150-07.pdf.

24. *See, e.g.,* KAN. STAT. ANN. § 66-1228 (2007).

25. J.A. Walker, T.N. Rauh & K. Griffin, *A Review of the Residential Conservation Service Program,* 10 ANNUAL REVIEW OF ENERGY 285 (1985).

26. Edna Sussman, *Reshaping Municipal and County Laws to Foster Green Building, Energy Efficiency, and Renewable Energy,* 16 N.Y.U. ENVTL. L. J. 1, 9 (2008).

Buildings" program is taking time to gain steam.[27] In the meantime, homeowners struggle to practically implement and understand strategies for energy efficiency. Energy audits may inform a homeowner to seal certain doors and windows, but the average American homeowner needs accessible information and lacks the financial resources to hire contractors and consultants to implement many changes. In addition, building owners exhibit reluctance to make large energy efficient investments since they often do not gain the life-cycle benefits of some investments due to relatively brief ownership. In other words, homeowners are often unwilling to take on short-term costs despite long-term gains.

From a policy perspective, many agree that "[t]he most direct and comprehensive way to drive greener building is through changing energy and building codes."[28] This is a way to influence individual behavior through action at the municipal or state government level. Establishing energy-efficiency standards through building codes would force all contractors and builders to understand how to implement energy-efficient building codes and require governments to produce information that homeowners can understand in doing their own home improvements.[29] Boston requires its affordable housing to be LEED certifiable.[30] Frisco, Texas, and Brookhaven, New York, require Energy Star home standards in new buildings.[31] Washington, D.C., requires that many publicly owned and operated buildings that are either newly constructed or substantially modified use Energy Star or LEED certification benchmarks.[32] With some exceptions, the state of Montana requires that all new homes meet the minimum requirements of the 2003 International Energy Conservation Code.[33] And California's Energy

---

27. Amy Cortese, *'Green' Buildings Don't Have to Be New*, N.Y. Times, Jan. 27, 2008.

28. Sussman, *supra* note 26, at 13.

29. *Cf.* Sarah B. Schindler, *Following Industry's LEED: Municipal Adoption of Private Green Building Standards*, 62 Fla. L. Rev. 285 (2010).

30. Patricia M. Burke, Galen Nelson & Wilson Rickerson, *Boston's Green Affordable Housing Program: Challenges and Opportunities*, 11 NYU J. Legis. & Pub. Pol'y 1 (2007/2008).

31. Sussman, *supra* note 26, at 12.

32. D.C. Code § 6-1451.02.

33. Mont. Admin. R. 24.301.160 (2008).

Efficiency Standards for Residential and Nonresidential Buildings, established in 1978, attempt to incorporate new energy efficiency technologies and methods.[34] California reports that its building efficiency standards (along with those for energy efficient appliances) have saved more than $56 billion in electricity and natural gas costs since their inception.[35]

Existing municipal building codes actually may hinder progress. It took more than a year to amend local zoning requirements so that former Vice President Al Gore could install solar panels on his Belle Meade, Tennessee, home. Due to noise and aesthetic concerns, zoning rules had permitted power-generating equipment only to be located on the ground level. Remedial efforts are also underway elsewhere to update outdated ordinances. State statutes in California and New Mexico prohibit any restrictions on the installation or use of a solar home energy system.[36] California went a step further. Consistent with early common law in England and the United States (which prohibited neighbors from blocking the sunlight into their neighbors' homes), California passed its Solar Shade Control Act so homeowners' solar panels could not be blocked.[37] Zoning and building codes could also require certain building geographical orientations as part of broader solar and wind power strategies.

Some municipal programs are quite ambitious. Aspen, Colorado, with an admittedly wealthy citizenry, has adopted a Renewable Energy Mitigation program to increase energy efficiency and meet home energy budgets. Under its municipal code, new homes and substantial renovations require owners to install a two-kilowatt solar photovoltaic system or an equivalent renewable energy system or, alternatively, pay a substantial fee ($5,000 for a home of more than 5,000 square feet, and $10,000 for a home of more than 10,000 square feet).[38] Mitigation fees (up to $100,000) and renewable energy system installation requirements in Aspen can even be higher when energy budgets are exceeded due to snowmelt systems, outdoor pools, and spas.

Comprehensive building and land development ordinances can also include provisions for green and light colored roofs, shade trees, solar hot water heaters, and green landscaping. Efforts like green landscaping can absorb carbon dioxide and reduce the heat island effect caused by heat reflection off hard and dark surfaces like roofs and parking lots. U.S. Forest Service data show the importance of urban forests, which store 700 million tons of carbon nationwide.[39]

To date, government programs generally have not been as focused on greenhouse-gas-generating products used at the home, such as lawn mowers, weed

34. Cal. Title 24, Part 6.

35. Cal. Energy Comm'n, *California's Energy Efficiency Standards for Residential and Nonresidential Buildings*, http://www.energy.ca.gov/title24/.

36. *See* CAL GOV'T CODE § 65850 (2008); N.M. STAT. § 3-18-32 (2008).

37. CAL. PUB. RES. CODE § 25982 (2008).

38. ASPEN & PITKIN COUNTY, CO., ENERGY CONSERVATION CODE § 311.1, 311.2 (2008), http:///www.aspenpitkin/pdfs/depts/7/Chapter3.pdf.

39. U.S.D.A. National Urban Forest Data Summary Statistics, http://www.fs.fed.us/ne/syracuse/Data/Nation/data_nation.htm.

whackers, and other tools found in the garage and shed. Fossil-fueled household tools are not subject to direct standards under the federal Clean Air Act, though states are free to regulate them in their own plans to meet national air quality standards. Like building design standards, emission or design standards can be created for lawn mowers and tractors, chain saws, blowers, and trimmers to lower their emissions. The danger in creating design standards, however, is that better designs and technologies may evolve over time, and the wide array of products available for household use would create administrative burdens for determining and enforcing design standards. While some minimal exhaust standards are in place, little direct regulation of greenhouse-gas-emitting household tools has taken place; instead, all levels of government have chosen to advise citizens how best to reduce their carbon footprint, usually focusing on lighting and energy-efficient appliances rather than on a broad array of home maintenance equipment.

However, leaf blowers are one household tool that has received some regulatory attention. They produce significant emissions of greenhouse gases and substantial noise, in exchange for relatively minor aesthetic value. Given the concerns over leaf blowers, the California Air Resources Board filed a report summarizing their negative health and environmental impacts.[40] Many states and cities are limiting their use during ozone action days, prohibiting their use for blowing debris into public roadways, and demanding their emissions conform to specific health standards.

In addition to using tools such as information dissemination and standard setting, governments can increase energy efficiency in the home and lower greenhouse gas emissions by creating economic markets for emissions and establishing both disincentives and incentives to limit fossil-fuel-burning devices in the home. Options include cap-and-trade programs, taxes, and tax credits. In a cap-and-trade program, an emission level is set or capped (and may be lowered over time), and emissions permits (totaling the amount of emissions under the cap) are distributed or auctioned off. This market solution attempts to monetize the proper value of polluting and creates a market for permits whereby individuals who limit their emissions will make money either by producing more efficiently or selling off excess permits. A cap-and-trade system currently is used in the U.S. Acid Rain Program for trading sulfur dioxide emissions permits and has been considered as an option for reducing greenhouse gas emissions in the United States. As discussed previously, states can develop their own statewide or regional trading systems, and these systems potentially could also cover emissions-producing products in the home.

In 1998 California's Bay Area Air Quality Management District proposed making carbon-emitting household tools part of an existing emission trading system. Under the plan, industry would help take out of service high-emitting farm, lawn, garden, utility, and construction equipment to use their emissions as credit

---

40. CAL. AIR RES. BD., A REPORT TO THE CALIFORNIA LEGISLATURE ON THE POTENTIAL HEALTH AND ENVIRONMENTAL IMPACTS OF LEAF BLOWERS (2000), *available at* http://www.arb.ca.gov/msprog/leafblow/leafblow.htm.

(known as an "offset") for other industrial emissions.[41] The final rule abandoned these offsets due to community concerns that offsets would increase pollution at a specific local source, in addition to agency concerns about requiring too many complicated offset rules. As a policy and implementation matter, another problem with addressing household sources through offsets rather than direct regulation is that offsets provide incentives for fraud by people who would claim credits for decommissioning units not actually in use.

Individual use of gas-powered tools can also be curbed through increased taxes or by providing tax credits or rebates. To encourage hand-powered mowers and cleaner lawn mowers, many states and regions have instituted lawn mower buy-back programs, offering citizens a rebate toward the purchase of a push mower or electric mower in exchange for turning in an old gas-powered lawn mower.[42] Financial incentives are also provided for installing energy efficient infrastructure in the home. For example, Maine provides a rebate for the installation of solar panels in the home.[43] The federal Energy Policy Act of 2005 provided tax credits for home efficiency improvements such as windows, doors, roofs, solar panels, and insulation in residential buildings. Under the American Recovery and Reinvestment Act of 2009, consumers who purchase and install specific products, such as energy-efficient windows, insulation, doors, roofs, and heating and cooling equipment in existing homes, can receive a tax credit for 30% of the cost, up to $1,500 for improvements "placed in service" starting January 1, 2009, through December 31, 2010.[44]

Thus, various government programs already exist that effectively influence individual behavior and promote home energy efficiency by providing consumer information; setting energy, building, and technology requirements; and using market and economic mechanisms. As discussed in the next section, in order to mitigate the environmental footprint of the home, government policy, often through legislation, also seeks to influence whether individuals can afford more energy efficient vehicles.

Affording the Hybrid Car

A number of government programs address the concern that the nation's dependence on oil is both costly at the gas pump and costly to the environment. Economic incentives remain an option in the United States to promote individual energy conservation in transportation choices. The federal government has provided tax deductions and tax credits for lesser polluting vehicles, though the dollar amounts are somewhat limited and face continual expiration. Individuals seeking financial

---

41. Bay Area Air Quality Management District, Public Workshop Notice, Proposed Regulation 2, Permits, Rule 9; Interchangeable Emission Reduction Credits (Jan. 27, 1998); *see also* CAL. CODE REGS. §§ 91500 et seq.
42. *See* U.S. EPA, *Lawn Mower Buyback Program Case Study*, http://www.epa.gov/air/recipes/mowers.html.
43. *See* ME. REV. STAT. ANN. tit. 35-A § 3211-C (2008); ME. CODE. R. 65-407-930 (2008).
44. U.S. Dep't of Energy, Consumer Energy Tax Incentives, http://www.energy.gov/taxbreaks.htm.

support for making environmentally friendly transportation choices, such as buying hybrid or alternative fuel vehicles, must try to understand complicated Internal Revenue Service rules.

The Energy Policy Act of 2005 provided a credit for taxpayers who purchased energy efficient and alternative fuel vehicles such as hybrids. The advantage of tax credits is that the credit is subtracted directly from the total amount of federal tax owed. However, under this program, hybrid car tax credits started to phase out and decrease in amount soon after 60,000 qualified manufacturers' vehicles were sold. Thus, tax credits ran out for the most popular hybrid cars. Federal environmental and tax policy regularly exhibit such irony. For example, the federal government encourages driving rather than using mass transit by providing $36 billion a year in parking subsidies, allowing employers a tax deduction for providing their employees with free or discounted parking as a business expense.[45]

Creating financial incentives to encourage the purchase of more fuel-efficient vehicles has been a primary policy mechanism for states to reduce individual transportation carbon footprints. Numerous states provide income tax credits, sales tax exemptions, and rebates for people who buy hybrid or alternative fuel vehicles.[46] To encourage the purchase of hybrid vehicles, states and municipalities also permit low-emission vehicles to use carpool lanes regardless of the number of passengers in the vehicle[47] and offer free or discounted parking for hybrid vehicles.[48] Even insurance companies have attempted to influence individual procurement power by providing auto insurance discounts for hybrid cars.

Yet, as a policy matter, an exclusive focus on improving personal vehicle technology would be misplaced. If walking, biking, jogging, or kayaking to the office, grocery store, or school is not an option and use of a motor vehicle is a must, then mass transit buses and trains or carpooling should be the next option. Unfortunately, across the nation, municipal and regional transportation systems are in financial distress. The current national transportation system is a patchwork model with significant economic, environmental, and organizational inefficiencies. Yet, the creation of a sustainable and coordinated national transportation system and urban train systems, apart from the interstate highway system, has been impeded by a

---

45. Oliver A. Pollard, III, *Smart Growth and Sustainable Transportation: Can We Get There From Here?*, 29 FORDHAM URB. L.J. 1529 (2002).

46. COLO. REV. STAT. ANN. § 39-22-516 (2008); CONN. GEN. STAT. ANN. § 12-412 (2008); Illinois Environmental Protection Agency, Illinois Green Reward Program, http://www.illinoisgreenfleets.org/ (last visited July 14, 2009); LA. REV. STAT. ANN. §§ 47:38, 47:287 (2008); N.M. STAT. ANN. 7-14-6 (2008); OR. REV. STAT. ANN. 316.116, 469.160 to 469.180, 801.375 (2008); WASH. REV. CODE ANN. § 82.08.809, 82.08.813 (2008).

47. AZ. REV. STAT. 28-2416, 28-737B, and Executive Order No. 2007-03, 2007; COLO. REV. STAT. 42-4-1012; FL. STAT. 316.0741; UTAH CODE 41-6a-702, 63-55-241.

48. Cities with such discounts include Los Angeles, Santa Monica, and San Jose, California; Manitou Springs, Colorado; New Haven, Connecticut; Baltimore, Maryland; Ferndale, Michigan; San Antonio, Texas; and Salt Lake City, Utah. *See* U.S. Dep't of Energy, List of State and Federal Incentives and Laws for Hybrid and Alternative Fuel Vehicles, http://www.afdc.energy.gov/afdc/incentives_laws.html.

lack of resources and political foresight to adapt to modern transit needs, as well as competing recommendations for the creation of such a system.[49]

These challenges have only been heightened by America's $787 billion economic stimulus and recovery package, formally known as the American Recovery and Reinvestment Act of 2009.[50] The Act provides monies for promoting energy efficiency and renewing the nation's transportation systems. However, despite funds for hybrid and electric vehicles and rail service, the Act still allocates far more money for roads and highways. For example, my home state of Vermont will spend 20 times more stimulus money on highways than on mass transit.[51] Similarly, of the $529 million in total stimulus money rewarded to my birth state of Wisconsin, nearly 20% will be spent on a single highway project, the reconstruction and expansion of Interstate 94.[52] Across the country, nearly four times more money will be spent on roads and bridges than rail service, $28 billion versus $8 billion in the first installment. The disparity is striking. It means that the infrastructure of sprawl will persist, and individual energy consumption and the risk of climate change are being hedged against the creation of carbon free automobile technology.

Regulating the Trash

Municipalities have long overseen solid waste removal, though this was not always the case. In the past, household waste was sorted and reused, with organic scraps used as fertilizer and animal feed. With early industrialization, the nature of waste disposal changed as city streets turned to filth and people burned garbage. Modern sanitation systems eventually evolved. Now, household waste moves from trashcan to curb to transfer station in preparation for a landfill or incinerator, or instead to a material recovery facility to sort items for recycling. With increased wealth and consumer spending, more is thrown away now than ever before.

Waste management programs have grown more complex in response. Some programs now include financial *disincentives* to produce garbage with a goal of waste reduction in mind, and many local governments have set up curbside recycling programs that vary in scope and complexity. Generally, many localities also rely on state and national legislation to address regulation of toxic and electronic waste, although some local programs have tackled these issues as well. Thus, a review of existing regulatory regimes demonstrates that current waste management policies consider (1) economic tools, (2) the effectiveness of local efforts, and (3) the appropriate level of government action.

---

49. *Compare* F. Kaid Benfield, *Running on Empty: The Case for a Sustainable National Transportation System*, 25 ENVTL. L. 651 (1995), *with* Cynthia J. McNabb, *Viability of a Sustainable and Feasible National Transportation System*, 26 TRANSP. L. J. 133 (1998).

50. One can find more information about The American Recovery and Reinvestment Act and news releases about its expenditures at Recovery.gov.

51. Vermont Agency of Transportation, *American Recovery & Reinvestment Act Transportation Stimulus*, online at http://apps.vtrans.vermont.gov/stimulus/ ("Vermont will receive some $125 million in highway and bridge money, as well as an additional $5.6 million in public transportation funding.").

52. Tom Held, *I-94 Gets Big Share of Stimulus*, MILWAUKEE JOURNAL SENTINEL, Mar. 3, 2009.

Municipal solid waste programs, while sending significant amounts of garbage to landfills, have helped stop individuals from burning trash and littering the streets, which results in disease and odor. The "backyard burning" of trash, historically common in rural communities and used to avoid paying waste collection fees, harms both human and environmental health by releasing dioxins, particulate matter, carbon monoxide, and nitrogen oxides into the air.[53] With few exceptions, most states and municipalities ban the outdoor burning of garbage, and weekly garbage pickup is the norm for most Americans.

Landfill waste, consequently, has proliferated. Governments, domestic and foreign, have sought to limit the volume of solid waste entering landfills through economic incentives, recycling programs, and composting initiatives; they have also attempted to regulate the disposal of harmful and hazardous substances such as plastic bags, car tires, oil, and batteries. States and municipalities have further developed programs designed to decrease consumption and promote the purchase of items with less packaging. One such plan adopted by communities is the U.S. Environmental Protection Agency's (EPA) Pay-As-You-Throw (PAYT) program, where residences are charged by the can, bag, or, less commonly, pound of garbage.[54] As seen in Figure E, some states have a significant number of PAYT communities.

These programs can reduce waste but also can create administrative burdens and require capital investments. In addition, potential concerns arise about illegal roadside dumping and the inability of poor households to pay. To successfully implement PAYT, localities must design an appropriate system in light of population, geography, and existing infrastructure. Related choices include whether to charge on the basis of weight or volume, how to price and bill, and what containers to use (bins, carts, pre-paid bags, or personal bags or cans with pre-paid tags or stickers). Regardless of program design, residents still need education and must change behavior to ensure effectiveness.

Perhaps the most clear-cut regulatory method to reduce landfill waste is a disposal ban on certain products.[55] For example, Nova Scotia, Canada, bans the following materials from landfills: electronics, corrugated cardboard, newsprint, used tires, auto lead-acid batteries, leaf and yard waste, post-consumer paint products, automotive antifreeze, low-density plastic bags and packaging, compostable organic material, redeemable beverage containers, and containers made from steel, tin, glass, and No. 2 plastic.[56] China and San Francisco, among other countries and

53. EPA provides information about backyard burning at http://www.epa.gov/msw/backyard/.
54. Information on the EPA's PAYT program is available at http://www.epa.gov/epaoswer/non-hw/payt/intro.htm.
55. *See, e.g.,* AZ. REV. STAT. ANN. §§ 44-1304, 44-1322, 49-803 (vehicle tire, lead-acid battery, and oil landfill disposal bans); IDAHO CODE ANN. §§ 6503, 6507 (disposal ban of tires); CONN. GEN. STAT. § 22a-208v (barring disposal of grass clippings); ME. STATE PLANNING OFFICE, 2006 MAINE TOWNS WITH WASTE BANS, http://mainegov-images.informe.org/spo/recycle/docs/data/2006data/2006mainetownswithwastebans.pdf.
56. Province of Nova Scotia, Materials Banned from Disposal Sites in Nova Scotia, http://www.

Figure E: United States Pay-As-You-Throw Communities

Pay-As-You-Throw at a Glance

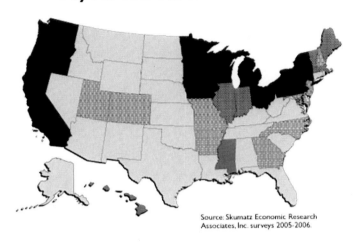

Source: Skumatz Economic Research
Associates, Inc. surveys 2005-2006.

Number of Communities with Pay-As-You-Throw

| 0 | 1-25 | 26-100 | 101-200 | 200+ |

Source: U.S. EPA, *Pay-As-You-Throw*, http://www.epa.gov/epaoswer/non-hw/payt/06comm.htm.

cities, have enacted bans on free plastic bags at stores (though enforcement in China has been variable at best),[57] and some stores like Whole Foods Market shifted to using only paper bags (though any legislation regulating grocery bags based on product material may be of little environmental value[58]). Recycling programs must supplement any disposal ban, for something must be done with the used materials.

Though more than 9,000 municipal curbside recycling programs existed in 2001, increasing rapidly from about 1,000 programs in 1988, curbside collection programs are now declining for financial reasons.[59] State governments often require municipalities to implement recycling and provide educational support. For example, Connecticut's Department of Environmental Protection provides extensive information on how to recycle consumer and household goods.[60] The

gov.ns.ca/nse/waste/banned.asp.
    57. Ian Urbina, *Pressure Builds to Ban Plastic Bags in Stores,* NY TIMES, July 24, 2007; Anthony Kuhn, *China Bans Free Plastic Bags* (NPR Radio Broadcast, Jan. 13, 2008).
    58. ULS REPORT, REVIEW OF LIFE CYCLE DATA RELATING TO DISPOSABLE, COMPOSTABLE, BIODEGRADABLE, AND REUSABLE GROCERY BAGS (June 2007).
    59. Phil Simmons et al., *The State of Garbage in America,* 4 BIOCYCLE 26 (2006).
    60. Conn. Dep't of Environmental Protection, Reduce/Reuse/Recycle at Home, http://www.ct.gov/dep/cwp/view.asp?a=2714&q=324852&depNav_GID=1645&depNav=|.

state, through municipal waste facilities, requires recycling of paper products, glass, scrap metal, rechargeable batteries, car batteries, and waste oil, as well as composting of leaves.[61] States have developed old tire collections and deposits on beverage containers to increase recycling.[62]

While recycling keeps waste out of landfills and allows for reuse of materials that otherwise would be taken from virgin sources, recycling is not a complete solution due to the financial and environmental costs of recycling itself. It takes a lot of energy to recycle, from the diesel-fueled collection trucks to the material recovery facilities, and recycling quality depends on significant market forces. People require the proper incentives to recycle, and markets must exist for the materials. No market for glass exists because glass is too cheap to make; and despite the obvious ability and ease in recycling paper, 50% of all paper ends up in landfills.[63] Finally, even the best-conceived recycling projects cannot keep up with the current rate of consumption and disposal. Ultimately, people must reduce consumption and, in turn, waste generation.

Four forms of household waste are particularly troubling, making decreased waste generation and increased recycling imperative—household hazardous waste, e-waste, organic waste suitable for composting, and plastics, especially from packaging. Many individuals are simply not aware of the impact of these waste streams. For example, during an Earth Day lecture to middle school students in 2008, when asked where they put their dead batteries, nearly every student said in the garbage can. The students did not realize that landfilling poses an environmental hazard since batteries contain hazardous materials including lead, mercury, and cadmium.

To achieve recycling goals for hazardous or any other waste, informational resources and convenient recycling points must exist so consumers know both that they should recycle and where to recycle. The U.S. Battery Management Act, largely enforced against manufacturers and sellers in an effort to change consumer behavior, requires that batteries have clear labeling so consumers know to recycle some battery types and mandates that some batteries be easily removable for recycling purposes.[64] The effectiveness of labeling for batteries seems questionable, while convenient and high visibility drop-off locations would provide the necessary and more effective tandem. By comparison, the European Union's directive on batteries is much more aggressive; it requires member countries to take necessary measures (including economic instruments) to promote and maximize separate waste collections and prevent batteries from being thrown away as unsorted municipal waste.[65] This mandate is accompanied by binding standards requiring collection rates of at least 25% and 45% by 2012 and 2016, respectively.

---

61. *See, e.g.,* CONN. GEN. STAT. § 22a-256a, 22a-241b-1 to 22a-241b-4.

62. *See, e.g.,* Iowa DNR Waste Management, Leave the Old When Buying New - Retire Your Tires, http://www.iowadnr.com/waste/recycling/tires/retire.html; IOWA CODE § 455C (bottle deposit system).

63. HEATHER ROGERS, GONE TOMORROW: THE HIDDEN LIFE OF GARBAGE 6-7 (2005).

64. 42 U.S.C. § 14301 et seq.

65. Council Directive 2006/66 2006 O.J. (L266) 1 (EC).

The state of California has taken the approach of promoting activity at the local level by offering grants to municipalities to educate citizens about and establish collection points for household hazardous waste.[66] Funded by these grants, Santa Clara County, in northern California, recruited three dozen retail stores and community centers to provide free collection of batteries and fluorescent lighting. The city of Los Angeles helped establish oil filter collection and exchange events at Kragen auto parts stores within the city limits. Within one year, collection of used oil filters in the city nearly tripled from 4,250 to more than 12,000, resulting in the recycling of 18,300 pounds of steel and 11,700 pounds of oil. Another convenience commonly available is municipal drop-off points where residents can leave household hazardous waste free of charge. Unfortunately, many residents are not aware of the existence or locations of these centers, and many others simply would not make it a priority to collect and deposit household hazardous waste such as oil, batteries, electronics, and paints in the first place.

Jurisdictions are still struggling to find effective approaches to address the comparatively new phenomenon of e-waste, which has been brought on by broad and rapid progress in modern technologies. Efforts to minimize e-waste, i.e., used electronics, have proliferated, with the European Union's efforts proving to be an ambitious model. The EU has banned hazardous substances in most electronic equipment and established collection, recycling, and recovery goals for electronics.[67] Under the EU e-waste directive, manufacturers bear responsibility for implementation through take-back programs. The United Nations, while lacking any binding authority to regulate e-waste, has created StEP, an initiative of various UN organizations with the overall aim to "solve the e-waste problem."[68] The initiative employs five task forces (policy and legislation, redesign, reuse, recycle, and capacity-building and public awareness) and promotes publications and projects to achieve its aim.

In the United States, household e-waste is not regulated at the federal level. The Resource Conservation and Recovery Act (RCRA) gives the EPA authority to regulate hazardous waste from "cradle-to-grave" (i.e., from production to use to disposal). However, RCRA allows household e-waste disposal to escape regulation, and concerns exist that applying RCRA to e-waste would be "overly burdensome and most likely cost prohibitive to the administration."[69]

66. *See* Cal. Integrated Waste Management Bd., Household Hazardous Waste Discretionary Grant Program, http://205.225.229.1/HHW/Grants/; CAL. RES. CODE § 47200 (2008).
67. Council Directive 2002/95 2002 O.J. (L37) 19 (EC) (also known as the Restriction of the Use of Certain Hazardous Substances ("RoHS")); Council Directive 2002/96 2002 O.J. (L37) 24 (EC) (Waste Electrical and Electronic Equipment (WEEE) Directive).
68. Solving the E-Waste Problem, http://www.step-initiative.org/ (last visited July 14, 2009).
69. 40 C.F.R. § 261.4(b)(1) (2008); 45 Fed. Reg. 33,084, 33,099 (May 19, 1980) (codified at 40 C.F.R. pt. 261); Heather L. Drayton, *Economics of Electronic Waste Disposal Regulations*, 36 HOFSTRA L. REV. 149, 163 (2007).

In the absence of federal e-waste policy, many states already have or currently are considering bans and recycling programs for electronic equipment.[70] State programs include labeling initiatives, manufacturer take-back requirements, and landfill bans. For example, Maine and Washington State have modeled their programs after the EU, requiring extended producer responsibility so that manufacturers pay for the recycling costs of e-waste collected by localities.[71] In contrast to consumer fee programs like California's, these e-waste policies are free to residents, businesses, schools, and government entities. California's Electronic Waste Recycling Act of 2003 utilizes an advance recovery fee whereby consumers pay for the disposal or recycling cost at time of purchase.[72] Japan maintains a similar program.[73] The effectiveness of these programs is evidenced by the much higher rates of recycling achieved in California and Japan.[74]

Overall, Americans recycle only 10% to 15% of their e-waste[75] and one-third of recyclable municipal solid waste.[76] Individuals face many impediments to improving the overall recycling rate: unreliable municipal recycling programs, confusion over what to recycle and how to dispose of certain items properly, and inconvenient drop-off locations and disposal fees. However, these are exactly the types of problems potentially better addressed by local government action, providing greater consumer education and targeting specific types of waste. Industry fears the costs of eco-friendly product research and design, and the potentially costly changes in existing infrastructure. Any successful waste reduction and recycling program, whether for e-waste, food containers, or hazardous waste, must decrease barriers

---

70. States with WEEE-type legislation include California, Connecticut, Illinois, Maine, Maryland, Massachusetts, Minnesota, Oregon, Rhode Island, Texas, Vermont, Virginia, and Washington.

71. ME. REV. STAT. ANN. tit. 38 § 1610; WASH. REV. CODE ANN. § 70.95N.030.

72. CAL. PUB. RES. CODE § 42464.

73. Under Japan's Home Appliance Recycling Law, consumers pay recycling fees (from Yen 2,500 to nearly Yen 5,000) to retailers, who must pass on the used appliance and the fees to the manufacturers to recycle. *A Stronger Recycling System*, JAPAN TIMES, Jan. 8, 2008.

74. Cal. Integrated Waste Management Bd., Disposal and Diversion Rate Statistics (2009), http://www.ciwmb.ca.gov/LGCentral/Rates/default.htm ("Californians diverted more than 50 million tons of solid waste away from landfills and into recycling, composting and transformation programs in 2006, for an estimated statewide diversion rate of 54 percent."); JAMES I. DAVEN & ROBERT N. KLEIN, PROGRESS IN WASTE MANAGEMENT RESEARCH 40 (2008) ("Japan recycles 65% of its MSW [municipal solid waste] into usable products and 40% of its waste paper into high quality paper."); Japan Ministry of Foreign Affairs, Kids Web Japan, Explore Japan: Protecting the Environment, http://web-japan.org/kidsweb/explore/environment/q4.html ("According to statistics for fiscal 2004, 87.1% of steel cans were recycled, as were 86.1% of aluminum cans and 90.7% of glass bottles. Also, 68.5% of newspapers and other used paper were recycled in 2004. Recycling of plastic bottles has also started. 46.4% of PET bottles were recycled in fiscal 2004 . . . ."); R.E. HESTER & ROY M. HARRISON, ELECTRONIC WASTE MANAGEMENT 91 (2008) ("Japan was one of the first countries to legislate for e-waste recycling through the Home Appliances Recycling Law (HARL), enacted in 2001. HARL covers only the four largest groups of appliances (TVs/monitors, refrigeration equipment, air-conditioning equipment and washing machines); recycling rates in Japan are between 64 and 84% depending on the category of waste.").

75. Drayton, *supra* note 69, at 153.

76. U.S. EPA, MUNICIPAL SOLID WASTE GENERATION, RECYCLING AND DISPOSAL IN THE UNITED STATES: FACTS AND FIGURES FOR 2007, http://www.epa.gov/epawaste/nonhaz/municipal/pubs/msw07-rpt.pdf.

for individuals to recycle and provide incentives for manufacturers to improve products and their packaging.

On the one hand, while consumer fee models force individuals to pay disposal or recycling costs in the retail price, these models may reduce incentives for industry to improve design. On the other hand, consumer fee programs or manufacturer take-back programs are good for recycling businesses that receive state or manufacturer payment and for second-hand component dealers receiving reusable and re-saleable materials. These recycling businesses hold recycling events and create convenient drop-off locations to lower costs for consumers. Even the U.S. Postal Service has attempted to decrease the daily costs of household environmentalism by establishing a pilot program that allows customers to recycle small electronics and inkjet cartridges by mailing them free of charge. Promoting a steady, lower cost flow of recyclable materials also has the benefit of creating a more robust domestic market for recycling.

Initial entrance into the recycling market is expensive. Currently, landfill disposal costs less, and processing e-waste requires difficult disassembly and intensive labor. Many recycling companies prosper financially by hiring cheap labor in countries with few environmental laws and worker safety regulations. In addition to the carbon footprint of shipping and export, this pattern creates a potential trade-off between waste reduction and social justice—recycling mandates of e-waste may result in its shipment overseas to developing countries. Exporting garbage, including e-waste and its accompanying contaminants, is now big business, garnering revenues of more than $1 billion.[77]

By comparison, programs to promote effective management of organic wastes are still in their infancy in the United States. The general practice is continued municipal disposal of organic waste, supplemented by the existence of relatively limited state and local composting programs. Many American states have, to varying degrees, educational and assistance programs to promote composting,[78] but these programs generally do not have comprehensive bans on throwing away compostable and biodegradable organic food and yard waste. Like recycling programs, the number of yard trimming composting sites in the United States has increased dramatically since the late 1980s.[79] Fortunately, large-scale composting projects also have increased, but such projects have maintained low numbers overall due to the challenges of keeping and processing food waste.

---

77. ROGERS, *supra* note 63, at 9.

78. For example, Iowa, Maine, and Georgia have educational programs promoting composting and mulching as key to waste reduction. Iowa DNR Waste Management, Organics and Composting, http://www.iowadnr.com/waste/recycling/organics/index.html; Maine State Planning Office, Waste Management and Recycling Program, http://www.maine.gov/spo/recycle/mainerecycles/composting.htm; Georgia Department of Community Affairs Home Composting Program, Composting at Home in Georgia, http://www.dca.state.ga.us/development/EnvironmentalManagement/programs/downloads/Composting.pdf.

79. Simmons, BIOCYCLE, *supra* note 59.

The EU has sought better results, requiring member states to reduce the amount of biodegradable waste that is landfilled to 35% of 1995 levels by 2016.[80] Composting can play a major role in this effort, and Europe has many voluntary composting programs at the local level.[81] The success of composting programs depends upon picking the correct waste to collect (usually kitchen and garden waste), providing an effective sorting system, having an adequate public relations and educational campaign, and determining whether the actual composting should happen in the home, in the neighborhood or community, or in a centralized municipal facility.

Finally, plastics, particularly those from packaging, potentially pose the most problems of all household wastes. Referred to as "Satan's Resin,"[82] plastics do not degrade, are filled with toxins, and will outlive any readers of this book. In the 1950s, "the accumulated scientific breakthroughs of two massive world wars finally hit civilian life in full force,"[83] resulting in a rapid increase in plastics used for food packaging and housewares. Nearly two decades later, a new ethic emerged when industry finally persuaded consumers that plastics were "disposable."

Plastics are inextricably linked to the general rise of disposable goods. Many use plastic milk jugs rather than reusable glass bottles, plastic cups rather than glass mugs, and individually wrapped foodstuffs rather than bulk items. With this change, plastics have filled landfills and our natural environment—the ocean contains, by mass, more plastic than plankton.[84]

Opportunities exist to turn back the clock on plastics. For example, one possibility would be to increase plastic bottle deposits with an eye toward returning to refillable glass bottle programs, as was the norm in the United States and remains so in Germany under its Packaging Ordinance, and specifically promote the purchase of refillable milk bottles. These choices have real economic consequences, as non-refillables allow larger, centralized and non-local production facilities, while refillables require retailers to meet redemption, sorting, and storage demands. Another policy dilemma is posed by the challenge of promoting bulk purchases and items with less packaging over individually wrapped personal containers. The CEO of Terracycle, a company that uses waste products to make finished retail products, has advocated ending single-use packaging, standardizing packaging and taxing non-standardized packaging, and creating a "bottle bill" for all packaging so packaging would be returned to the manufacturer, creating incentives to reduce or recycle packaging.

While existing law and other public policy measures influence the household waste and carbon footprint, future challenges exist in directly addressing the relationship between individual behavior and environmental harm. Implementing

---

80. Council Directive 1999/31 1999 O.J. (L182) (EC).

81. The following contains some "success stories" of voluntary composting programs at the local level: http://ec.europa.eu/environment/waste/publications/pdf/compost_en.pdf.

82. ELIZABETH ROYTE, GARBAGE LAND: ON THE SECRET TRAIL OF TRASH 176 (2005).

83. ROGERS, *supra* note 63, at 103.

84. C.J. Moore, S.L. Moore, M.K. Leecaster & S.B. Weisberg, *A Comparison of Plastic and Plankton in the North Pacific Central Gyre*, 42 MARINE POLLUTION BULL. 1297 (Dec. 2001).

everyday environmentalism at home requires understanding the lesser-known and aggregate consequences of consumer choice as discussed earlier in Part A. It also necessitates activating eco-friendly social and cultural norms through evolving legal systems and community initiatives.

C. Everyday Environmentalism at Home

The United Nations' Agenda 21 and the Rio Declaration on the Environment recognize the unsustainable consumption levels of industrialized nations and the importance of an informed and active society in limiting consumption.[85] However, while these United Nations actions, especially Agenda 21,[86] have suggested implementation goals for countries, little progress has been made in changing the overall trends of specific individual behavior patterns. Developing policies and approaches to improve activities and choices made in the home may be a key to promoting sustainable consumption and everyday environmentalism, helping to alter the impact of individual action on the natural environment. The following discussion considers what public policy can do to promote changes in individual behavior and household infrastructure.

Public awareness, government action, information dissemination, market incentives, targeted audiences, and community initiatives are the six broad categories of decision-making tools that may be useful in designing policy to influence individual behavior, as discussed in the Introduction. Some of these tools are already being used and are having some effect in existing policy programs. Going forward, the primary avenues to change the individual carbon and waste footprint appear to be through (1) direct government regulatory techniques, specifically focusing on economic tools that can shift consumer choice and standard-setting where consumers lack the resources to initiate change, and (2) the development of eco-friendly social and cultural norms at the community level, especially through information generation and dissemination.

Regulatory techniques can include bans, standards for pollution levels or product performance, market-based and economic incentives, and information disclosures,[87] but determining the relative effectiveness of regulatory options becomes far more complicated when seeking to influence the divergent preferences and responses of individual actors.

> Recognition that everyday economic activities have negative environmental impacts could revolutionize the way we approach environmental problems, both philosophically and managerially. Traditional policy measures—technology-based, centralized,

---

85. JOHN DERNBACH, STUMBLING TOWARDS SUSTAINABILITY 21 (2002).

86. U.N. CONF. ON ENV'T AND DEV., AGENDA 21, U.N. Doc. A/CONF.151/6/Rev. 1 (1992), *reprinted in* 31 I.L.M. 881 (1992), *available at* http://www.un.org/esa/dsd/agenda21/.

87. Kesan & Shah, *supra* note 21, at 327.

command-and-control regulation on large, stationary, "point" sources—are poorly suited for managing reductions from diffuse sources of pollution.[88]

The challenge is identifying which environmental planning and policy mechanisms will "address the cumulative effect of many small, dispersed, and ubiquitous emission sources that could have global impact."[89] As opposed to traditional centralized environmental law, direct government regulation should focus on using those regulatory tools that can reach a diffuse market (e.g., carbon tax, informational labeling) or address circumstances where consumers lack appropriate incentives or ability to change infrastructure (e.g., emissions standards, housing codes, recycling facilities). Fortunately, given the challenges of regulating individual behavior, support is growing for efforts to activate social and cultural norms for environmentally friendly behaviors to deal with the "democratization of pollution sources"[90] in the home and elsewhere in daily life.

Government Action & Economics

Direct government regulation should be pursued both where the regulation can reach diffuse markets through economic inducements or disincentives and where consumers lack appropriate incentives or resources to change existing infrastructure. The traditional avenue for regulating environmental harm through directly limiting emissions and setting design standards will remain necessary since individuals need efficient consumer goods in order to exert their procurement power. The key will be for old regulatory ideas, like taxes and economic subsidies, to take new form.

The true environmental costs of household consumption are not revealed quickly. An option is to make these costs immediate—a carbon tax for individuals. During his Nobel Prize speech, Al Gore stated:

> And most important of all, we need to put a price on carbon—with a CO_2 tax that is then rebated back to the people, progressively, according to the laws of each nation, in ways that shift the burden of taxation from employment to pollution. This is by far the most effective and simplest way to accelerate solutions to this crisis.[91]

Despite its flexibility and potential for immediate effect, the carbon tax, even at the industrial level and especially at the individual level, is unpopular among many politicians. Yet, an individual carbon tax, implemented through an increased gasoline tax and through home utility bills coupled with rebate coupons or tax credits for the poor, would go a long way toward changing consumer behavior. In 2006 Boulder, Colorado, became the first U.S. city to impose such an energy tax

---

88. Timothy P. Duane, *Environmental Planning and Policy in a Post-Rio World*, 7 BERKELEY PLAN-NING J. 27, 31 (1992).

89. *Id.* at 27.

90. *Id.*

91. Al Gore, Speech on Acceptance of Nobel Peace Prize (Dec. 10, 2007).

on its citizens' municipal utility bill. The average household monthly bill increased by only $1.33.

Furthermore, not all economic incentives need to be negative. Positive subsidies also are an option, and they can effectively harness consumer purchasing power to lower the carbon footprint from small-ticket items. For example, in Montpelier, Vermont, through a subsidy designed by the non-profit group "Efficiency Vermont," people can purchase a compact fluorescent light bulb for as little as 99¢ at the local hardware store.

Consumer decision-making could be further eased with the creation of even more rigorous energy efficiency standards for appliances, tools, and homes. For example, EPA has recently promulgated emission standards for small engines.[92] In addition, the Department of Energy is moving to create dramatically improved energy efficiency standards for appliances and to meet required revision deadlines from both the Energy Policy and Conservation Act of 1975 and more recent legislation that had not previously been met.[93] In light of the vast number of fossil-fuel-powered appliances and tools in the home, defining and enforcing emissions standards for an enormous number of household items may prove costly and burdensome, but the effectiveness of such regulation will need to be evaluated.

The need for standard setting by government entities may even be more compelling in areas where buyers cannot make the necessary choices. For example, renters do not install appliances, and buyers of existing homes cannot ensure energy efficient construction and may not be able to afford retrofitting. Design standards or energy efficiency requirements for entire homes (potentially including household tools and vehicles), implemented through federal, state, or municipal building codes or market incentives to upgrade home efficiency, can both reduce energy usage and create better building norms.

Similarly, since consumers cannot control product designs, to reduce the household landfill footprint, extended producer responsibility is now used for e-waste in many states and in Europe and could be extended to all forms of products and packaging materials.[94] Since manufacturers' own costs, or the costs they choose to pass to consumers, would reflect the costs of having to collect and recycle all used and unwanted consumer products, this system would build incentives to design and to make products with little waste that will last longer.[95]

Norms & Information

Customs, norms, traditions, and everyday rituals matter. They signal what society values or, at minimum, evince the expectations (whether good or bad for

---

92. *See* U.S. EPA, *Lawn and Garden (Small Gasoline) Equipment*, http://www.epa.gov/OMS/equip-ld.htm#consumer.

93. Ian Talley, *Obama Mandates New Appliance-Efficiency Standards*, WALL STREET J., Feb. 5, 2009.

94. *Cf.* Jon Felce, *European Union Food Labeling and Packaging: The Need to Strike a Balance*, 63 FOOD DRUG L.J. 113 (2008).

95. For more information on how to reduce waste from packaging, read Dan Imhoff's *Paper or Plastic: Searching for Solutions to an Overpackaged World* (2002).

the environment) of our social and cultural lives. Energy inefficiency should be anticipated when society values energy consumption. In 1959 Richard Nixon announced proudly that "44 million families in America own 56 million cars, 50 million television sets, 143 million radio sets, and ... 31 million of those families own their own homes."[96] One has to wonder how different this would be if we consumed less and took more pride in how much we walked each week or how little we threw away. From a policy perspective then, the key question becomes whether and how can everyday social and cultural norms be changed and activated to embody environmentally friendly decision-making.

Professor Michael Vandenbergh has suggested that traditional legal regulation and economic incentives should be supplemented with legal changes that help change individual behavior by activating environmental norms.[97] Prescriptive laws and taxes, levied on individual action, can be intrusive, inefficient, expensive, unpopular, and difficult to enforce. However, law still must play an integral role in activating individual environmental norms. In terms of shifting values, law helps to change beliefs by recognizing problematic behavior such as dumping hazardous waste or smoking. Law can embody social consensus, and it can provide information when political will does not permit direct regulation. In other words, law can both generate and symbolize stronger environmental norms.[98] One way to do this is by providing consumers with greater and more accurate information regarding their choices. Consumers need easy access to understandable information where and when decisions are made, and they need education about how to use that information. Improved government-sponsored programs must require trustworthy and attention-grabbing labels, especially to counteract "green washing," the business practice of disingenuously marketing products as environmentally friendly.

Yet, informational tools cannot accomplish the job on their own. Eco-labeling, the practice of labeling products with environmental data, remains ineffective unless price and quality can compete with other goods. Absent a carbon tax on manufactured goods, economic subsidies and tax incentives are needed to offset the increased cost of environmentally friendly goods. The problem is not that current information efforts are all-around weak and unavailable (e.g., Energy Star, "Reduce, Reuse, Recycle"); rather, the challenge is in crafting how informational efforts can integrate with traditional regulation.[99] Unfortunately, individual choice steeply discounts long-term savings from energy efficiency and prefers the quick fix.[100] Individuals, as well as public service announcements, "tend to overemphasize the energy-reducing value of behaviors that have perceptible effects, such as turning off lights, and to discount behaviors that are less perceptible but have much

---

96. RICHARD NIXON, SIX CRISES 259-260 (1962).
97. Michael Vandenbergh, *The Individual as Polluter*, 35 ELR 10723 (2005).
98. Vandenbergh & Steinemann, *supra* note 3, at 1738.
99. *Id.* at 1704.
100. *Id.* at 1725.

greater effects on energy saving, such as improving the efficiency of heating and cooling systems."[101] Environmental policy needs to work to counter this trend.

Direct information about the energy efficiency (e.g., how much electricity a product uses) and construction of a product (e.g., the extent to which it is made of recycled materials and manufactured sustainably) can be coupled with textured knowledge about the environmental consequences of consumer choice. To activate norms, individuals need to know that environmental problems caused by their actions can have significant consequences.[102] For example, "many people have only a vague sense of where their discards go."[103] Books like Elizabeth Royte's *Garbage Land* effectively teach that garbage does not simply disappear and instead fills landfills the size of small mountains, which harm our waterways and natural landscape.

More and better information on consumer products can help implement environmentalism at home, but mechanisms also must exist for individuals to take greater responsibility and accounting of their daily behavior. Paying attention to one's choices changes future decision-making, but sometimes it is difficult to know what one actually is choosing. What is the carbon footprint of my car, and am I using too much energy in the home? Vandenbergh advocates the creation of an "Individual Carbon Release Inventory" (ICRI) as an amendment to the federal Emergency Planning and Community Right-to-Know Act, created by national survey data about household energy usage.[104] This information could be reported in the news to make individuals aware of the potentially heavy carbon footprints of their everyday activities. The ICRI would resemble the successful Toxics Release Inventory, a publicly available database containing information on toxic chemical releases and waste management activities as reported by industry. Making toxic releases public has improved waste practices because corporations wish to avoid the adverse publicity.

However, despite administrative burdens, perhaps individual households should fill out ICRI forms themselves—an environmental census with follow-up information explaining how one's household compares with others in the region and nationwide, rather than using random-sample survey data. This program, however conceived, could be administered through EPA or the EIA as suggested by Vandenbergh, or the U.S. Census Bureau, which, for example, does housing surveys for the U.S. Department of Housing and Urban Development. Individuals would list the number of hours of powered lawn equipment use, miles driven, and bags of solid waste thrown away, among other things (perhaps through a weekly or monthly survey). Already, household carbon footprint calculators are available on the Internet to educate and motivate consumers. While these individual self-

---

101. *Id.*
102. Michael P. Vandenbergh, *Order Without Social Norms: How Personal Norm Activation Can Protect the Environment*, 99 N.W. UNIV. L. REV. 1101, 1123 (2005).
103. ROGERS, *supra* note 63, at 11.
104. Vandenbergh, *supra* note 101, at 1148.

assessments might actually prove more costly and create less reliable data, the environmental census, like the environmental impact statement in the National Environmental Policy Act, could harness the power of process to evoke substantive change at the household level.

In deciding between using a national environmental survey versus a national environmental census, one must weigh the implementation costs, including administrative burdens and political perception (e.g., would individuals view an environmental carbon footprint census like the population census or like taxes?), the quality of data received, and, perhaps most importantly, the benefits of having individuals pay attention to and understand their personal household carbon footprints. Studies indicate that information can trigger environmental norms. For example, increased awareness of consequences of individual transportation behavior has a positive effect on willingness to reduce personal car use.[105]

Another important component to establishing norms of household environmentalism is creating new technological infrastructure that disseminates consumer information. Technologically driven information can change behavior. Imagine a device that records and visually displays home electricity usage in real time, or a digital readout on vehicles that displays carbon emissions on an ongoing basis.[106] Admittedly, figuring out the most energy-efficient products is difficult. The options will become greater with time, though for now consumers can look for Energy Star-labeled products and rely upon the EPEAT (Electronic Product Environmental Assessment Tool) system which was developed with a grant from EPA to help buyers compare and select electronics based on their environmental attributes.[107]

In addition, community initiatives and grassroots relationships also have influenced environmental norms by prompting changes in local behavior by making it easier for individuals to reduce fuel usage and reuse what might otherwise end up in a landfill. While costly in terms of time intensity and manpower, face-to-face community norm campaigns can effectively raise environmental awareness and apply social pressure to change behavior.[108] Just as, if not more, effective has been building online relationships among consumers via websites like Freecycle and Craigslist that provide information on unwanted goods to be had for free or sale. Due to ever-increasing energy costs, grassroots cooperative fuel and car-pooling groups are also on the rise.

Environmentally friendly norm activation is not without constraints. It is far easier to change norms when you can afford it. Financial and social costs, cultural history, physical effort, and mental energy all constrain norm transformation.[109] Cars run more efficiently when the gas tank is full, yet many fill up only $10 or

---

105. Annika M. Nordlund & Jorgen Garvill, *Effects of Values, Problem Awareness, and Personal Norm on Willingness to Reduce Personal Car Use*, 23 J. ENVTL. PSYCHOL. 339, 345 (2003).

106. Vandenbergh & Steinemann, *supra* note 3, at 1732.

107. EPEAT, http://www.epeat.net/ (last visited July 14, 2009).

108. *See* Vandenbergh, *supra* note 101, at 1133.

109. *Id.* at 1121.

$15 at a time because they lack the cash on hand. Hybrid cars are more expensive, especially with rebates dwindling. Due to the efficiency of industrial food produc- ers, it remains less expensive to buy food shipped from long distances rather than locally grown produce. And never underestimate the power of habit and routine.[110] If batteries, food scraps, or plastics have gone in a family's trash for the past two decades, making an intentional change requires mental energy.

So, given the promise of creating environmental norms while recognizing constraints, where do we start? The overall recommendation is to pick the "low hanging fruit," a term now used by academics and actors alike to refer to the easiest behaviors and infrastructure to change to lessen the carbon footprint. Low hanging fruit, like carpooling and using CFLs, are more easily influenced than some behaviors by accessible information, mobilizing community action, and effective economic subsidies. These simple solutions may shift existing norms and should not be dismissed as trivial. During his campaign, President Obama suggested that if all Americans inflated their tires properly and took their cars for scheduled tune-ups, the oil savings would equal the amount of oil produced by expanding offshore drilling. While this statement was mocked by the opposi- tion party, the suggestion was accurate. These simple behaviors would reduce oil demand in the U.S. by several percentage points.[111] Such solutions for individu- als are simply sensible and avoid an "over-emphasis on technical solutions and a neglect of cultural ones."[112] The most sensible low-hanging fruit: stop engine idling, reduce standby power use, buy CFLs, turn down the thermostat by two degrees, decrease household water temperature, keep proper tire pressure, and change car air filters.[113] In the United States, these actions alone would reduce carbon dioxide emissions 150 million tons by 2014, the equivalent of removing 26 million cars from the road.[114]

110. Vandenbergh, *supra* note 101, at 10786.

111. Michael Grunwald, *The Tire-Gauge Solution: No Joke*, TIME (Aug. 4, 2008).

112. Bradley A. Harsch, *Consumerism and Environmental Policy: Moving Past Consumer Culture*, 26 ECOLOGY L. Q. 543, 545 (1999).

113. Michael P. Vandenbergh, Jack Barkenbus & Jonathan M. Gilligan, *Individual Carbon Emissions: The Low Hanging Fruit*, 55 UCLA L. REV. 1701 (2008). *See also* Grace Renshaw, *The Campaign to End American Idle*, 37 VAND. LAW. 16 (2010).

114. *Id.* at 1706.

CHAPTER FOUR

Food

For once, I was able to pay the full karmic price of a meal.

Michael Pollan, *Omnivore's Dilemma* 9 (2006)

For most, the price of food is the amount paid at the supermarket register. However, the low prices at the supermarket do not adequately reflect the environmental costs of the modern food system—notably, the health and ecological consequences of pesticide use and the greenhouse gas emissions from the livestock industry, processing plants, and food distribution systems. Nor are most consumers aware of these costs. Further, even those consumers who are aware and wish to make more environmentally friendly choices will find it difficult to secure and evaluate information about the environmental impacts of different foods. As with other aspects of everyday environmentalism, the key will be to develop effective policy and regulatory tools that will promote informed decision-making on the part of individuals and shift social and cultural norms to promote more environmentally friendly food production and consumption patterns, thereby reducing the aggregate environmental impact of individual food choices.

Part A of this chapter considers how existing federal law affects current American food production and choices through agricultural subsidies, pesticide regulation, and food labeling. As discussed in Part B, public policy and economic realities in the United States have influenced the creation of overlapping food markets that provide consumers with different choices and induce varying levels of environmental harm. These first two parts demonstrate the need for greater awareness of the ecological costs of food choice and for greater understanding of the existing role of government in influencing these choices. Part C considers the various policy and regulatory tools that might be used to influence individual behavior and food choices based on environmental effects. Specifically, in light of the six decision-making tools discussed in the Introduction, Part C advocates decreasing the ecological footprint of food production, distribution, and consumption through (1) creation and use of more comprehensive eco-labeling for food that will make the environmental costs of food more visible and understood, (2) promoting and creating broader access to a local organic food market through both local initiatives and state regulation and programs, and (3) providing consumers with additional information about the aggregate impacts of food choices in order to shift social and cultural norms and change food purchases in ways that will decrease the carbon and ecological footprint of individual food choices.

A. Food and the Law

Contrary to claims that the American food industry is driven merely by consumer tastes and demands, American law directly influences which foods get produced, how foods are produced, and which foods people eat. While new initiatives are necessary to modify consumer food choices in the United States, as discussed in Part C, the federal government already influences what farmers grow and further impacts consumer choice through informational labeling.

The U.S. Farm Bill and accompanying agricultural subsidies create incentives for farmers to produce large amounts of commodity grain, especially soybeans and corn. These incentives lead to monoculture, habitat loss, large industrial farms, and increased pesticide usage. Federal legislation does, however, regulate pesticide usage and provide labeling laws attempting to inform consumers about how food is produced. Most recently, government-regulated organic food labeling, domestically and abroad, has influenced the structure of the modern food system. Thus, existing policy already has made decisions regarding the level of government action and information dissemination in creating the American food market. Future policymakers must evaluate these efforts before specifically proceeding towards further regulation aimed at individual food choices.

Agricultural Subsidies—The Farm Bill

"Every five to seven years, the president of the United States signs an obscure piece of legislation that determines what happens on a couple hundred million acres of private property in America, what sort of food Americans eat (and how much it costs), and as a result, the health of our population."[1] The legislation is the "Farm Bill." The Farm Bill's power was installed by President Franklin D. Roosevelt and approved by the U.S. Supreme Court decision *Wickard v. Filburn*, which gave Congress broad authority to regulate commercial prices under the Commerce Clause of the U.S. Constitution.[2] The Farm Bill continues to exert significant impact on the nation's economic, environmental, and health status.

The Farm Bill centralized farm policy in an effort to support farmers through the Dust Bowl and the Great Depression. Technological advances in farm equipment and fertilization resulted in crop overproduction and accompanying low crop prices. The Farm Bill, which has held various names over the years, provides agricultural subsidies for commodity crops to farmers and promotes production-control measures.[3]

---

1. Michael Pollan, *Foreword* to DANIEL IMHOFF, FOOD FIGHT: THE CITIZEN'S GUIDE TO A FOOD AND FARM BILL (2007).
2. 317 U.S. 111 (1942).
3. The U.S. government adopts employment of soil conservation measures as the rationale for

After World War II, farming evolved through the adaption of war technologies into fertilizer mixtures and equipment and the advent of pesticides and genetically modified organisms. Meanwhile, farm debt grew, crop diversity decreased, and families left the farm. Farm sizes boomed as family farms evolved into factory farms. The Farm Bill's role has dramatically changed from supporting farming to the subsidization of industrial agriculture, all with disastrous environmental consequences.[4] The agribusiness lobby, representing businesses such as Cargill and Archer Daniel Midland, helped create a Farm Bill that supports the growth of cheap and plentiful soybeans and corn. Agribusiness wants cheap raw commodities for livestock feed and processed ingredients. Subsequently, with heavy lobbying efforts, direct subsidies to farms have risen dramatically, reaching $32 billion in 2000.[5]

The large subsidies create incentives for putting new fields into production whenever possible and boosting crop yields through increased use of pesticides, herbicides, and fertilizers rather than through integrated pest management, green fertilizers, and crop rotation, which farmers fear may lead to lost production.[6] Massive grain subsidization creates further and significant health and environmental costs. With corn so inexpensive and abundant, the prevalence of value-added products,[7] led by high fructose corn syrup and fatty meats created by animal feed made from processed corn, makes it difficult to make healthy food products. The U.S. factory farm and the industrial food model's environmental costs include concentrated water and air pollution, biodiversity loss due to increased monoculture, large-scale wetlands and habitat loss in their conversion to farmland, runoff from concentrated animal feeding operations, and an increase in "food miles" (transportation miles needed to get food from the farm to the dinner table). Corn's dominance also has led to ill-conceived and inefficient ethanol production, which fails to reduce greenhouse gas emissions, converts food-producing cropland,

---

supplemental payments to farmers. These are attempts to restrict production through conservation easements, wetlands reserves, wildlife habitat improvement, grasslands protection, and conservation plans for highly erodible lands. Conservation programs blended with commodity supports may go only so far, and the ecological success of these conservation measures is unknown.

4. *See* William S. Eubanks, *A Rotten System: Subsidizing Environmental Degradation and Poor Public Health with Our Nation's Tax Dollars*, 28 STAN. ENVTL. L. J. 213 (2009).

5. John H. Davidson, *The Federal Farm Bill and the Environment*, 18 NAT. RES. & ENVT. 3 (2003).

6. Integrated pest management (IPM) is "the coordinated use of pest and environmental information with available pest control methods to prevent unacceptable levels of pest damage by the most economical means and with the least possible hazard to people, property, and the environment." U.S. EPA, *Pesticides and Food: What "Integrated Pest Management" Means*, http://www.epa.gov/pesticides/food/ipm.htm. Rather than pesticides, IPM uses mechanical trapping devices, natural predators (e.g., insects that eat other insects), insect growth regulators, mating disruption substances (pheromones), and if necessary, chemical pesticides. *Id.* Green fertilizer is organic or natural fertilizer. Crop rotation is the practice of growing different crops in the same area to avoid pest build-up common to a monoculture.

7. Value-added products are created when raw products, like corn, are processed to become another product with a higher value.

removes land from conservation programs, and leads to deforestation elsewhere as international markets respond to produce soy and grain as corn prices skyrocket.[8]

Pesticides

Farmland accounts for roughly half of the land in the lower 48 states, and, not surprisingly, farming practices are linked directly to ecological change. Chemical use has perhaps the most direct environmental impact of any agricultural practice. Pesticides intentionally cause environmental harm by killing living organisms. They also prevent pest damage to potentially a third of the nation's crop, help food preservation, and result in cheaper food production. Still, pesticides have enormous costs. They kill beneficial insects, potentially poison wildlife and their reproductive systems, impair water quality, and, ironically, create pesticide-resistant pests that, in turn, require application of new or more toxic chemicals in order to be killed.

Pesticides reach and have the ability to harm people. Pesticides applied in the field can remain on or in harvested domestic or imported crops that people eventually eat either directly or indirectly through animals that eat those crops. Processors or packers may intentionally apply chemicals to protect food. Testing has confirmed that no longer used or banned pesticides persist in the natural environment.

Defining pesticides generally as "safe" or "unsafe" in common language has little meaning, as the science for evaluating effects is quite complicated. Toxicity levels and health effects from chemical exposure have extreme variation. In other words, a chemical pesticide may have different effects on adults, children, or the elderly. Harms may take effect incrementally, mirroring pesticide amounts, or only once a specific concentration is reached, and pesticides may react differently in humans when consumed on raw versus cooked produce. Human health and environmental risks from pesticides may pose an even greater risk when considering emissions and toxics from the production process and chemical exposures to production workers and field hands. As early as 1987, the U.S. Bureau of Labor Statistics found that agricultural workers suffered the highest rate of chemically related illness of any occupational group.[9] In 1992 EPA estimated that farm workers experienced tens of thousands, and perhaps as many as 300,000, illnesses each year due to pesticide exposure.[10]

Widespread use of synthetic pesticides, derived from war weapons research, began after World War II and has since become a global phenomenon.

Estimates of global pesticide use are staggering. More than 1,600 types of pesticides are currently available. More than five billion pounds of pesticides, with a value of over thirty billion dollars, are used annually in the world. Pesticide use in the United States

8. Jebediah Purdy & James Salzman, *Corn Futures: Consumer Politics, Health, and Climate Change*, 38 ELR 10851 (2008).

9. U.S. Bureau of Labor Statistics, 52 Fed. Reg. 16050, 16059 (1987).

10. General Accounting Office, *Hired Farmworkers: Health and Well-Being at Risk* 13 (1992); U.S. EPA, *Summary of Risk-Benefit Analysis for Worker Protection Standard*, 57 Fed. Reg. 38105 (1992).

accounts for 27 percent of global pesticide usage, with U.S. exports to other countries exceeding 450 million pounds of pesticides per year.[11]

With the publication of Rachel Carson's *Silent Spring*, the pesticide issue helped spark the environmental movement.[12]

Pesticides—herbicides, insecticides, and fungicides, which kill plants, bugs, and fungi, respectively—have varying toxicity levels. Insecticides like DDT have low toxicity levels but remain in foods and soils for a long time. By contrast, another pesticide type, called an organophosphate, while more toxic, breaks down rapidly and is unlikely to contaminate food unless applied close to harvest. However, some pesticides are applied to food *after* harvest, leaving residue on the food product. The most common example: shipped strawberries are sprayed with fungicides after harvest to prevent fungi or mold.[13]

Most pesticide legislation focuses on health impacts and neglects broader eco-system concerns, as evinced by the actions of those federal agencies that regulate pesticides in foods. EPA registers pesticides, assesses the risk of pesticides, and establishes maximum residue limits (or "tolerances") for quantities in food. The Food Safety and Inspection Service of the U.S. Department of Agriculture monitors and enforces pesticide tolerance levels in meat and poultry. The Food and Drug Administration enforces tolerance levels in imported and domestic food, primarily fruits and vegetables.

The Federal Insecticide, Fungicide, and Rodenticide Act (FIFRA), first known as the Insecticide Act of 1910, began as a labeling and consumer protection statute attempting to abate false claims about pesticide effectiveness. Its modern formula-tion, passed in 1947 and significantly amended in the 1970s, mandates pesticide registration and the setting of tolerance levels for pesticide in food. To date, EPA has registered more than 17,000 pesticides; without such registration, their sale and distribution is prohibited.[14] FIFRA directs EPA to register pesticides only to the extent that their use will not cause "unreasonable adverse effects on the envi-ronment," where "environment" includes "water, air, land, and all plants and man and other animals living therein, and interrelationships which exist among these."[15] Registration encompasses providing proper labeling and directions for use. Thus, under FIFRA, pesticides are assessed both procedurally (e.g., registration) and substantively (e.g., tolerance levels) on a one-time nationwide basis. Unfortunately, in the field, many registered pesticides are over-applied or otherwise improperly used, resulting in higher risks.

---

11. Mary Jane Angelo, *Embracing Uncertainty, Complexity, and Change: An Eco-pragmatic Reinven-tion of a First-Generation Environmental Law*, 33 ECOLOGY L. Q. 105, 145 (2006).

12. *See id.* at 108; RACHEL CARSON, SILENT SPRING (1962) (an early criticized book but ultimately a best-seller about the harmful effects of pesticides that motivated the American public to become con-cerned about pesticides and environmental degradation).

13. MARVIN J. LEVINE, PESTICIDES: A TOXIC TIME BOMB IN OUR MIDST 67 (2007).

14. *Id.* at 1.

15. FIFRA § 2(j); 7 U.S.C. § 136(j); FIFRA § 3; 7 U.S.C. § 136(a).

Risk determination under FIFRA does not exist in a vacuum. EPA will not register a pesticide under FIFRA unless the applicant receives tolerance-level approval or an exemption from establishing tolerance under the Federal Food, Drug and Cosmetic Act (FFDCA). Under the FFDCA, EPA sets tolerances for pesticide residues on food. Food is deemed unsafe, and its role in commerce prohibited, unless it has a tolerance level that provides "reasonable certainty that no harm will result from aggregate exposure to the pesticide chemical residue, including all anticipated dietary exposure."[16]

However, the Delaney Clause in the FFDCA states that no food additive "shall be deemed to be safe if it is found to induce cancer when ingested by man or animal."[17] Read literally, the Delaney Clause sets a "zero risk" standard for any pesticide that induces cancer during animal testing, even if there is little risk to humans due to weak cancer inducing potential or low incidence of human exposure. The U.S. Court of Appeals for the Ninth Circuit, in the case *Les v. Reilly*, upheld this textualist and literal reading, holding that no de minimis risk (i.e., miniscule amount) exception to the Delaney Clause existed.[18] While legally appropriate, this decision faced criticism on practical grounds, given that advanced technology allows for the detection of small cancer effects when animals receive large doses of active pesticide ingredients.

Food processors and agricultural business grew concerned that many pesticides often found in trace amounts in food would be banned. Congress responded with the Food Quality Protection Act of 1996 (FQPA), which lifted any potential bans by no longer defining pesticides as "food additives" subject to the Delaney Clause.[19] Thus, cancer-inducing chemicals in raw and processed food are permissible and considered "safe" so long as there is a "reasonable certainty of no harm." But does legal equal safe? This is a particularly challenging question to answer, and risk determination is a difficult proposition for both regulators and consumers.

Regulators must determine whether the pesticide residue has a threshold effect (i.e., whether adverse impacts occur only when a specific dosage is achieved), the arc of the dose-response curve (i.e., showing the relationship between the pesticide amount and the response of the individual), and how pesticide residues may impact various individual characteristics (e.g., type of diet, adult versus child). Consumers, in turn, face yet another layer of difficult risk evaluation—namely trying to measure and compare pesticide risk to other dietary risks. In other words, if an apple contains pesticide residue at a certain level and that level is determined unsafe, should individuals shift their consumer purchases to other less healthy, but pesticide-free, snack foods? Would it be healthier to eat a pesticide-free but fatty meal from the local burger franchise or an apple grown using pesticides? These are

---

16. FFDCA § 408, 21 U.S.C. § 346a(b)(2).
17. FFDCA § 409, 21 U.S.C. § 348(c)(3)(A).
18. 968 F.2d 985 (9th Cir. 1992).
19. Pesticides are excluded from the definition of food additive in section 210(s) of the FFDCA, and they are no longer subject to the Delaney Clause in section 409. FQPA § 3219(s).

difficult questions. Neither federal statutes nor regulatory risk assessment proce-
dures provide consumers with the information needed to address these trade-offs
or enable them to make proper choices that promote not only human health but
also the natural environment.

Food Labeling

As noted above, absent rigorous substantive regulation of food production processes, consumers are left to make their own choices about which products meet
sustainable criteria. However, governments are in a position to help provide necessary information to make these choices through labeling programs. "The main
objective of eco-labeling programs is to harness market forces and channel them
towards promoting more environmentally friendly patterns of production."[20] However, quality eco-labeling of food requires accurate and verifiable information, and
it must provide life-cycle information on production, processing, and distribution.
Consumers must have information about chemical additives, land stewardship
practices, and the fossil-fuel consumption required to bring any food to market.

Under the Organic Foods Production Act (OFPA) and the National Organic
Program (NOP), the U.S. government creates production, handling, and labeling
standards for organic agricultural products.[21] Individuals buy organic products to
promote sustainable and chemical-free agriculture, as well as to keep their bodies
free of synthetics and pesticides. OFPA establishes a national organic certification
program where agricultural products may be labeled as organic if produced and
handled without the use of synthetic substances. The program prohibits using
synthetic fertilizers and growth hormones and antibiotics in livestock and adding synthetic ingredients during processing.[22] Agricultural practices must follow
an organic plan approved by an accredited certifying agent and the producer and
handler of the product.[23]

OFPA creates process-based standards but does not implement standards or
require tests for actual chemical content in food and also does not assess overall
land use practices. Thus, certified organic labeling, using the USDA Organic label
shown below, informs consumers about the food production process, but does not
directly describe food quality or a lack of land degradation, though organic food
still is likely to have fewer chemicals than conventional counterparts.[24]

---

20. Surya P. Subedi, *Balancing International Trade with Environmental Protection: International
Legal Aspects of Eco-Labels*, 25 BROOKLYN J. INT'L. L. 373, 375 (1999).
21. Organic Foods Production Act of 1990, 7 U.S.C. § 6501 et seq.
22. 7 U.S.C. §§ 6508(b)(1), 6509(c)(3), 6510.
23. 7 U.S.C. §§ 6504, 6505.
24. Michelle T. Friedland, *You Call That Organic?—The USDA's Misleading Food Regulations*,
13 N.Y.U. ENVTL. L. J. 379, 398-99 (2005). However, "because food produced in accordance with
the NOP regulations will not be intentionally sprayed with pesticides or intentionally grown or raised
using genetically engineered seed or other inputs, the likelihood of the presence of pesticide residue or
genetically engineered content will clearly be lower than in foods intentionally produced with pesticides
and genetic engineering techniques. But organic food will not be free of such contamination. Evidence
clearly indicates that both pesticides and genetically engineered plant materials often drift beyond their

So what counts as organic? For many, the organic label means healthy, environmentally friendly, safe, and pesticide free. While in some cases these characteristics are true, they are not elements of the legal definitions of organic. And legal definitions matter. The NOP created under OFPA creates a four-tiered labeling system for organic foods.[25] All organics are not created equally.

Table 2: Categories of USDA Organic Foods

Content of Organic Ingredients	Organic Seal?	Permitted Label Phrases
100%	Yes	"100% Organic"
95%-99%	Yes	"Organic"
70%-94%	No	"Made with Organic Ingredients"
69% or less	No	Can only list organic ingredients

First, a product can be labeled "100 percent organic" and carry the U.S. Department of Agriculture and certifying agent seals if it contains 100% organically produced ingredients as defined by OFPA (e.g., without synthetic substances).[26] Second, a product must contain at least 95% organic ingredients to be labeled simply "organic" and use the USDA and private certifying agent seals.[27] Third, a product with at least 70% organically produced ingredients (or perhaps better stated, with *only* 70% organic ingredients) can be labeled "made with organic ingredients" and carry the seal of a private certifying agent.[28] For products containing less than 70% organic ingredients, organic ingredients may be listed on the label, but neither

---

intended applications, and organic food, like any food, may be accidentally contaminated." *Id.* at 399-400.

    25. 7 C.F.R. § 205.301. In addition to looking for "organic" labeled foods, consumers can look at five-digit PLU codes. Organic foods all start with 9.

    26. 7 C.F.R. § 205.301(a); 7 C.F.R. § 205.303. OFPA defines "synthetic" as "a substance that is formulated or manufactured by a chemical process or by a process that chemically changes a substance extracted from naturally occurring plant, animal, or mineral sources, except that such term shall not apply to substances created by natural occurring biological processes." 7 U.S.C. § 6502(12); 7 C.F.R. § 205.2.

    27. 7 C.F.R. § 205.301(b); 7 C.F.R. § 205.303.

    28. 7 C.F.R. § 205.301(c).

the word "organic" nor any seal can be used. Thus, consumers of organic products should look for the USDA seal over the sole seal of other certifying agents, including state governments, because it guarantees at least 95% organic content. Although individual U.S. states have the right to seek approval of stricter standards, to date, none have exercised this right.

Two key and related questions arise in determining the effectiveness of organic labeling. First, when a consumer sees the word "organic" on a label, are the different meanings of organic clear to the average consumer? And second, does "certified organic" mean what consumers think it means? Potentially adding to the confusion, agribusiness has sought watered-down definitions of "organic" so they can cash in on the growing popularity of organic products. Lobbied by industry to loosen the standard for organic, the Secretary of Agriculture created rules allowing non-organic feed to be used in dairy cattle herds that were transitioning to an organic diet and permitting the use of synthetic substances in the handling of products labeled as organic.

The U.S. Court of Appeals for the First Circuit in *Harvey v. Veneman* declared these rules in contravention of the plain language of the OFPA.[29] Despite this, producers can use chemicals in the production and handling stages if the synthetics are not harmful and are necessary because no natural substitute exists.[30] For example, carbon dioxide can be used in post-harvest activities like ripening.[31] That said, and despite attempts to the contrary, current NOP rules ban genetically modified organisms, sewage sludge, and irradiation in certified organic foods.[32] The organic brand also excludes poultry, eggs, and milk from animals raised with antibiotics or growth hormones.

---

29. Harvey v. Veneman, 396 F.3d 28 (1st Cir. 2005).
30. 7 U.S.C. § 6517.
31. 7 C.F.R. § 205.605(b).
32. Friedland, *supra* note 24, at 384, 388. The regulations also prohibit most uses of ionizing radiation, the application of sewage sludge as fertilizer, and the use of drugs or hormones to promote growth in livestock. 7 C.F.R. § 205.105(f), § 205.105(g), § 205.237(b)(1).

Besides organic certification, other private food labeling schemes exist to inform consumers. For example, the blue Marine Stewardship Council label certifies sustainable fisheries and seafood businesses.[33] Similarly, co-op grocers often sell food with labels such as "locavore region" (grown or produced within 100 miles) and "locally grown" (made within the county).

However, a look at the food labeling programs of other governments, notably the European Union, demonstrates the benefits of establishing much more comprehensive organic product legislation, including labeling programs. Compliance with EU organic farming regulations permits display of the EU's own organic food logo (shown above). New EU regulations on organic production and labeling, at least on their face, exhibit a broader and more ambitious model than their U.S. counterparts.[34] The EU organic model offers a holistic paradigm considering animal welfare, environmental pollution, and biological diversity, in addition to chemical and synthetic inputs.

The Europeans are ahead of the curve in terms of food labeling and production. For example, egg labeling is compulsory. All eggs produced in the EU must be stamped with a code to show whether they arrived from a free-range environment, a barn, or a caged battery, and egg packing must indicate the method of production.

The French government has also successfully improved chicken production and labeling through its "Label Rouge" poultry system.[35] Label Rouge attempts to offset the difficult dualism of providing quality production coupled with adequate distribution. Poultry from a specific region in France can receive the "Red Label" quality seal so long as its growth does not rely on chemical feed additives or high-growth genetics and it meets criteria for taste and agricultural practice. Label Rouge offers a model for middle-sized production that can produce high-quality foods and have significant distribution.

Despite increased interest in food labeling, effective global labeling programs are complicated by World Trade Organization regulations seeking to break down barriers to international trade. At the same time, there continues to be strong interest and action to increase food labeling. The United Nations' Agenda 21 states, "Governments, in cooperation with industry and other relevant groups, should encourage expansion of environmental labeling and other environmentally related product information programs designed to assist consumers to make informed choices."[36] Eco-labels, affixed to far more than food, provide information about the environmental costs of consumer choice. They assess a product's life-cycle: the raw materials used, the production process, distribution, use, and disposal, including consideration of pollution, waste, and carbon footprint. Such information

---

33. *See* Marine Stewardship Council, http://www.msc.org/get-certified.

34. Council Regulation (EC) No. 834/2007 (Jun. 28, 2007). *See* http://eur-lex.europa.eu/LexUriServ/LexUriServ.do?uri=OJ:L:2007:189:0001:0023:EN:PDF.

35. For information on "Label Rouge," see G.W. Stevenson & Holly Born, *The 'Red Label' Poultry System in France*, in C. CLARE HINRICHS & THOMAS LYSON, REMAKING THE NORTH AMERICAN FOOD SYSTEM (2007); http://www.poultrylabelrouge.com/.

36. NICHOLAS A. ROBINSON, ed., AGENDA 21 & THE UNCED PROCEEDINGS at 38, para. 4.21 (1993).

is important for conscientious consumers, especially in the United States where food production, from the farm to the store, accounts for 20% of overall fossil-fuel consumption.[37]

B. The Food System

The modern American food system can best be described as being divided into three types of overlapping markets—industrial, organic, and local. These markets are defined by what and where products are purchased and have different ecological consequences. These markets are also defined by how food is produced, especially the energy source for food production that has changed from solar energy to fossil fuels. Most Americans participate in the industrial food market by shopping at large grocery stores, eating processed foods, and taking advantage of nearly every possible produce and protein regardless of season and location.

Meanwhile, the organic food market has become bifurcated. The "big organic" or "industrial organic" market allows people to buy raw and processed organic foods on the same scale as non-organic foods. Retail grocers sell organic cereals, produce, and milk produced all over the world, often in the same food section as their traditional counterparts or in a special natural section of the grocery store. The "small organic" market produces chemical and synthetic-free foods without the benefit of large-scale production or nationwide marketing and distribution systems. The local food market offers a range of small-scale buying venues, like farmers' markets, community supported agriculture programs, and local co-ops, and locally and regionally food grown through a diverse array of agricultural practices, including pesticide-intensive production and sustainable organic farming.

Choosing between industrial, organic, or local food has significant environmental consequences. These markets differ in terms of agricultural inputs (e.g., petroleum-based pesticides versus legume fertilization), food availability (e.g., extent of processing, more than seasonal food availability), and carbon footprint (e.g., due to transportation and processing).

Industrial Food

Michael Pollan's book *In Defense of Food: An Eater's Manifesto* counsels consumers: "Eat food. Not too much. Mostly plants."[38] However, Pollan's advice is heeded with great difficulty because of the industrial food model that permeates the American diet. The weekly grocery ad lists mostly processed foods like frozen pizzas and burritos, soda, premade meals, and sugary breakfast cereals. These items are certainly not plants, and one can legitimately question whether they are "food" at all. The industrial food model is defined by cheap commodity grain, value-added factory processing, produce grown with pesticides, and large production

---

37. DAN IMHOFF, PAPER OR PLASTIC: SEARCHING FOR SOLUTIONS TO AN OVERPACKAGED WORLD 102 (2002).

38. MICHAEL POLLAN, IN DEFENSE OF FOOD: AN EATER'S MANIFESTO 1 (2008).

and distribution systems powered by fossil fuels. The environmental and public health consequences of this food system are potentially severe. The economics of commodity food production have led to even more advertising and more processed goods, resulting in less consumption of whole non-processed foods, high-input farming practices to produce larger and cheaper yields, more plastic and paper packaging, increased pollution from factories and trucking, and larger grocery chains with sizable parking lots that cause storm runoff.

With the transition of grain from a food item to an agricultural commodity, as discussed in Part A,[39] agribusiness has sought inexpensive raw materials to make money on industrially processed foods. Think Kellogg's Corn Flakes and Pop Tarts for breakfast rather than pancakes and eggs. "The reason Nestle considered instant coffee in the first place wasn't that consumers were desperate for fast coffee, but that coffee beans had become too cheap to sell in their raw form."[40] In the industrial model, food is now the commodity, produced at the lowest possible costs and shipped to destinations of highest value. Cooking has moved from the kitchen to the factory. The United States, with only 5% of the world's population, accounts for 40% of global consumption of frozen food, ready meals, and soup.[41] Processed foods have the highest profit margins and are the most heavily marketed. The cost of raw materials (mostly grain) is only a fraction of a retail price driven by profit margin, production, packaging, and distribution. In addition, American foods lack an eco-label, and nutritional labeling facts do not provide complete or understandable information, especially given the ease with which producers can identify ingredients by stating, "May include one or more of the following."

The industrial food system also employs high-input farming featuring petroleum-based pesticides and fertilizers. For example, in 2004 nearly 500 million pounds of pesticides were used in the United States.[42] These inputs have the potential, through runoff, to pollute groundwater and streams. A 2006 study by the U.S. Geological Survey released the following findings:

> At least one pesticide was detected in water from all streams studied and ... pesticide compounds were detected throughout most of the year in water from streams with agricultural (97 percent of the time), urban (97 percent), or mixed-land-use watersheds (94 percent). In addition, organochlorine pesticides (such as DDT) and their degradates and by-products were found in fish and bed-sediment samples from most streams in agricultural, urban, and mixed-land-use watersheds—and in more than half the fish from streams with predominantly undeveloped watersheds. Most of the organochlorine pesticides have not been used in the United States since before the [National Water-

---

39. *See also* WILLIAM CRONON, NATURE'S METROPOLIS: CHICAGO AND THE GREAT WEST (1992); MICHAEL POLLAN, OMNIVORE'S DILEMMA (2006).

40. PAUL ROBERTS, THE END OF FOOD 35 (2008).

41. *Id.* at 34.

42. Craig Osteen & Michael Livingston, *Pest Management Practices*, in AGRICULTURAL PRODUCTION MANAGEMENT (2006), *available at* http://www.ers.usda.gov/publications/arei/eib16/Chapter4/4.3/.

Quality Assessment] studies began, but their continued presence demonstrates their persistence in the environment.[43]

The large production and distribution systems of industrial agriculture and commercial processing rely on questionable land use practices and are powered by fossil fuels. Industrial farming techniques such as over-tilling and a lack of crop rotation mine the soil of its natural nutrients and increase erosion. Finally, petroleum remains the single most important component in the modern food system, used as fuel for transportation and production of food, fertilizers, and pesticides.

Organic and Local Food

The American organic food market is booming. Organic products are available in more than 20,000 natural food stores and more than three-quarters of conventional grocery stores.[44] The total number of certified organic growers increased from 3,587 in 1992 to more than 8,000 in 2006.[45] The total number of farmland acres devoted to organic production, including both cropland and rangeland, has exploded from 935,450 acres in 1992 to more than 4 million acres in 2005.[46] While organic production *may* cost more and *may* yield less than conventional agriculture (though some data suggest with proper practices yields can be equivalent), organic products sell for 50% to 100% more. Organic is a valued-added label allowing for a much greater selling price, taking advantage of consumer perceptions that "organic" is better for personal and environmental health.[47]

The perceived environmental benefits of organic production and agriculture primarily consist of better and fewer inputs (e.g., organic fertilizers and no pesticides) and a lower carbon footprint. The basic premise of the organic food system is the absence of chemical and synthetic substances in the food production process. Organic farmers do not use petroleum-based chemical pesticides, occasionally relying instead on naturally created pesticides found in plants and roots. Pesticides contaminate the environment, pose health hazards to farm workers, and arguably do not work in the long term because pests over time can develop immunity to them.

43. U.S. GEOLOGICAL SURVEY, PESTICIDES IN THE NATION'S STREAMS AND GROUND WATER, 1992–2001—A SUMMARY (2006), *available at* http://pubs.usgs.gov/circ/2005/1291/.

44. Catherine Greene & Carolyn Dimitri, U.S. Dept. of Agriculture, *Organic Agriculture: Gaining Ground*, AMBER WAVES, Economic Research Service (2003), *available at* http://www.ers.usda.gov/amberwaves/feb03/findings/organicagriculture.htm.

45. U.S. Dept. of Agriculture, Table 2. U.S. certified organic farmland acreage, livestock numbers, and farm operations, at http://www.ers.usda.gov/Data/Organic/index.htm#tables; U.S. Census Bureau News Press Release, http://www.census.gov/Press-Release/www/releases/archives/miscellaneous/007871.html.

46. U.S. Dept. of Agriculture, Table 2. U.S. certified organic farmland acreage, livestock numbers, and farm operations, at http://www.ers.usda.gov/Data/Organic/index.htm#tables.

47. *See* Faidon Magkos, Fotini Arvaniti & Antonis Zampelas, *Organic Food: Nutritious Food or Food for Thought? A Review of the Evidence*, 54 INT'L J. FOOD SCIENCES & NUTRITION 257 (2003) (finding evidence that organic food is healthier on the margin, but that inadequate information is available and suggesting that there are some human health benefits (higher ascorbic acid content and higher quality protein) in organic vegetables).

The scope of some pesticide usage is quite harmful to the environment as illustrated by the problem of excessive application of pesticides to the nation's strawberry crop. Conventional strawberry farming uses nearly three times more chemical pesticides than cotton growing, which itself is considered pesticide intensive due to the significant harm the cotton crop faces from pests.[48]

Organic farms typically fertilize the soil with legume cover crops, facilitating a symbiotic relationship with bacteria in the soil to convert nitrogen in the air to useable form, and compost, providing phosphorous and potassium.[49] This minimizes the presence of contaminants in agricultural runoff. By contrast, factory-produced synthetic fertilizers are water soluble, a characteristic that is good for plants and bad for streams. Agricultural runoff from areas where these fertilizers are used results in a build-up of excess nutrients in water bodies that create algae blooms, which use up oxygen and essentially suffocate fish and shellfish populations. One of the largest "dead zones" is in an enormous area of the Gulf of Mexico at the base of where the Mississippi deposits high-nutrient runoff.

The organic market, because of its very success, has its own ecological consequences. The popularity of organic products has led to the creation of a large-scale "industrial organic" market. On the one hand, this change should be welcomed. More land is farmed with fewer chemicals, and more consumers have access to chemical-free food products. On the other hand, as discussed in greater detail below, the industrial organic market relies on fossil fuels for food processing and delivery, employs questionable agricultural techniques, and potentially dilutes the meaning of the organic brand with so many available products. The desire for pre-packaged ready-to-eat produce and concerns about contaminated food may lead to new environmentally problematic regulations such as requiring fences or bare dirt borders around organic fields, setting up poison stations to keep out wildlife, and removing or killing living organisms from streams—all in an effort to keep away animals that might carry pathogens.[50]

The popularity of organic food has led to the increased availability of not only organic apples and carrots but also popular processed foods made with organic ingredients. Organic Kellogg's Rice Krispies and Kraft Organic Macaroni and Cheese Dinner are on the grocery store shelves. Large manufacturers have recognized the potential revenue stream in products that are both processed and certified organic. For example, Kraft Foods owns the "natural" cereal producer Back to Nature, and Kellogg owns Kashi. Archer Daniels Midland, Coca-Cola, Dole, General Mills, H.J. Heinz, Kellogg, Mars, Kraft, Sara Lee, Tyson Foods, and many other large food companies have acquired or partnered with organic food brands or companies or have started their own organic lines.

---

48. PAMELA C. RONALD & RAOUL W. ADAMCHAK, TOMORROW'S TABLE: ORGANIC FARMING, GENETICS, AND THE FUTURE OF FOOD 20 (2008).
49. *Id.* at 16-17.
50. Barry Estabrook, *The Greens of Wrath,* GOURMET, Nov. 2008.

Industrial factories, fueled by nonrenewable energy, are making organic meals, and organic processed foods and organic fresh fruits, vegetables, and meats are shipped long distances via fossil-fuel-powered trucks and airplanes. Demand for both organic produce and fresh produce in general has ended seasonal variations in availability, as overnight delivery from multiple climate zones in climate-controlled containers has become commonplace.

Large organic farms also engage in potentially degrading agricultural techniques. Over-tilling, which can disrupt the soil and cause erosion and nutrient loss, is commonly used to offset the lack of pesticide usage and high instance of monoculture. Overplanting, as well as waste from excess use of water resources and discard of fresh food, is part of the process by which farms meet overnight delivery numbers. Organic farms are sometimes fertilized with off-site manure trucked in from other farms, further increasing the carbon footprint.

These impacts undermine the ideal view of "small organic" agriculture—locally produced and regionally distributed fresh and chemical-free produce and meats— and potentially the informational value of the organic label itself. A local *and* organic food movement avoids a number of the environmental problems of the traditional industrial food and industrial organic models. Local food has a much lower carbon footprint due to its smaller scale, lack of large processing facilities, smaller distribution schemes, and non-traditional sales outlets, including farmers' markets, community-supported agriculture programs, and small co-ops. However, while local food has a decreased carbon footprint, local food is not necessarily produced through sustainable, low-input, and organic agricultural techniques. Local farmers often use chemical pesticides and fertilizers.

Thus, organic labels and local outlets do not in and of themselves guarantee local organic food. But the benefits of local food, sometimes called civic agriculture, are clear. The local food market localizes production and sales, reduces food miles, favors smaller well-integrated farms helping the local economy, and competes on quality rather than least cost of production.[51]

The key question is this: how can public policy increase consumer awareness of better food choices that will ultimately decrease the environmental costs of food and decrease the carbon footprint of food production, distribution, and consumption? Part C suggests models for informational labeling for food, encouraging local food systems through government action, and facilitating a shift from protein sources with a higher carbon footprint through consumer awareness.

C. Improving Consumer Food Choices

Governments shape consumer food choices through legislation like the Farm Bill, pesticide regulation, and food labeling. Public policy plays a role in determining what food is produced, how food is produced, and what food is consumed. To date,

---

51. HINRICHS & LYSON, *supra* note 35, at 19-28.

these determinations have promoted an industrial food model that values least-cost production technologies, experimental biology to increase output, and large farms. This model, supported by government regulation, agribusiness, and large agricultural universities, has had significant and negative environmental consequences. At the same time, the modern American diet has become a product of processed foods, fossil fuels, chemicals, and land degradation.

But the traditional model is beginning to evolve. Certainly, the industrial organic food model has gained significant traction. With increased popularity of certified organic foods and grocers like Whole Foods Market, and Americans' growing fear of chemical residues in their diet and in nature, large-scale organic production will continue to emerge with a larger share of America's food market. Organic food has almost quadrupled its market share in the last decade,[52] and organic food sales have grown from $1 billion in 1990 to more than $20 billion as of 2008.[53]

While this is a promising trend, further action is needed to avoid ongoing environmental harm from detrimental farming, food production, and food distribution practices. Of the six decision-making tools identified in the Introduction for promoting everyday environmentalism, the most effective steps for doing so with respect to food are: (1) informational labeling that (2) also enables identification of environmentally detrimental foods, (3) greater governmental support of local organic food markets, and (4) actions to promote increased public awareness in order to change personal decisions and behavior. Accordingly, this section advocates: better consumer product choice made easier through eco-labels that evaluate chemical and fertilization techniques, production location, carbon footprint, and product life-cycle information; programs that make it easier to buy less-processed, artisanal, seasonal, and local products; and greater awareness of the benefits of a more plant-heavy diet.

Organic v. Locavore: A Successful Eco-labeling System

> Wavering in the produce section of a Manhattan grocery store, I was unable to decide between an organic apple and a nonorganic apple (which was labeled conventional, since that sounds better than "sprayed with pesticides that might kill you"). It shouldn't be a tough choice—who wants to eat pesticide residue?—but the organic apples had been grown in California. The conventional ones were from right here in New York State.[54]

Environmentally conscious consumers often face this type of dilemma.[55] These choices would be easier if consumers had better information regarding chemical

52. ORGANIC TRADE ASS'N, EXECUTIVE SUMMARY, ORGANIC TRADE ASSOCIATION'S 2007 MANUFACTURER SURVEY, http://www.ota.com/pics/documents/2007ExecutiveSummary.pdf (stating that organic food sales accounted for 0.8% of total food sales in 1997, and 2.8% in 2006).
53. ORGANIC TRADE ASS'N, The Organic Industry, http://www.ota.com/pics/documents/Mini%20fact%201-08%20confirming.pdf.
54. John Cloud, *Eating Better Than Organic*, TIME, Mar. 2, 2007.
55. For suggested answers to food conundrums like this, see Marion Nestle's book *What to Eat* (2006).

and fertilization techniques, production location, carbon footprint, and product life-cycle information. An effective eco-labeling system would, at least for grocery store or co-op purchases, inform consumers about the environmental costs of their food purchase and provide a baseline comparison for food in different production categories.

Admittedly, any labeling system, whether an eco-label or certified organic label, can disadvantage small and local producers if large agribusiness can afford to comply with requirements more easily. Under any legislative requirement, farmers and food processors would need to spend time, effort, and money to compile labeling information. Small producers clearly may need public resources to help them generate and convey information used for the eco-label.[56]

An eco-label seal should be available for products within a food category determined by defined environmental criteria. Eco-labels would be based on a technocratic assessment of a product's life-cycle, providing consumers with a visual seal. Products also could list descriptive information of interest such as location of production and chemicals used in the production process. (As of 2009, the U.S. Department of Agriculture was beginning to implement the Country of Origin Labeling Law for foods.[57]) Disclosure of such basic information on an eco-label, in addition to a seal or rating for excellent products, would be a useful tool in comparing brands.

The NOP regulations operate by controlling the use of the word "organic" in food labeling and marketing, and those who wish to label their products "organic" may do so only if they comply with the regulations' detailed requirements.[58] But these types of regulations often are co-opted by special interest lobbyists, and the actual meaning of the organic label may be misaligned with what consumers think it means. Thus, technocrats should decide the environmental criteria for eco-labels, addressing two preliminary questions to create a successful eco-label: (1) Will the eco-label provide accurate information, and (2) will the eco-label lead to a more environmentally friendly consumer choice?

An eco-label informational and certification scheme can provide engaged consumers with a measurable analysis created by experts and also provide a single point of product comparison for the less-engaged consumer. How would an eco-labeling scheme potentially work?[59] First, a group of experts must pick food categories to target, identified by the scope of their adverse environmental impacts,

---

56. The National Organic Production rules allow small farmers and handlers who follow the national organic standards to sell their product as organic if, and only if, they sell less than $5,000 worth of organic agricultural products per year and follow the national standards for production, labeling, and record keeping. 7 C.F.R. § 205.101(a)(1).

57. The Farm Security and Rural Investment Act of 2002, Pub. L. No. 107-171, § 10816, 116 Stat. 134, 533 (codified at 7 U.S.C. § 1638 (2006)).

58. Organic Foods Production Act of 1990, 7 U.S.C. § 6501 et seq.; 7 C.F.R. § 205 et seq.

59. For a discussion of a potential eco-label model, see JULIAN MORRIS, GREEN GOODS?: CONSUMERS, PRODUCT LABELS AND THE ENVIRONMENT 30-34 (1997).

where eco-labels would make a significant improvement to the environment.[60] These categories might include meats and seafood, pesticide-intensive produce like berries, spinach and potatoes, and heavily processed foods. Second, objective scientific criteria to evaluate products must include a full life-cycle analysis. A life-cycle analysis would include consideration of natural resource and chemical use (starting at the production process or raw extraction stage), as well as emissions and pollution generated during the production, distribution and use, and disposal stages. The key is to inventory the materials that make up the food and allow for food production as well as the resulting environmental impact, something that is more difficult to determine. Third, products would be evaluated according to those scientific criteria and a seal awarded. Fourth, in light of technology and agricultural innovation, production selection criteria would be consistently reviewed.

An eco-label for food certainly provides more points of information than does the current organic label. For example, the European Union's voluntary flower logo program indicates that those products are more environmentally friendly than conventional products based on a life-cycle ecological assessment.[61] The key is to determine what factors influence the success of any eco-labeling program. It is hard to overemphasize the importance of first targeting those food categories whose regulation would help the environment if their carbon, chemical, and waste

---

60. Outside the food context, Europe has led in the creation of eco-labels with the Nordic Council Program (of Norway, Sweden, and Finland), Germany's Blue Angel Program, and the European Union's Eco-Label Award Scheme. In Germany's Blue Angel Program, an environmental label jury, composed of representatives from environmental groups, science organizations, consumer associations, industry, trade unions, and the media, review life-cycle reports to determine whether the "Umweltzeichen" ("environmental label") is appropriate. Surya P. Subedi, *Balancing International Trade with Environmental Protection: International Legal Aspects of Eco-Labels*, 25 BROOKLYN J. INT'L L. 373, 378 (1999).The European Union uses five administrative layers to implement its eco-label scheme, developing product groups and ecological criteria to harmonize environmental labeling in its member countries. JULIAN MORRIS, GREEN GOODS?: CONSUMERS, PRODUCT LABELS AND THE ENVIRONMENT 59 (1997). The eco-label can be affixed to those products that meet established product group criteria for the entire life-cycle of the product.

61. *See* European Union Eco-label, http://ec.europa.eu/environment/ecolabel/index_en.htm.

footprints were reduced. What is also known is that government eco-labels are more effective than private ones, and simple and transparent seal-of-approval logos and labels have generally shaped consumer behavior more than the complex information-disclosure labels.[62] In addition, eco-labels require a good quality assurance scheme (which also would benefit from governmental ownership of the label) and a successful marketing program.[63]

For example, Sweden has recently embarked upon an ambitious carbon labeling and information program for food.[64] Foods in grocery stores and on restaurant menus will list the amount of carbon dioxide produced per kilogram of the product. National recommended dietary guidelines will now give equal weight to climate impacts and public health. This is an important combination, merging health and ecology in a holistic fashion. In determining which products and populations to target, which is an important decision-making tool in changing individual behavior, policymakers need to make sure that environmental concerns do not lead to less healthy eating habits. For example, the conventionally grown, but otherwise very nutritious, piece of fruit should be considered superior to foods with less nutritional value even if they are local, organic, and have a low carbon footprint. This is an especially important consideration for populations and areas where nutrition can be an overriding concern like school lunch programs and developing regions of the world. The Swedish dietary program makes clear how to make healthy food trade-offs in exchange for better environmental impacts.

Scandinavia's organic certification program will begin requiring farmers to convert to low-emissions techniques if they want to display the organic seal. "The Swedish effort grew out of a 2005 study by Sweden's national environmental agency on how personal consumption generates emissions. Researchers found that 25 percent of national per capita emissions—two metric tons per year—was attributable to eating."[65] While the impact of the new program will not be known for some time, Sweden has proved to be a leader in greenhouse gas emission reductions, and the United States may be able to learn from its efforts.

Food Miles: Improving the Local Organic Food Model

The "should I buy local or should I buy organic" debate is a false choice. Instead, public policy should help increase access to local organic food, providing a vigorous artisan and seasonal supplement to the developing industrial organic norm. In fact, developing a more local food system may even prove more important than an eco-labeling program since local food will be raw and less processed while

---

62. Abhijit Banerjee & Barry D. Solomon, *Eco-Labeling for Energy Efficiency and Sustainability: A Meta-Evaluation of US Programs*, 31 ENERGY POLICY 109 (2003).

63. *See also* Helen Nilsson, Burcu Tunçer & Åke Thidell, *The Use of Eco-Labeling Like Initiatives on Food Products to Promote Quality Assurance—Is There Enough Credibility?*, 12 J. CLEANER PRODUCTION 517 (2004).

64. For the details on Sweden's initiative see Elisabeth Rosenthal, *To Cut Global Warming, Swedes Study Their Plates*, N.Y. TIMES GLOBAL (Oct. 22, 2009).

65. *Id.*

processed and packaged foods are the ones that traditionally have significant informational labeling.

Local food has fewer "food miles," the distance food travels from where it is grown or raised to where it is ultimately purchased. Local food is produced closer to where you live, does not require as much ground and air transportation to get to your local market, and encourages more seasonal eating. And local foods, compared with other products, are generally not subject to the same level of energy-intensive processing and packaging. Compare the meat, eggs, produce, jam, cider, and cheese purchased at your local farmers' market with those products available at your industrial food grocery store. One will find that farmers' markets usually provide fresh locally grown produce from within a two-hour drive, include many farmers that engage in organic practices with no pesticides even if not certified organic, and supply products that contain no color additives, no preservatives, and are hand-made rather than factory processed.

In a study of Iowa food production, university researchers found that the "conventional system used four to 17 times more fuel than the Iowa-based regional and local systems, depending on the system and truck type. The same conventional system released from five to 17 times more carbon dioxide from the burning of this fuel than the Iowa-based regional and local systems."[66] For these and many other reasons, legal and social regimes should promote access to local food. First, any remaining barriers to farmers' markets and outdoor direct vending must disappear. As early as 1976, Congress passed the Farmer-to-Consumer Direct Marketing Act, charging the Secretary of Agriculture to coordinate with state agencies to facilitate direct marketing from farmers to consumers, leading to the promotion of farmers' markets, community gardens, and direct marketing to school lunch programs.[67] More recently, farmers' markets have been increasing in number and popularity. According to the U.S. Census of Agriculture, the number of farms selling directly to consumers rose 30% from 1992 to 2002.[68]

Second, on-farm food processing should be encouraged, increasing limits on the amount of goods that can be processed on the farm and providing user-friendly site inspections by governmental regulators. In the interest of food safety, the federal government and some states have shown great reluctance to allow on-site meat processing and cutting, much to the dismay of some farmers who believe they

---

66. LEOPOLD CENTER FOR SUSTAINABLE AGRICULTURE, FOOD, FUEL AND FREEWAYS: AN IOWA PERSPECTIVE ON HOW FAR FOOD TRAVELS, FUEL USAGE, AND GREENHOUSE GAS EMISSIONS 2 (2001). "The conventional system represented an integrated retail/wholesale buying system where national sources supply Iowa with produce using large semitrailer trucks. The Iowa-based regional system involved a scenario modeled after an existing Iowa-based distribution infrastructure. In this scenario a cooperating network of Iowa farmers would supply produce to Iowa retailers and wholesalers using large semitrailer and midsize trucks. The local system represented farmers who market directly to consumers through community supported agriculture (CSA) enterprises and farmers markets, or through institutional markets such as restaurants, hospitals, and conference centers. This system used small light trucks." *Id.* at 1-2.

67. 7 U.S.C. § 3001.

68. HINRICHS & LYSON, *supra* note 35, at 28.

can process meat cleaner and better without having to drive animals for miles to permitted processing facilities.

Third, social networks should encourage subscription farming, commonly known as community-supported agriculture (CSA). CSA farmers offer weekly, often organic, produce and locally processed foods, often along with local area delivery, for an upfront payment or, sometimes, in exchange for farm labor. One becomes a member or shareholder in a farm, reaping the benefits of a good harvest as well as taking the risk of a rough season, all while building a direct connection with the farm and farmer. A CSA member typically will receive carrots, potatoes, and greens, and, depending on the farm, can also receive eggs, artisan cheeses, grass-fed and free-range meats, fresh-baked bread, and the opportunity to take part in farm activities and demonstrations.

Fourth, local grocers and co-ops should be encouraged to carry more local options. For example, co-op supermarkets, often already providing a member discount, should expand this program to include a locavore incentive. And fifth, local farmers and processors themselves must better market their food. Local food can deliver a unique and higher-valued product, and its niche market must be exploited. As of 2007, more than 12,000 farms were marketing products through community-supported agriculture,[69] and overall direct farm sales to individuals, while relatively small, had grown.[70]

Admittedly, despite advocacy to promote CSAs and local distribution, there is currently little empirical understanding of the long-term potential of CSAs as an alternative to a more industrial food model. Thomas Jefferson's agrarian dream, as discussed in Chapter One, may be just that. Even though becoming a "locavore" is all the rage in some social circles, a serious problem remains. Most produce at local markets is not organic or labeled, forcing consumers to wonder what they are buying. "I don't know what local means. Do they use local pesticides?"[71] But at least many consumers can talk to their local farmers about their agricultural techniques (an option certainly not available in the grocery store).

The Merits of Vegetarianism

Local food does reduce the carbon footprint of your diet. However, the findings of Weber and Matthews in *Food-Miles and the Relative Climate Impacts of Food Choices in the United States* suggest that making a dietary change would better lower an average household's food-related carbon footprint than buying local.[72] Buying local will reduce greenhouse gas emissions by 4% to 5%, but shifting one

---

69. USDA, 2007 CENSUS OF AGRICULTURE 606 tbl.44, *available at* http://www.agcensus.usda.gov/Publications/2007/Full_Report/Volume_1,_Chapter_2_US_State_Level/st99_2_044_044.pdf.

70. USDA, 2007 CENSUS OF AGRICULTURE 9 tbl.2, *available at* http://www.agcensus.usda.gov/Publications/2007/Full_Report/Volume_1,_Chapter_1_US/st99_1_002_002.pdf.

71. John Cloud, *My Search for the Perfect Apple*, TIME, Mar. 12, 2007 (quoting Joseph Mendelson III, Legal Director of the Center for Food Safety).

72. Christopher L. Weber & H. Scott Matthews, *Food-Miles and the Relative Climate Impacts of Food Choices in the United States,* 42 ENVIRON. SCI. TECHNOL. 3508 (2008).

day per week of protein from meat or dairy to vegetables, or even another protein source (fish, chicken, eggs), has the same effect as buying all household food from local providers. A *completely* local diet saves the equivalent of 1,000 miles per year driven, but a *one day per week* protein shift from red meat to chicken, fish, or eggs saves 760 miles per year, and a *one day per week* shift to veggies saves 1,160 miles per year.[73]

Americans raise and kill more than 10 billion animals a year for food, more than 15% of the world's total. Individuals choose a vegetarian diet for varying reasons, including health (usually to avoid red and fatty meats), ethical (to protest animal treatment), and environmental reasons. However, the ecological impacts alone of eating meat can be quite persuasive on the road to a vegetarian diet. The livestock industry has an immense carbon footprint, contributes to waste runoff and water pollution, creates potentially harmful ecosystem effects, and presents some "unnatural" developments in food production (e.g., carnivorous salmon and cattle with digestive systems designed for grass are both fed corn).

According to the United Nations Food and Agriculture Organization, meat production accounts for 18% of the world's total greenhouse gas emissions.[74] All transportation forms combined, in contrast, represent 13%. As discussed in Chapter Two, the U.S. Environmental Protection Agency is moving forward to regulate greenhouse gases under the Clean Air Act. As evidence of the large carbon footprint of livestock farms, which emit carbon dioxide from machinery and trucks as well as methane from cattle manure, a beef industry group was one of the first to challenge the EPA ruling that greenhouse gas emissions endanger human health.[75]

The livestock industry's concern about greenhouse gas regulation should come as no surprise, given the industry's consumption of significant amounts of energy. Pasture-fed cattle eat grass, their growth fueled by the sun's energy. Concentrated animal feed operations (CAFOs), an arm of the industrial food model, want to produce meat quickly and cheaply. Thanks to government subsidies, cattle now are fed cheap grain instead of their natural preference of grass. Corn feed production uses fertilizer and requires delivery, so animal growth is now fossil-fueled. Natural inefficiency is coupled with practical inefficiency, compounding the emissions problems, as it takes 20 pounds of grain to produce a pound of beef, 4 pounds of chicken, or 7 pounds of pork.[76] Processing plants making everything from hamburger patties to chicken nuggets emit greenhouse gases, as do the cattle themselves in the form of methane.

The waste stream from CAFOs and processing plants contributes to damaging runoff and water pollution. Hogs, chickens, and cows produce mounds of manure,

---

73. *Id.* at 3512-13.

74. Claudia Deutsch, *Trying to Connect the Dinner Plate to Climate Change*, N.Y. TIMES, Aug. 29, 2007.

75. Timothy Gardner, *Beef Group Challenges U.S. EPA Climate Finding*, Dec. 29, 2009 (Thomson Reuters).

76. ROBERTS, *supra* note 40, at 210.

requiring the creation of "poop lagoons" and leading to a high nutrient load in run-off. Land simply cannot absorb enough nitrogen and phosphorus, so precipitation washes these nutrients into streams, rivers, and underground aquifers. The nutrients foster the growth of algae, which sucks oxygen from the water and consequently endangers other species. Similarly, livestock can overgraze land, and ranchers kill prairie dogs to protect land for grazing. Consequently, livestock production can hurt other species populations and destroy the land.

In the seafood industry, operating in a forum ripe for a "tragedy of the commons," overproduction has decimated some fisheries, and unintended "bycatch" has harmed other marine populations. For example, scallop fishers can kill or injure turtles.[77] Shrimp trawling scrapes the ocean floor.

Modern feeding mechanisms have unnatural results, despite their efficiency. "Whereas a 1970s-era broiler needed ten weeks to reach slaughter weight, today's model does it in forty days, which means an enterprising chicken farmer can raise two more crops each year and thus increase his annual output by 40 percent."[78] Cows and fish are naturally happy to forage and eat on their own with no need for stored and cut grains. The unnatural feeding of farm animals does not end with fish and cows eating corn rather than the meat and grass for which their digestive systems were designed. For example, farmed salmon eat corn and red dye, instead of the pink krill eaten in nature that makes salmon flesh pink. Cows, natural herbivores, also have been fed poultry manure and, prior to the mad cow scare, "rendered" beef innards—nature manipulated yet again.

The current organic label does not address this unnatural feeding problem. Federal law mandates that "organic livestock" eat "organically produced feed" that contains no "plastic pellets for roughage; manure refeeding; or ... urea," and no "growth promoters and hormones" "in the absence of illness."[79] Yet, "organic livestock" as defined by federal law are not organic throughout their entire life-cycle. Poultry farmers must use organic methods by the second day after hatch to carry the organic label. For livestock, the counting begins during the last third of gestation.[80]

Important questions remain unaddressed. Is an animal really organic after it is exposed to a chemical substance at any point in its life-cycle? Must cattle be "allowed to graze on pasture much of the year, or may they be confined in pens, fed organic grain, and allowed to graze only as required by the animal's stage of production?"[81] Should we certify as organic wild fish, potentially high in heavy metals and whose diet is not known, or farmed fish, whose environment can be

---

77. Katherine Renshaw, *Leaving the Fox to Guard the Henhouse: Bringing Accountability to Consultation under the Endangered Species Act,* 32 COLUM. J. ENVTL. L. 161, 193-194 (2007).

78. ROBERTS, *supra* note 40, at 69.

79. 7 U.S.C. § 6509.

80. *See* Claire S. Carroll, *What Does Organic Mean Now? Chickens and Wild Fish are Undermining the Organic Foods Production Act of 1990,* 14 S.J. AGRIC. L. REV. 117, 128 (2004).

81. Chad M. Kruse, *The Not-So-Organic Dairy Regulations of the Organic Food Production Act of 1990,* 30 S. ILL. U. L. J. 501 (2006).

controlled? And perhaps most importantly, can a viable organic and local low-carbon meat market be developed?

***

A more information-transparent food labeling system is needed since, at some level, all categorical labels and preferences are unhelpful. Current food label categories are simply proxy measures for some series of set legal criteria or general public preferences. These can be improved by making them more user-friendly, comprehensive, and accurate. Individual action and government regulation are both necessary to create more effective labeling programs and the public awareness and understanding that are needed to make more environmentally conscious food choices.

Eco-labels are a more accurate alternative to the "certified organic" label, which says both too much and not enough. The organic seal seems to advertise a completely chemical-free product but often does not, and it does not address the carbon footprint of food and potentially harmful agricultural practices. Eco-labels that include life-cycle analysis would help fill in the informational gap. Both individuals and society as a whole often put diets in categories such as omnivore, meat-eater, organic, vegetarian, vegan, or locavore. These categories project perceived benefits and values like health conscious, ethical, foodie, environmentalist, real American, and many more. Yet, these categories can be unhelpful since they mask the complexity of the actual environmental trade-offs and overlook the potential benefits of smaller, even meal-by-meal individual environmental decision-making. Locally grown and pasture-fed meat can be chosen if and when it is available, and those focusing on organic produce need to remember that it can have a huge carbon footprint when eating out of season.

At the end of the day, categories are helpful only to the extent they provide accurate information allowing consumers to make smart, ecological choices. At best, local farmers at the outdoor market can be asked exactly how they produce, process, and distribute their food. Farmers are happy to have this conversation. At minimum, industrial organic should become the norm, improved by government-sponsored, expanded eco-label criteria and a more accessible local food market.

CHAPTER FIVE

Sprawl

> Sprawl has been denounced on aesthetic, efficiency, equity, and environmental grounds and defended on choice, equality, and economic grounds. Sprawl has become the metaphor of choice for the shortcomings of the suburbs and the frustrations of the central cities. It explains everything and nothing.
>
> George Galster, Royce Hanson, Harold Wolman, Stephen Coleman & Jason Freihage, *Wrestling Sprawl to the Ground: Defining and Measuring an Elusive Concept,* 12 HOUSING POLICY DEBATE 681 (2001)

The dominant American residential landscape is now suburban, sprawling further from downtown and converting rural landscape into low-density residential developments.[1] This development pattern comes with significant ecological, social, and cultural costs. The numerous environmental harms of sprawl include losses of carbon sinks (i.e., natural resources, like wetlands and forests, that store greenhouse gases), increased air pollution and storm water runoff, diminished water quality, increased water consumption, habitat loss, and biodiversity loss.

This chapter examines the ecological impacts of sprawl and suburbanization on natural resources, as well as the government programs and social and cultural values that support sprawl and suburbanization. Throughout the chapter, particular attention is paid to wetlands, as one illustration of both the ecological effects of sprawl and the limited ability of current policies and practices to mitigate the impacts of sprawl. Wetlands are lands with water-saturated soils that perform important ecological functions—water purification, climate regulation, flood protection, wildlife habitat, and much more—and also have a history of being destroyed in the face of development interests.

Accordingly, Part A describes the phenomenon and the ecological costs of sprawl, with a particular focus on wetlands destruction. Part B then reviews the various current land use practices, land use planning mechanisms, and regulatory programs that seek to manage and limit both sprawl and wetlands destruction. These first two parts are intended to generate awareness of the ecological costs of land use development patterns and provide greater understanding of the existing roles of government policy and publicly supported infrastructure that both sup-

---

1. DOLORES HAYDEN, BUILDING SUBURBIA: GREEN FIELDS AND URBAN GROWTH, 1820–2000, at 3 (2003). *See generally* KENNETH T. JACKSON, CRABGRASS FRONTIER: THE SUBURBANIZATION OF THE UNITED STATES (1987).

port and inhibit sprawl. In determining which regulatory and policy tools can best address the environmental effects of sprawl, Part C concludes that the existing land use planning model must be modified through (1) increased inter-governmental coordination at all levels of government, (2) mechanisms that value the natural services provided by natural resources threatened or lost due to development, and (3) practical initiatives to improve land use planning at the local level. In addition, new programs are needed to (4) use informational mechanisms to create awareness of the costs and impacts of sprawl and (5) establish financial incentives to change individual behavior patterns.

A. The Consequences of Sprawl

Whatever one's specific definition of suburban sprawl, it represents the most destructive pattern of developmental growth. Sprawl consumes undeveloped land outside of already-developed urban centers, often converting open space into expansive low-lying development reflecting little land use planning. These suburban communities are characterized by "low-density residential development interspersed with strip commercial and retail development linked by a vast street and highway system that overemphasizes automobile use and de-emphasizes mass transit."[2] With sprawl comes increased freshwater demands,[3] and, as discussed in Chapter Three, sprawling development has significantly increased the household carbon footprint since individuals drive farther to work and live in communities where driving is required to get from one place to another.

The Rise of Suburban Development

Modern-day suburbia rose out of a post-World War II driving culture fueled by newly built roads and bridges and the government-funded interstate highway system, as well as the economic boom of edge cities that began in the 1950s and '60s. Suburbanization reflected the developing American norm of owning a single-family home with a yard, the relatively low economic costs of development outside city centers, and cultural preferences for living outside the city. The current landscape

---

2. Eric M. Braun, *Smart Growth in North Carolina: Something Old or Something New?*, 35 Wake Forest L. Rev. 707, 708 (2000). *See also* Patrick Gallagher, *The Environmental, Social and Cultural Impacts of Sprawl*, 15 Nat. Resources & Env't. 219 (2001) (defining sprawl as "uncontrolled development that expands outward from city centers and consumes otherwise undeveloped land"); Randolph R. Lowell, *Coastal Smart Growth*, 22 Pace Envtl. L. Rev. 231, 234 (2005) (citation omitted) ("Sprawl embodies the most destructive and all-encompassing product of unmanaged growth."). Suburban sprawl is "the pattern that takes over when, with little coordinated planning, people and businesses desert established communities to develop the open countryside." Patricia E. Salkin, *Smart Growth at Century's End: The State of the States*, 31 Urb. Law. 601, 604 (1999) (quoting *Smart Growth Bills Bow to Reality: Fight Sprawl or Watch it Get Worse*, Buff. News, May 3, 1998, at H2). "Sprawl is largely a consequence of numerous government policies and subsidies that encourage low-density development and results in problems ranging from air pollution to wetland degradation." Rachel L. Schowalter, *Reuse, Restore, Recycle: Historic Preservation as an Alternative to Sprawl*, 29 Envtl. L. Rep. 10418, 10419 (1999).

3. *See, e.g.*, Peter Annin, The Great Lakes Water Wars (2006) (discussing whether water should be pumped out of the Great Lakes basin to suburban communities outside the basin).

illustrates how nature has been modified in the interests of development and the increased encroachment of suburbanization on rural areas.[4] New Orleans and central Florida, described below, are iconic examples.

In New Orleans, a sizable portion of which lies below sea level, wetlands once teemed with live oaks, cypress trees, moss, waterfowl, alligators, and fish. Extensive drainage of those wetlands fostered development in the Crescent City and created subsidence and flooding problems in Jefferson Parish and east New Orleans.[5] Modern development on even lower ground required protection from a man-made levee system, due to the city's location on a section of land between Lake Pontchartrain and the Mississippi River along Bayou St. John. Ironically, these supposedly protective engineering feats thwarted wetlands' vast ecosystem services and contributed to the devastating flooding after Hurricane Katrina in 2005. Wetlands no longer existed to provide necessary flood protection, and natural buffer areas between land and water had been destroyed.

In Central Florida, development proponents worked hard to enable Walt Disney World to be built, including exempting Disney from land use laws. Disney also made the Orlando area the home of Celebration, its planned suburban development community. "Disney poured $2.5 billion into transforming an unpromising wetland into a large and handsome town center—dredging an artificial lake, building roads, parks, and bridges as well as downtown shops."[6] Despite the destruction of acres of wetlands and its distance from workplaces, some have viewed the Celebration development as a positive reaction to sprawl. While Celebration is suburban, it is a walkable community with parks, shops, restaurants, schools, a fire department, and a post office in close proximity. Yet, the fundamental pattern of development and the magnitude of land conversion, in New Orleans, Florida, and elsewhere pose major problems. Population now trends toward suburban growth, with the number of suburbanites increasing on average 7.3 times faster than city dwellers.[7] More than a million acres of rural and undeveloped land are converted annually to suburban use in the United States. And the growth of suburbs exceeds that of the cities by a ratio of six to one, with the nature of suburban development making matters worse.

The single most destructive aspect of suburbia is low-density development exemplified by spacious residential lots, and, due to its emphasis on automobile use, accompanying large roads and huge parking lots. Even in suburbs with a reasonable residential density of three to four single-family units per acre, land conversion rates are high (and population densities appear low) because of the amount of paved surface (about 67% in suburbs compared with less than 30% in small towns).[8] The rate of land use conversion in the suburbs far exceeds the rate

---

4. HAYDEN, *supra* note 1, at 4–5, 183.

5. For more information on New Orleans, see CRAIG E. COLTEN, AN UNNATURAL METROPOLIS: WRESTING NEW ORLEANS FROM NATURE (2006).

6. HAYDEN, *supra* note 1, at 210.

7. For suburban growth and density trend data, see G.S. Kleppel, *Urbanization and Environmental Quality: Implications of Alternative Development Scenarios*, 8 ALB. L. ENVTL. OUTLOOK J. 37, 44 (2002).

8. Kleppel, *supra* note 7, at 49–50.

of population growth, and developing land does more than hurt wetlands; it also creates a host of other environmental problems.

The Diverse Impacts of Sprawl

The basic characteristics of sprawl create multiple economic, cultural, social, and ecological problems. In particular, sprawl is identified by development patterns that overemphasize the automobile and low-density residential neighborhoods.[9] The social, cultural, and economic consequences of sprawl are pronounced. Sprawl increases the economic burden on suburban municipalities and outlying urban areas since such developments cost more to service due to distance between dwellings, commercial structures, and central services, and infrastructure must be created from scratch when establishing new developments. In addition, sprawl can contribute to economic voids in central cities, economic and racial segregation, and destruction of community.

Table 3: Consequences of Sprawl

Ecological Harms	Social and Cultural Harms
Increased air pollution	Loss of community
Harmful agricultural land conversion*	Decline of central city
Diminished water supply and quality*	Increased gasoline usage and driving miles
Wetlands loss*	Increased vehicular traffic
Increased carbon footprint*	Longer commutes
Aesthetic landscapes lost*	Loss of pedestrian amenities
Increased water consumption	Loss of open space
Groundwater mining	Economic segregation
Prevention of groundwater recharge*	Racial segregation
Disruption of hydrological cycles*	
Water pollution*	
Biodiversity loss*	

*related to wetlands loss

Sources: MILLENNIUM ECOSYSTEM ASSESSMENT, ECOSYSTEMS AND HUMAN WELL-BEING: WETLANDS AND WATER SYNTHESIS, tbl. 1 (World Resources Institute 2005); Christina A. Klein, *The New Nuisance: An Antidote to Wetlands Loss, Sprawl, and Global Warming*, 48 B.C. L. REV. (2007); Randolph R. Lowell, *Coastal Smart Growth*, 22 PACE ENVTL. L. REV. 231 (2005); Jeremy R. Meredith, *Sprawl and the New Urbanist Solution*, 89 VA. L. REV. 447 (2003).

As seen in Table 3 above, the environmental costs are numerous. The effects of sprawling development patterns include loss of sensitive lands, agricultural land

---

9. For discussions of the negative consequences of sprawl, see Lowell, *supra* note 2; Jeremy R. Meredith, *Sprawl and the New Urbanist Solution*, 89 VA. L. REV. 447 (2003).

conversion, increased energy consumption due to larger homes, polluted runoff from impervious surfaces, deforestation due to development, and species loss due to land development, temperature increases, flooding, and drought. Sprawl promotes ground water and fresh water depletion due to high per household water usage and increases water pollution, air quality degradation, and carbon dioxide emissions, and, as discussed in the greatest detail in this chapter, wetlands destruction.

Sprawl increases water consumption and demands for water from more distant sources. The sprawl lifestyle, which often includes large lawns, car washes, and swimming pools, contributes to overdraft of water resources across the country. For example, the expansion of urban areas in southwestern Sunbelt states is taking a toll on the once mighty Colorado River. Additionally, the "mining" of ground water, as it is known in Arizona, represents a serious threat to long-term aquifer productivity in many regions. Sprawl's impact on water supply, however, arises not just by overuse of surface and ground water, but also by interference with ground water recharge: sprawl means pavement, and a paved area will prevent ground water recharge.[10]

Suburban communities are often located in areas with limited water supplies. Some communities, thus, have sought to receive water from outside natural water basins. For example, the City of Waukesha, a sprawling suburb west of Milwaukee, has long sought Lake Michigan water to provide water for a part of the community that lies outside the Great Lakes Basin, meaning that water used in the community would not flow back into the Great Lakes. And even states in the West and Southeast, where sprawl is a major problem, have long desired to pump water from the Great Lakes.[11]

With development focused on the automobile as the primary transportation mechanism, water quality has suffered, as has air quality with the accompanying increases in greenhouse gas emissions. Many of the environmental problems of sprawl are "inextricably linked with automobile travel."[12] The amount of pavement needed for parking lots and roadways prevents the land from absorbing precipitation and instead delivers it, along with sediment, litter, and chemicals such as gasoline and pesticides, into waterways. And "[r]esidents must rely on automobile travel for even the simplest trips, because sprawled development creates large distances between residential and commercial areas."[13] The distance of suburbs from the city centers, combined with the still very limited public transportation systems in the United States, helped vehicle use soar from 1 trillion to 2 trillion miles per

---

10. Patrick Gallagher, *The Environmental, Social and Cultural Impacts of Sprawl*, 15 NAT. RESOURCES & ENV'T 219, 220 (Spring 2001).

11. Such a diversion is regulated by the Great Lakes Compact, which requires the consent of the governors of states bordering the lakes before a diversion outside the basin can commence.

12. Meredith, *supra* note 9, at 464.

13. *Id.* at 465 (citing Andres Duany et al., SUBURBAN NATION: THE RISE OF SPRAWL AND THE DECLINE OF THE AMERICAN DREAM 24-25 (2000)).

year from 1970 to 1990,[14] while population increased by 22%.[15] Individuals also live increasingly farther from work. "From 1960 to 1990, the number of people with jobs outside their counties of residence grew over 200% to 27.5 million."[16] All these travel patterns have resulted in increased traffic congestion, causing idling emissions and wasted fuel, and air pollution resulting in smog, respiratory problems in humans, and harm to crops.

Sprawl implicates a host of ecological concerns, but wetlands prove a useful example of the magnitude of the problem, as discussed below. Like other natural resources implicated by sprawl, the benefits of wetlands are often underappreciated, and the fact that development creates the environmental harm is often unknown to consumers (in this case home buyers). Thus, creating awareness of wetlands destruction and the other adverse impacts of sprawl will need to be an important part of future policy initiatives.

Wetlands & Sprawl

The average person might call a wetland a bog, a swamp, or a marsh. The scientist might describe a wetland by discussing its hydrological role or the ecosystem services it provides. The hunter might see a wetland as habitat for waterfowl, and farmers as potential cropland in need of drainage. And developers might consider wetlands an impediment to construction or an amenity for potential purchasers.

Early Christians and Puritans viewed wetlands as evil and the devil's playgrounds, and later settlers shared this disdain, associating wetlands with muck, mosquitoes, and disease.[17] This view towards wetlands mirrors the historical trends of natural resource consumption discussed in Chapter One. Even literature invoked wetlands as dangerous and scary places. The headless horseman first appears near a swamp in Washington Irving's *The Legend of Sleepy Hollow*. And Charles Dickens, while visiting southern Illinois in 1842, described a wetland as a "dismal swamp" filled with "rank, unwholesome vegetation" that was a "hotbed of disease, an ugly sepulcher, a grave uncheered by any gleam of promise: a place without one single quality, in earth or air or water, to commend it . . . ."[18]

Today, by contrast, from an ecological perspective, wetlands are recognized as necessary ecosystems where water saturates or floods the soil. They vary widely in their soil types, topography, climate, water chemistry, hydrology, and vegeta-

---

14. F. KAID BENFIELD ET AL., ONCE THERE WERE GREENFIELDS: HOW URBAN SPRAWL IS UNDERMINING AMERICA'S ENVIRONMENT, ECONOMY AND SOCIAL FABRIC 30 (1999).

15. According to the U.S. Census Bureau, the U.S. population was 203,211,926 in 1970 and 248,709,873 in 1990.

16. Meredith, *supra* note 9, at 465 (citing Fed. Highway Admin., U.S. Dept. of Transp., Journey to Work Trends in the United States and its Major Metropolitan Areas, 1960-1990 (1993)).

17. ANN VILEISIS, DISCOVERING THE UNKNOWN LANDSCAPE: A HISTORY OF AMERICA'S WETLANDS xi, 33-35 (1997) (noting the early Puritan and Christian notions that swamps are evil, devilish and "sinful").

18. CHARLES DICKENS, AMERICAN NOTES: A JOURNEY 171 (Fromm Int'l Publ'g Corp. 1985) (1842) (as cited in J.R. MCNEILL, SOMETHING NEW UNDER THE SUN: AN ENVIRONMENTAL HISTORY OF THE TWENTIETH-CENTURY WORLD 186 (2001); HUGH PRINCE, WETLANDS OF THE AMERICAN MIDWEST: A HISTORICAL GEOGRAPHY OF CHANGING ATTITUDES 121 (1997)).

tion; they are permanent, seasonal, or even ephemeral. Wetlands are best described through their important environmental functions, characteristics not respected by religious text or understood by early settlers. They filter pollutants and excess nutrients, reduce flooding, retard stormwater runoff, recharge aquifers, and provide habitat for fish, waterfowl, and wildlife. To reflect these values, ecologists embraced the term "wetland" instead of "swamp" in the 1950s.[19]

Society enjoys numerous—and quite valuable—benefits from wetlands. As seen in Table 4, wetlands purify water and perform a variety of lesser-known services, such as absorbing carbon from the environment.

Table 4: Wetland Ecosystem Services

Water purification	Waste detoxification
Climate regulation	Food
Freshwater	Fiber and fuel
Biochemical materials	Genetic materials
Water regulation and hydrological flow	Erosion regulation
Natural hazard regulation	Pollination
Soil formation	Nitrogen cycling
Storm surge reduction	Flood protection
Animal habitat	

Sources: MILLENNIUM ECOSYSTEM ASSESSMENT, ECOSYSTEMS AND HUMAN WELL-BEING: WETLANDS AND WATER SYNTHESIS, tbl. 1 (World Resources Institute 2005); Christine A. Klein, *The New Nuisance: An Antidote to Wetlands Loss, Sprawl, and Global Warming*, 48 B.C. L. REV. 1155 (2007).

Wetlands also provide real financial benefits. For example, EPA reported that the wetlands of South Carolina's Congaree Bottomland Hardwood Swamp operate as a $5 million wastewater treatment facility.[20] The total economic value placed on the services performed by freshwater marshes is more than double that of drained marshes used for agriculture.[21] Individual communities receive in excess of $1 million in benefits from wetlands' ability to purify water.[22] Draining 5,000 acres of wetlands wipes out natural flood control valued at $1.5 million annually.[23] And destroying wetland habitats harms the fishing, hunting, bird watching, and wildlife photography industries, valued at billions of dollars annually in the United States.[24]

19. VILEISIS, *supra* note 17, at 7, 209 (noting the term "wetlands" entered into the American vocabulary in the 1950s).

20. Lowell, *supra* note 2, at 250 (citing EPA, Wetlands and People, available at http://www.epa.gov/OWOW/wetlands/vital/people.html (last updated March 23, 2005)).

21. *See* MILLENNIUM ECOSYSTEM ASSESSMENT, *supra* note 3, at 2.

22. Christine A. Klein, *The New Nuisance: An Antidote to Wetlands Loss, Sprawl, and Global Warming*, 48 B.C. L. REV. 1155, 1200 (2007).

23. *Id.* at 1201 (citing EPA, FUNCTIONS AND VALUES OF WETLANDS (2001)).

24. *Id.* (citing EPA, FUNCTIONS AND VALUES OF WETLANDS).

Despite wetlands' benefits (underappreciated in the past), people have historically destroyed wetlands for economic, moral, utilitarian, agrarian, and aesthetic
reasons,[25] and the destruction has been rampant. The original religious desire to
rid the land of unhealthy marshes and wicked swamps was replaced by the simple
notion that wetlands stood in the way of commercial progress. In line with traditional
consumption behavior, settlers intensively logged wetlands, which, once empty of
extractable resources, served only to hinder agricultural and urban development.
Early urban development exacted a steep toll on the land. Marshes and swamps
were filled along the east coast, upper Midwest, and Mississippi Delta to develop
cities and early suburbs now within city borders. The cities of Boston, Chicago,
Milwaukee, and New Orleans are built upon wetlands. By 1645, Bostonians had
already manipulated all natural wetlands that initially existed within their small
city's boundaries.[26] Early Boston's low-lying outskirts, like Back Bay, would be
filled, and before long the city's "sprawling suburbs would soon swallow up the
critical natural landscapes."[27] Wetland destruction allowed for the construction
of New Orleans. Trees and bottomland forests were cut, levees built, and ditches
dredged to eliminate swamps, stop flooding, and make room for development and
channels of commerce. By 1727, New Orleans was home to a levee more than a
mile long and 18 feet wide to keep floodwaters out.[28]

Wetlands drainage, ironically known as "reclamation," "could magically create valuable lands from worthless lands, a prospect that matched expectations of
unsurpassing opportunity in America."[29] Wetlands drainage is one of the oldest
land modification techniques, and reclamation projects were commonplace in
twentieth century Europe and North America. Farm journal advocacy and education
encouraged people to view natural wetlands as profitable farmland, drained to make
fertile agricultural lands. Wetlands transformed into farmlands in the valleys of
California, the upper Midwest, the Florida Everglades, and Mississippi. "Between
the mid-1950s and the mid-1970s alone, 458,000 acres of wetlands—an area half
the size of Rhode Island—had been whittled away *each year*. Agriculture accounted
for 87% of those losses."[30] From 1985 to 1995, the net amount of wetlands lost
dropped to 117,000 acres per year, with agriculture claiming the most acreage but
with development accounting for more loss than in earlier decades.[31]

From the 1780s to the 1980s, 60 wetlands on average were destroyed each hour,
a stunning rate that decimated more than half the wetlands in the lower 48 states,
according to the U.S. Geological Survey.[32] More than 220 million acres of wetlands

---

25. ANN VILEISIS, DISCOVERING THE UNKNOWN LANDSCAPE: A HISTORY OF AMERICA'S WETLANDS
75 (1997).
26. VILEISIS, *supra* note 25, at 32.
27. *Id.* at 243.
28. VILEISIS, *supra* note 25, at 44–45.
29. *Id.* at 67.
30. *Id.* at 273.
31. BENFIELD ET AL., *supra* note 14, at 70–71.
32. *Id.* at 70.

habitat once covered the nation's land. As of 2006, just over 100 million acres of wetlands remain across an American landscape dominated by suburbs.[33] Sprawling suburban subdivisions, commercial strip malls, big box stores with huge parking lots, and other types of development accounted for 61% of the net freshwater wetlands lost in the United States between 1998 and 2004.[34] Now, wetlands are in more danger from sprawl than agriculture.[35] "Because riverine networks, lakes, wetlands, and their connecting groundwaters, are literally the 'sinks' into which landscapes drain, they are greatly influenced by terrestrial processes."[36] Wetlands are uniquely and significantly harmed by suburban sprawl, with tens of thousands, and perhaps hundreds of thousands, of acres of wetlands lost each year.[37] "Almost half of all annual wetland losses are caused by sprawl development, attributable in part to increased development in coastal areas."[38] Land conversion can directly destroy wetlands and cause biodiversity loss and hydrology changes.

Loss of wetlands parallels a loss in biological resources. Wetlands are a "cradle of life" providing habitat for waterfowl, fish, birds, mammals, plant life, and endangered species.[39] One-half of the animals and one-third of the plants listed as endangered or threatened depend on wetlands.[40] Industrialization and urbanization took their toll on wetlands by the 1930s, resulting in a decline of wildlife populations, especially fish and waterfowl, and "flyways" used by migratory

---

33. For wetlands acreage data, see T.E. DAHL, U.S. FISH & WILDLIFE SERV., STATUS AND TRENDS OF WETLANDS IN THE CONTERMINOUS UNITED STATES 1998 TO 2004 (2006), http://wetlandsfws.er.usgs. gov/status_trends/national_reports/trends_2005_report.pdf; VILEISIS, *supra* note 25, at 4, 11. Worldwide over the twentieth century, people drained 15% of perhaps 10 million square kilometers of wetlands, an area the size of Canada. J.R. MCNEILL, SOMETHING NEW UNDER THE SUN: AN ENVIRONMENTAL HISTORY OF THE TWENTIETH-CENTURY WORLD 188 (2001); *see also* MILLENNIUM ECOSYSTEM ASSESSMENT, ECOSYSTEMS AND HUMAN WELL-BEING: WETLANDS AND WATER SYNTHESIS 3 (2005), *available at* http:// www.millenniumassessment.org/documents/document.358.aspx.pdf ("More than 50% of specific types of wetlands in parts of North America, Europe, Australia, and New Zealand were converted during the twentieth century.").

34. DAHL, *supra* note 33, at 16.

35. *See* Ryan M. Seidemann & Catherine D. Susman, *Wetlands Conservation in Louisiana: Voluntary Incentives and Other Alternatives*, 17 J. ENVTL. L. & LITIG. 441, 482 (2002).

36. Jill S. Baron et al., *Meeting Ecological and Societal Needs for Freshwater*, 12 ECOLOGICAL APPLICATIONS 1247, 1247 (2002).

37. *See* Craig Anthony Arnold, *Clean-Water Land Use: Connecting Scale and Function*, 23 PACE ENVTL. L. REV. 291, 198–99 (2006) ("Wetlands have been lost to land development at alarming rates: More than half of the wetlands in the coterminous United States have been lost since 1700, and the loss continues to exceed 50,000 acres per year, but down from nearly 300,000 per year in the 1980s."); *see also* Nancy Kubasek & Alex Frondorf, 32 REAL EST. L.J. 246 (2003) ("Furthermore, 100,000 acres of wetlands are destroyed every year due to urban sprawl."); Jerry L. Anderson, *The Environmental Revolution at Twenty-Five*, 26 RUTGERS L.J. 395, 401 (1995) ("Wetlands are still vanishing at an almost unbelievable rate of hundreds of thousands of acres every year....") (citing Robert D. Sokolove & P. Robert Thompson, *The Future of Wetland Regulation is Here*, 23 REAL EST. L.J. 78, 78 (1994) (estimating loss at 300,000 acres per year); Lettie M. Wenner, *Wetlands Preservation in the United States: A Case of Fragmented Authority*, 13 N. ILL. U. L. REV. 589, 595 (1993) (100,000 to 200,000 acres of wetlands filled per year in the 1980s)).

38. Gallagher, *supra* note 10, at 221.

39. BENFIELD ET AL., *supra* note 14, at 70.

40. *Id.* ("About half of the animals and one-third of the plant species listed as endangered or threatened are dependent on wetlands.")

birds. Given how wetlands destruction hurts game animals, it should come as no surprise that sportsmen and hunting clubs promoted early attempts to regulate and protect wetlands.

Changing water flow patterns, increased flooding, decreased groundwater recharge, loss of natural water filtering mechanisms—all are grim consequences of wetlands destruction. Wetlands absorb excess rainwater and snow melt and abate potential flooding problems. More roads, parking lots, and homes mean fewer permeable surfaces, which causes increased runoff into the limited remaining wetlands. These areas are unprepared for the increased flow and nutrient loads,[41] and the result often is flooding in low-lying areas unsuited for the water flow. Thus, development pressures remaining healthy wetlands by forcing them to absorb more water flow and runoff pollutants to compensate for the wetlands that development destroyed. So, wetlands loss perversely destroys and damages the ability of remaining wetlands to provide effective ecosystem services.

B.   Regulating Sprawl and Wetlands

The environmental costs of sprawl—water consumption and pollution, energy consumption, wetlands loss, among many others—generally have been subject to traditional environmental regulation issued under statutes that deal with each specific natural resource. Therefore, Part B discusses wetlands regulation to show how the ecological consequences of sprawl have been traditionally dealt with in a detailed manner on a resource-by-resource basis (and not with the initial intention of mitigating sprawl effects).

While wetlands loss has slowed, the review of current wetlands programs below confirms that this approach has not been effective in addressing the effects of sprawl. Only more recently has legislation been passed to mitigate the costs of sprawl directly, commonly known as "smart growth" or "growth management" legislation. On the one hand, in the absence of any national land use legislation or policy, most land use decisions are made at the local level. On the other hand, sprawl or smart growth legislation, in its relative infancy, has been promulgated by state governments. The following section reviews common elements of these current smart growth programs as part of a new effort to address and mitigate sprawl.

Sprawl & the Law

"Land use is the forgotten agenda of the environmental movement."[42] This is because while the harms associated with land use are well known, sprawl "evades a...clear solution."[43] As discussed previously, national policy has historically

---

41. James D. Wickham et al., *Geographic Targeting of Increases in Nutrient Export Due to Future Urbanization*, 12 ECOLOGICAL APPLICATIONS 93, 93–94 (2002).

42. John Turner & Jason Rylander, *Land Use: The Forgotten Agenda*, in THINKING ECOLOGICALLY: THE NEXT GENERATION OF ENVIRONMENTAL POLICY 61 (1997).

43. Meredith, *supra* note 9, at 448.

promoted American sprawl through federal transportation and housing policy.[44] Federal transportation policy provides for near full subsidization of highways compared with the low funding of mass transit. The Federal Housing Administration provides selective insurance for home mortgages and has a preference for home construction rather than repair. The American promotion of "single family housing has often driven suburban planning by default."[45] Thus, at the federal level, no land use policy or program recognizes or addresses the negative impacts of sprawl.

In part, this may be due to the established pattern in the United States of land use decisions being the purview of local governments. On the one hand, at the local level, municipalities generally have dealt with sprawl by focusing on practical tools to maintain traditional neighborhood structures and influence the pattern and pace of development.[46] On the other hand, local governments often support sprawling development due to the short-term economic gains such development can provide for municipalities.

States began to recognize that some broader perspective was needed in order to coordinate development and planning on a broader geographic basis. At the state level, Hawaii first passed land use legislation in 1961, and now, over the last two decades, the vast majority of states have passed some sort of "smart growth" or "growth management" legislation.[47] Smart growth legislation hopes to be the antithesis to sprawl by institutionalizing the pragmatic goals of compact, high-density, mixed-use development and by creating transportation choices besides the automobile.[48]

Hawaii's Land Use Law empowers a state agency to determine the location, use, and timing of new development across the state with the objectives of preserving environmentally sensitive areas and preventing haphazard development. In 1970, Vermont Act 250 established a statewide development permitting system over major projects through local and regional planning commissions. Oregon enacted legislation in 1973 that included growth management over urban boundaries and state oversight of local planning, with these states pioneering an effort that now includes nearly every other state in the Union.

While there is variation from state to state, state smart growth approaches generally have common elements. Using economic initiatives, states have eliminated subsidies that promote sprawl and have targeted spending and infrastructure to designated growth areas. Smart growth plans promote infill development (i.e., building on property or vacant lots within an already developed area) and preserve

---

44. Meredith, *supra* note 9, at 475-76.

45. Hayden, *supra* note 1, at 4.

46. Jay Wickersham, *Legal Framework: The Laws of Sprawl and the Laws of Smart Growth* in David C. Soule, REMAKING AMERICAN COMMUNITIES: A REFERENCE GUIDE TO URBAN SPRAWL 39 (2007).

47. For discussion of state growth management legislation, see Ed Bolen, Kara Brown, David Kiernan and Kate Kunschnik, *Smart Growth: A Review of Programs State by State*, 8 HASTINGS WEST-NORTHWEST J. OF ENVTL. L. & POL'Y 145 (2001); Wickersham, *supra* note 46, and Jerry Anthony, *Do State Growth Management Regulations Reduce Sprawl?*, 39 URBAN AFF. REV. 376 (2004).

48. Wickersham, *supra* note 46, at 34.

critical natural resources, open space, and areas of environmental and recreational value. Much state legislation is a reaction to the fact that local governments have traditionally dominated land use decisions. In response to the reality of local control, states encourage or require local governments to plan in ways that consider the above elements. States provide oversight of local planning, ensure consistency between local land use plans and zoning with state goals, and review and approve major development projects. Finally, states are supporting local planning by providing incentives and technical assistance to local governments and encouraging them to enter into regional planning agreements.

The environmental costs of sprawl are clear. Yet, smart growth legislation has proven to, at best, have limited effectiveness in containing or preventing sprawl in general. But, to what extent has state growth management legislation proven successful to protect natural resources implicated by sprawl by protecting them on a resource-by-resource basis? Wetlands prove a useful example to addressing this inquiry.

Wetlands & the Law

Wetlands protection is not the default rule under federal, state, or local law. Wetlands permitting processes generally are designed to allow development to proceed, even if wetlands are lost. While the rate of wetlands loss has declined in recent years, a review of current federal, state, and local laws confirms that environmental laws targeted to protect a single resource lack the more holistic perspective needed to protect wetlands and other resources against a diffuse source of impacts, such as sprawl. As discussed below, several different layers of governmental regulation play a role in determining whether development that destroys wetlands can proceed, despite the loss of ecological benefits. Yet, there exist few policies to help individuals refrain from living in sprawling developments, and none to help consumers understand that their housing may have been built upon a previously functioning wetland. While this may seem removed from everyday life, individual procurement power can influence development growth. By understanding regulatory structure and the ecosystem services of wetlands, people are better positioned to make eco-friendly choices when deciding where to live.

Little land use or water regulation protected wetlands before the 1970s. Suburban growth prospered, with state wetlands law and municipal zoning in their infancy and without a sophisticated understanding of the importance of wetlands. At the federal level, the U.S. Army Corps of Engineers (the Corps) concerned itself with building dams and levees to control the waters of marshy areas, and conversion of land into farmland remained economically important. Not until the 1960s and 1970s did Corps scientists begin to appreciate and understand the importance of wetlands and their services. For example, the decision to preserve wetlands along the Charles River in Boston saved the state of Massachusetts $17 million in potential flood damage.[49]

---

49. Regina McMahon, Comment, *The Lucas Dissenters Saw Katrina Coming: Why Environmental Regulation of Coastal Development Should Not Be Categorized as a "Taking,"* 15 PENN. ST. ENVTL. L. REV. 373, 380–81 (2007); *see also* VILEISIS, *supra* note 25, at 24–43.

Now, all levels of government struggle to determine the appropriate scope of wetlands protection in the face of overwhelming development interests.

At the national level, the Clean Water Act (CWA) subjects wetlands to federal regulatory jurisdiction.[50] The CWA operates as a cooperative arrangement between the Corps and EPA to share authority to regulate the nation's waters. The CWA gives EPA the authority to regulate pollutant discharges into waters[51] and prohibits the "discharge of dredged or fill material into the navigable waters" without an appropriate permit from the Corps.[52] With the help of the Corps, EPA issues guidance discussing the wetlands permitting process.[53] In determining whether to issue wetlands filling permits, the Corps must consider whether practicable alternatives to the activity exist, determine whether the activity is water dependent, and conduct a public interest review.[54] The Corps, exerting its significant discretion, has liberally granted wetlands filling permits. In other words, permits are granted to fill in wetlands with dirt for the purposes of development.

The historical position of the Corps, like that of other agencies such as the Bureau of Reclamation during the era of westward expansion, was to help promote agricultural, commercial and economic growth, and development. Nearly by definition, any public works project (including those satisfying the Corps' mission to build infrastructure) involves some destruction of the natural environment.

Exerting a greater presence after the Civil War in an effort to support river navigability, the Corps opened shipping channels, blocked sloughs, built revetments, removed snags, and dredged shallow areas.[55] Over a century later, the Corps approved dredge-and-fill permits under the CWA at a staggering rate, denying only around 1% of permit applications and resulting in an average annual wetlands loss of more than 50,000 acres.[56] The Corps' willingness to build flood-control dams and issue permits has encouraged extensive homebuilding on downstream floodplains and wetlands.

---

50. Such jurisdiction exists pursuant to the Federal Water Pollution Control Act Amendments of 1972 (and prior to that the Rivers and Harbors Act of 1899) meant to keep waterways clear for navigation. Rivers and Harbors Act of 1899 § 10, 33 U.S.C. § 403 (2006).

51. Clean Water Act § 402, 33 U.S.C.§ 1342 (2006).

52. Clean Water Act § 404, 33 U.S.C. § 1344 (2006).

53. Clean Water Act § 404(b)(1), 33 U.S.C.§ 1344 (b)(1) (2006).

54. 33 C.F.R. § 320.4(a) (2008); 40 C.F.R. § 230.10 (2008), *see also* William F. Pederson, *Using Federal Environmental Regulations to Bargain for Private Land Use Control*, 21 YALE J. ON REG. 1, 20 (2004) (footnotes omitted).

55. VILEISIS, *supra* note 25, at 112.

56. Between 1977 and 1980, the Corps had 76,000 dredge-and-fill permit applications; many received general permits, and the Corps denied only 960—less than 1.3 percent. VILEISIS, *supra* note 25, at 264; *see also* Brandee Kethcum, Note, *Like the Swamp Thing: Something Ambiguous Rises from the Hidden Depths of Murky Water—The Supreme Court's Treatment of Murky Wet Land in* Rapanos v. United States, 68 LA. L. REV. 983, 1014–15 (2008) ("The current mechanisms to regulate water quality have not totally fulfilled the CWA's statutory mandate. Even with the permitting program, average annual loss of wetlands still amounts to more than 58,000 acres per year. This figure is down eighty percent from the previous decade. In addition, of the nine states that reported to EPA sources of recent wetland losses, four indicated that filling and draining, residential development, and urban growth were among the highest causes." (footnotes omitted)).

The Corps' nationwide permit (NWP) program has also accelerated wetlands loss.[57] The program grants permits for filling in a wetland so long as the wetland meets some standardized criteria, and it does not require the permit applicant to demonstrate that the proposed site is the best alternative to minimize damage.[58] For example, NWP No. 29 (there are about 50 nationwide permitting programs available in all) permits any residential development, including single homes, multi-unit developments, and suburban subdivisions, so long as wetlands loss does not exceed one-half acre.[59] In addition to homes, the permit applies to building foundations, parking lots, garages, yards, and recreation facilities. Even worse, prior to the creation of current NWP No. 29, much development proceeded under the old NWP No. 26, which permitted wetlands fill so long as a project would not cause a loss of more than three acres.

Over the last 40 years or more, the Corps' understanding and appreciation of wetlands has increased, and the agency recognizes that protecting the environment is an explicit part of its mission. This enlightenment, driven by the passage of the CWA and the role of EPA, led to a decline in wetlands loss and an increase in efforts to create more mitigation-driven wetlands. However, the Reagan Administration challenged wetlands gains by expanding the general permitting program and failing to require individualized review for isolated wetlands measuring fewer than 10 acres.[60] Subsequently, preservation of wetlands became a higher priority, as reflected by President George H.W. Bush's "no net loss" wetlands campaign platform.[61]

While "no net loss" became a clear change in wetlands policy, adopted by subsequent presidents as well, no administration has exerted the full authority of EPA to significantly cut back the Corps' permitting of fill activities or end the nationwide permitting program altogether. EPA maintains veto authority over Corps' permitting under the CWA and can deny a permit if the discharge "will have an unacceptable adverse effect on municipal water supplies, shellfish beds and fishery areas (includ-

---

57. Clean Water Act § 404(e), 33 U.S.C. § 1344(e) (2006).

58. U.S. Army Corps of Engineers, Nationwide Permits Information, http://www.usace.army.mil/CECW/Pages/nw_permits.aspx.

59. Under NWP No. 29, "[t]he discharge must not cause the loss of greater than 1/2-acre of non-tidal waters of the United States, including the loss of no more than 300 linear feet of stream bed, unless for intermittent and ephemeral stream beds this 300 linear foot limit is waived in writing by the district engineer. This NWP does not authorize discharges into non-tidal wetlands adjacent to tidal waters." U.S. ARMY CORPS OF ENGINEERS, DECISION DOCUMENT NATIONWIDE PERMIT 29, http://www.usace.army.mil/CECW/Documents/cecwo/reg/nwp/NWP_29_2007.pdf (Mar. 1, 2007).

60. VILEISIS, supra note 25, at 275-279.

61. Actually, the idea of "no overall net loss of nation's remaining wetland base" first appeared in a 1988 National Wetlands Policy Forum report during the Reagan Administration. See Oliver A. Houck, Federalism in Wetlands Regulation: A Consideration of Delegation of Clean Water Act Section 404 and Related Programs to the States, 54 MD. L. REV. 1242, 1301 (1995) (citing CONSERVATION FOUND., PROTECTING AMERICA'S WETLANDS: AN ACTION AGENDA—THE FINAL REPORT OF THE NATIONAL WETLANDS POLICY FORUM 4 (1988)).

ing spawning and breeding areas), wildlife, or recreational areas."[62] EPA, though, has exercised this authority only sparingly.

Despite the seemingly broad scope and purposes of the CWA, namely to "restore and maintain the chemical, physical, and biological integrity of the Nation's waters,"[63] courts have limited the federal government's basic jurisdiction to regulate wetlands. Under the CWA, the Corps can regulate fill into "navigable waters," with "navigable waters" being defined as "the waters of the United States." Supreme Court precedent, *United States v. Riverside Bayview Homes* (1985), suggested that the federal government could protect a broad set of wetlands as "waters of the United States."[64] The Court concluded that federal agencies' regulatory powers should be construed broadly in determining "where water ends and land begins" because the term "navigable" is of limited import given its broad statutory definition.[65] Therefore, for more than 15 years, the common understanding of *Riverside* was that Congress had exercised the full scope of its constitutional powers in protecting the nation's wetlands through passage of the Clean Water Act. However, the scope of federal jurisdiction over wetlands became more limited following the Court's decision in *Rapanos v. United States* (2006).[66]

In *Rapanos*, three groups of justices differed on a standard to determine whether a wetland is subject to federal jurisdiction. Justice Scalia's plurality opinion argues that the CWA meant to assert jurisdiction over relatively permanent, standing, or flowing bodies of water, not intermittent and ephemeral wetlands, with a continuous surface connection.[67] In concurring with the decision (but based on a different rationale), Justice Kennedy's opinion asserts that the Corps maintains jurisdiction over wetlands that possess a "significant nexus" to navigable or potentially navigable waterways.[68] Wetlands possess this significant nexus "if the wetlands, either alone or in combination with similarly situated lands in the region, significantly affect the chemical, physical, and biological integrity of other covered waters more readily understood as 'navigable.'"[69] Justice Stevens's *Rapanos* dissent argues that Congress intended the CWA to "be given the broadest possible constitutional interpretation."[70] As a result, wetlands now face more limited federal protection

---

62. Clean Water Act, § 404(c), 33 U.S.C. § 1344(c) (2006).

63. 33 U.S.C. § 1251 (2006).

64. 474 U.S. 121 (1985).

65. *Id.* at 133.

66. 547 U.S. 715 (2006). An earlier decision, *Solid Waste Agency of Northern Cook County v. U.S. Army Corps of Engineers (SWANCC)*, 531 U.S. 159 (2001), first limited the Corps's wetlands jurisdiction and laid the groundwork for the Court to decide *Rapanos*. The *SWANCC* Court, relying on the word "navigable" in the statute despite its seemingly broad definition and seeking to avoid Commerce Clause concerns, held that isolated intra-state wetlands are not subject to federal jurisdiction based solely upon their use as habitat by migratory birds. Thus, developers would not need a federal permit to fill them.

67. *Rapanos*, 547 U.S. at 732–33, 742.

68. *Id.* at 779 (Kennedy, J., concurring).

69. *Id.* at 780.

70. Id. at 809–10 (Stevens, J., dissenting); *SWANCC*, 531 U.S. at 181 (Stevens., J. dissenting) (citing to S. REP. NO. 92-1236, at 144 (1972)).

and confusing jurisdictional standards that have resulted in the destruction and pollution of U.S. waterways.[71]

In light of the federal government's limited wetlands jurisdiction post-*Rapanos* and the Corps' permitting track record, the role of states and municipalities in wetlands protection has become even more important. States clearly retain the authority to regulate all wetlands in a state, but both the scope and level of state wetlands protection remain quite varied.[72] Some states lack laws allowing them to regulate wetlands left unprotected by the federal regulatory gap, and relatively few states have taken advantage of opportunities to fill the gap following the wave of judicial decisions about wetlands.[73]

Figure F: Map of States that Closed the Wetlands Regulatory Gap

Source: State Wetland Protection: Status, Trends & Model Approaches 10 Fig. 2-B (ELI 2008), http://www.elistore.org/Data/products/d18__06.pdf.

Those states that did fill the regulatory gap, like Wisconsin, asserted state jurisdiction over "non-federal wetlands," i.e., those wetlands no longer subject to federal authority, as well as over other wetlands in the state. Many of these

---

71. Charles Duhigg & Janet Roberts, *Rulings Restrict Clean Water Act, Hampering E.P.A.*, N.Y. Times (Feb. 28, 2010).

72. For perhaps the best and most thorough summary of state wetlands regulation, see *State Wetlands Protection: Status, Trends & Model Approaches,* a 50-state study by the Environmental Law Institute, available at http://www.elistore.org/reports_detail.asp?ID=11279 (March 2008).

73. Six states did adopt regulations that assert jurisdiction over geographically isolated wetlands: Indiana, North Carolina, Ohio, Tennessee, Washington and Wisconsin.

wetlands are located in suburban, exurban, and rural areas highly susceptible to sprawl. Wisconsin conservation and environmental groups (such as Sierra Club, Wisconsin Wetlands Association, Wisconsin Waterfowl Association, Rivers Alliance, National Wildlife Federation) urged quick adoption of legislation to restore regulatory authority over these wetlands, and other groups (such as the Wisconsin Homebuilders Association, Farm Bureau, Alliance of Cities) argued against enacting more stringent regulations than the federal regulations. After public debate and hearings, Wisconsin Governor Scott McCallum, a Republican, called a special legislative session in which both the Senate and Assembly unanimously adopted a bill signed into law on May 7, 2001. The legislation, known as 2001 Wisconsin Act 6, asserts Department of Natural Resources authority over non-federal wetlands using all the previously used federal criteria.[74] By using the same past federal standards to determine wetlands delineation and exemptions, the bill garnered support from both industry and environmental interests. Wisconsin thus became the first state to adopt a comprehensive response to the lack of federal jurisdiction over some wetlands.

In addition to asserting greater jurisdiction over wetlands as was done in Wisconsin, states can increase the scope of protection by developing more rigorous requirements than those of the federal government to maintain water quality standards and to limit wetlands degradation. In practical circumstances, state agencies can place conditions on nationwide permits and can veto any Corps permit if it violates state water quality standards.[75] State statutory law and constitutional provisions provide for further wetlands protections.[76] For example, Wisconsin's Chapter 30 statutory provisions regulate activities on the beds and banks of navigable waters, including wetlands, and the state's administrative code sets water quality standards that mandate consideration of whether wetlands projects are water dependent, whether alternatives exist, and whether significant problems will result.[77] All of these conditions limit the ability to develop residential housing in currently undeveloped areas near resources that provide valuable ecosystem services.

Some states are also building on a history of state protection of wetland resources that predates modern regulatory regimes. The Wisconsin Constitution protects navigable waters and wetlands by specifying that "the river Mississippi and the navigable waters leading into the Mississippi and St. Lawrence, and the carrying places between the same, shall be common highways and forever free, as well as

---

74. 2001 Wis. Act 6 (codified at WIS. STAT. § 231.36); WIS. ADMIN. CODE NAT. RES. §§ 351, 352 (2005).

75. State agencies can place conditions on NWP and veto any permit issued by the Corps under the CWA. 33 U.S.C. § 1341 (2006); 33 C.F.R. § 320.3(a) (2008). Nationwide permits can also be replaced by state and regional permitting systems made in conjunction with the Corps' Regional office. See, e.g., St. Paul District, U.S. Army Corps of Eng'rs, Regulatory (Permits): Highlights, http://www.mvp.usace. army.mil/regulatory/ (last visited Feb. 3, 2009).

76. Paula J. Schauwecker, Shifting the Focus of Wetlands Protection to State and Local Governments, 22 NAT. RESOURCES & ENV'T 66, 67 (2008) (citing JON KUSLER, MODEL STATE WETLAND STATUTE TO CLOSE THE GAP CREATED BY SWANCC (2001), available at www.aswm.org/swp/model-leg.pdf).

77. WIS. ADMIN. CODE NAT. RES. § 103 (2005).

to the inhabitants of the state as to the citizens of the United States."[78] This provision embodies Wisconsin's public trust doctrine, protecting the public's right to use navigable waters. The state, serving as trustee, holds title to navigable waters in trust for the benefit of citizens of the state and the nation.

Under this provision, sportsmen and hunting clubs initiated early efforts to protect Wisconsin's wetlands, which provide habitat for many game animals.[79] Similarly, state courts recognized the importance of wetlands. According to the Wisconsin Supreme Court in *Just v. Marinette*:

> Swamps and wetlands were once considered wasteland, undesirable, and not picturesque. But as people became more sophisticated, an appreciation was acquired that swamps and wetlands serve a vital role in nature, are part of the balance of nature and are essential to the purity of the water in our lakes and streams. Swamps and wetlands are a necessary part of the ecological creation and now, even to the uninitiated, possess their own beauty in nature.[80]

While state statutes can limit construction on or near wetlands, the public trust doctrine protects both the public's right to use the state's waterways and wetlands from environmental and aesthetic degradation.

As noted, in light of federal policy and court decisions, "more of the burden for regulating and protecting wetlands will shift to state and local governments,"[81] as already is the case for most land use planning. Like their state partners, local governments can employ a range of tools to protect wetlands, including zoning laws, subdivision and site-plan regulations, wetlands provisions in development ordinances, and separate wetlands ordinances.[82] Local governments can integrate protection of isolated wetlands into their larger water quality and watershed regulation efforts, can work to preserve wetlands by adopting local real estate tax incentives and by acquiring fee or conservation easement interests, and can establish buffer requirements for land next to wetlands.[83]

In fact, court decisions have prompted some local governments across the nation to adopt or amend their regulations to protect wetlands. For example, officials in Lake County, Illinois, located north of Chicago, amended their watershed development ordinance to protect more than 3,800 acres of wetlands in their jurisdiction

---

78. WIS. CONST. art. IX, § 1.

79. In *Diana Shooting Club v. Husting*, the Wisconsin Supreme Court recognized the public nature of navigable waters and held that the state's navigable waters "should be free to all for commerce, for travel, for recreation, and also for hunting and fishing, which are now mainly certain forms of recreation." 145 N.W. 816, 820 (1914).

80. *Just v. Marinette County*, 201 N.W.2d 761, 768 (Wis. 1972).

81. Schauwecker, *supra* note 76.

82. JON KUSLER & JEANNE CHRISTIE, ASS'N OF STATE WETLAND MANAGERS, COMMON QUESTIONS: THE SWANCC DECISION; ROLE OF THE STATES IN FILLING THE GAP 11 (2006); JON KUSLER, ASS'N OF STATE WETLAND MANAGERS, COMMON QUESTIONS: LOCAL GOVERNMENT WETLAND PROTECTION PROGRAMS 2 (2006); John R. Nolon, *In Praise of Parochialism: The Advent of Local Environmental Law*, 23 PACE ENVTL. L. REV. 705, 705–06 (2006).

83. KUSLER, *supra* note 82, at 2–4.

no longer subject to federal jurisdiction.[84] These make up about 45% of Lake County's remaining wetlands.[85] Under Lake County's rules, developers who want to build on these wetlands must establish a larger amount of wetlands elsewhere on the development site or they must pay someone an average of $60,000 an acre to establish them.[86] In nearby Kane County, Illinois, county officials revised their recently adopted storm water ordinance to protect wetlands by requiring developers to obtain local permits to build on sites containing wetlands not under federal jurisdiction.[87] The ordinance calls for buffers of varying sizes and the mitigation of some wetland losses, either through the creation of new wetlands in the county or payments in lieu of wetlands creation.[88] These are but two local examples, but many others exist in places like Escambia County, Florida; Dutchess County, New York; Attleboro and Melrose, Massachusetts; Snohomish County, Washington; and Bozeman and Lake Counties, Montana.[89]

As seen in this Part B, the federal government has failed to develop a national land use policy and provide enough oversight to ensure wetlands protection. Local

---

84. Erik Johnston, Nat'l Ass'n of Counties, *Innovative County Ordinances Save Money and Wetlands*, 37 COUNTY NEWS 1, 1 (2005); John Keilman, *Counties Embrace Wetlands Protection*, CHICAGO TRIB., Oct. 28, 2001, at 1.

85. Nat'l Ass'n of Counties, Wetlands Fact Sheet, http://www.naco.org/Template.cfm?Section=new_ technical_assistance&template=/ContentManagement/ContentDisplay.cfm&ContentID=18434 (last visited Feb. 3, 2009).

86. Keilman, *supra* note 84, at 1.

87. Kane County, Ill., Stormwater Mgmt. Ordinance §§ 414–18 (Jan. 1, 2005), *available at* http://www.co.kane.il.us/kcstorm/ordinance/adoptord.pdf; Kane County, Kane County Response to Flooding, http://www.co.kane.il.us/kcstorm/flood/response.htm (last visited Feb. 3, 2009).

88. Kane County, Ill., Stormwater Management Ordinance §§ 414–18.

89. Sheila Ingram, *Wetlands Ordinance Gets County Approval*, PENSACOLA NEWS J., Aug. 3, 2001, at 1A (county officials approved an ordinance requiring people to obtain a county permit before filling or otherwise affecting any wetlands and giving people the option of mitigating potential environmental damage by protecting wetlands elsewhere or by contributing to an environmental trust fund); Lynette Wacker, *Wetland/Waterbody/Watercourse Protection Catching On*, PLAN ON IT: A DUTCHESS COUNTY PLAN. FED'N NEWSL. 5 (2003), *available at* http://www.co.dutchess.ny.us/CountyGov/Departments/Planning/PlanOnIt1003.pdf (four towns in Dutchess County, New York, approved laws to cover wetlands otherwise left unprotected by state and federal laws); *see also* Dan Shapley, *Communities Act to Protect Wetlands*, POUGHKEEPSIE J., Nov. 29, 2003, at 1A; City of Attleboro, What is Protected by the Attleboro Wetlands Ordinance?, http://www.cityofattleboro.us/conservation/realpg2.htm (last visited Feb. 3, 2009) (the city approved a wetlands protection ordinance that requires a twenty-five-foot buffer zone around isolated wetlands); Melrose, Mass., Wetlands Protection Ordinance (May 7, 2007), *available at* http://www.cityofmelrose.org/departments/Conservation/adoptedordinance.htm (city officials approved an ordinance that prohibits anyone from removing, filling, dredging, building upon, degrading, discharging into, excavating, clearing, landscaping, polluting, draining, or changing the "physical, chemical, vegetative or biological characteristics" of any wetland, "whether or not they border surface waters," and requires buffers ranging from 100 feet to 200 feet around the wetland); Jeff Switzer, *Water and Wetlands Get More Protection*, DAILY HERALD (Everett, Wash.), Aug. 2, 2007, *available at* http://heraldnet.com/article/20070802/NEWS01/708020347 (county officials approved stricter rules to preserve wetlands, streams, and lakes in unincorporated parts of the county and to require buffers of up to 100 feet); JANET H. ELLIS, 2006 UPDATE OF CASE STUDIES FOR A PLANNING GUIDE FOR PROTECTING MONTANA'S WETLANDS AND RIPARIAN AREAS 2 (2006) (Bozeman city officials used zoning and subdivision regulations to regulate isolated wetlands measuring more than 400 square feet and smaller isolated wetlands providing habitat for rare animals or plants and where Lake County officials enacted density standards to help protect wetlands, streams, and rivers).

governments have proven to be poorly suited to deal with land use concerns given their focus on short-term economic interests. Accordingly, to date, sprawl has primarily been addressed directly through state legislation that seeks to modify development patterns and through federal, state, and local legislation that takes on a particular resource. Yet, growth management legislation has struggled to take effect, and development preferences and implementation problems have overwhelmed complex regulatory structure in environmental law. In order to effect change, policy must continue to focus on modifying existing infrastructure and legislation but also attempt to activate changes in individual behavior, something to this point that has not been attempted. Focused efforts will be needed to help consumers become more aware or receive more information about the environmental costs of sprawl, whether land use degradation or water scarcity, of their geographic and residential choices. By working from both ends of the hierarchy, from improved legal rules at all levels of government and from more active and informed individual choice, perhaps sprawl's momentum will stop pushing outward.

C. Limiting the Costs of Sprawl

As discussed above, no national land use policy exists to deal with the environmental costs of sprawling development. Most land use planning is done at the local level, and the environmental problems caused by sprawl have been traditionally dealt with through legislation that targets specific natural resources as opposed to development as a whole. Only recently have state governments passed "smart growth" or "growth management" legislation. In addition, individual choices about where to live promote development that can disturb natural resource functions. While sprawling developments have proved popular since the rise of the automobile, and while large tracts of land remain available in the United States, the choices to live in and permit development of these areas do not reflect the full environmental and even economic costs of development. Ultimately, however, ending sprawling land use practices will require significant revisions to traditional land use planning practices, as well as changes in individual preferences.

Efforts to mitigate the effects of sprawl should certainly address changing infrastructure and government policy since these seem to be drivers of sprawl. Surveys suggest that the suburban lifestyle may not be a top preference as a desired residential location and that people may like mixed-use development, may not necessarily prefer low-density communities, and may prefer compact business centers to malls.[90] Thus, going forward, land use policy and regulation should strive to influence individual behavior by activating these preferences or overcoming the influence of existing infrastructure and policy. In addition, perhaps consumer

---

90. Jeremy R. Meredith, *Sprawl and the New Urbanist Solution*, 89 VA. L. REV. 447, 472 (citing Robert G. Shibley, *The Complete New Urbanism and the Partial Practices of Placemaking*, 9 UTOPIAN STUD. 80, 82 (1998); Reid Ewing, *Counterpoint: Is Los Angeles-Style Sprawl Desirable?*, 63 J. AM. PLAN. ASS'N 107, 111 (1997)).

choice can be modified through providing greater information about the ecological costs of development and by creating financial incentives for individuals to live in dense neighborhoods near transit hubs and close to work.

In order to promote everyday environmentalism, public policy can directly influence individual behavior by, among other initiatives, providing consumers with knowledge of the environmental costs of their choices and by providing incentives to change behavior. However, traditional regulation and historical policy often still dictate infrastructure that influences and limits consumer choice. This book attempts to promote environmentally conscious decision-making in daily life and limit the negative ecological footprint of individual behavior. Earlier chapters explain that consumers have the ability to play a direct role by making eco-friendly choices by, for example, engaging in energy conservation. The earlier chapters also demonstrate that law can facilitate these choices through, for example, informational regulation like eco-labeling. But in the case of land use, are there limits to changing individual behavior?

In fact, in the case of sprawl, there are compelling arguments that there are significant limits to the individual behavior and consumer choice model promoted in Chapter Three (the household carbon and waste footprint) and Chapter Four (food choices). First, most development occurs prior to individual choices about where to live. Second, the informational burdens to understanding the true costs of choosing to live in a suburban development are heavy due to the complexities of land use—wetlands loss is a chief concern as are water scarcity, vehicle miles driven, and habitat loss. Third, the entrenched incentives for sprawl remain, the greatest being government subsidization of highway construction. And fourth, local land use planners have institutional limitations and resource constraints. Thus, most literature addressing the prevention of further sprawl has not focused on the individual, but instead has suggested changes to the traditional land use planning model, use of more creative direct land use regulation like the growth management legislation, and expansion of the jurisdiction of resource-by-resource environmental law, discussed above in Part B.

The role of individual behavior in preventing sprawl has been a largely untapped topic. Consumers should know more; and perhaps public policy can better inform customers of land degradation resulting from their potential residential development, as well as the increased carbon footprint and pollution of their choice. In addition, it is not clear that people actually prefer to live in the suburbs. Instead, people are shepherded towards sprawl and suburbanization through policy and infrastructure because they are either too burdened to acquire information or have no knowledge of how to activate true preferences.[91] In other words, it is simple to choose sprawl. This suggests that suburbanites may not know or not consider the true costs of sprawl. If so, then education may play a role in consumer choice by shifting preferences and influencing decisions at the local planning level.

---

91. *Cf.* Meredith, *supra* note 90, at 472.

This all leads to two important, but to this point unaddressed, empirical inquiries. First, if informational burdens are lowered and consumer knowledge increased about the environmental costs of sprawl, are individual residential choices subject to modification? Second, even if these goals can be accomplished, can these changed norms overcome the existing land use planning system and infrastructure that promotes sprawl?

The earlier chapters argue that activating changes in individual behavior is key, but the hurdle for accomplishing this is higher for sprawl; hence, the usual focus has been on changing current land use planning programs rather than directly influencing individual choice. As discussed below, changing existing land use management through sprawl legislation remains an attractive option (and popular among scholars and policymakers), even though the barriers to changing the existing land use model are steep. At the same time, this circumstance greatly underscores the need for a complementary model that seeks to directly influence individual behavior.

In short, going forward, two categories of changes are necessary to limit the true costs of sprawl: (1) traditional land use practices and planning processes that create sprawl must be changed as individuals are clearly driven by pre-existing infrastructure and options created by the existing legal regime, and (2) consumer preferences and behavior need to be modified through informational programs and economic incentives that can be shown to be effective. Dual tools are necessary since, even if different and more environmentally friendly preferences can be activated, land use planning and infrastructure choices must provide affordable places for people to live that would mesh with these new and changing environmental norms. In other words, of the necessary decision-making tools for influencing the environmental effects of everyday behavior discussed in the Introduction, mitigating sprawl will necessitate giving significant and equal weight to (1) changing traditional government action in addition to advancing more cutting-edge (2) informational labeling, (3) economic incentives, and (4) personal norm activation tools.

Improving the Existing Land Use Planning System

The familiar chorus among scholars—that the existing land use planning system and related infrastructure must be improved—rings true. The existing land use model of government incentives and local land use planning that promotes sprawl through highway construction and low-density development must pursue more progressive options. As discussed in Part B, while traditional resource-by-resource regulation addresses some ecological costs of sprawl, and while emerging growth management regulation is a necessary first step, additional changes to the existing land use regulatory structure must be made to mitigate the costs of sprawl, including better protection of wetlands. Necessary improvements include better inter-governmental coordination in land use planning, better understanding of the financial worth of ecosystem services provided by natural resources in doing development cost-benefit analyses, and implementing practical planning ideas to create a new more dense and sustainable agenda for local land use planning.

The path towards smart growth management is an excellent first step, but unfortunately sustained and effective anti-sprawl measures have been a rarity.[92] Professor Jerry Anthony researched the effectiveness of state growth management laws in controlling sprawl by examining the change in urban densities in 49 states over a 15-year period.[93] Anthony found that state growth management regulations have not made a significant impact in reducing sprawl. He was surprised by this finding given, at least on paper, the potential effectiveness of state smart growth laws. State programs have struggled for at least three reasons. First, limited support exists at the local level for actually limiting sprawl where land use decisions are made. Local governments' resources and technical understanding are too limited to effectively stop sprawl, and many local leaders simply do not want to limit sprawl given the short-term economic gains of development. Thus, the role of everyday environmentalism and making individuals understand the consequences of sprawl and their living choices is an even more important key to curbing sprawl. Second, Professor Anthony argues that states should not only create growth management legislation but must undertake a greater implementation role. Third, while regional planning approaches are preferable, as local decisions do not reflect greater geography and environmental concerns, no effective model of regional administration exists, in part due to ongoing control in local governments and lack of regional governmental power.

Thus, the following discussion offers further suggestions to change traditional regulatory land use practices that focus on sprawl directly and on individual natural resources, again using wetlands as an example. Necessary improvements include better inter-governmental coordination in land use planning, better understanding of the financial worth of ecosystem services provided by natural resources, and creating a new high-density development and sustainable agenda for local land use planning through practical initiatives.

First, there are problems with the existing structure of land use planning that, admittedly, will be difficult to change. The federal government has driven sprawl through highway construction and mortgage policy and has done little to limit sprawl. Local governments remain in control of most land use planning. Overall, far better inter-governmental coordination is needed to limit sprawl and protect the natural resources it implicates. This is a difficult proposition. Professor William Buzbee writes:

> Well established legal presumptions and traditional roles of federal, state, and local government make difficult any significant new attempts to alleviate and prevent harms associated with urban sprawl's cross-jurisdictional effects and roots. Sprawl

---

92. William W. Buzbee, *Urban Sprawl, Federalism, and The Problem of Institutional Complexity*, 68 FORDHAM L. REV. 57, 136 (1999).

93. See Anthony, *supra* note 47.

and current legal frameworks are mismatched. Local governments traditionally make land use choices, yet sprawl arises out of dynamics, causes, and effects that tend, at a minimum, to be regional. Any shift away from state and local governments' primacy in regulating land use, however, would be a major change in allocations of governmental responsibilities.[94]

Many argue for a greater federal role in land use planning by making better use of government taxes, conditional spending, and funding rewards to multi-jurisdictional entities, especially to create planning schemes that direct development to urban centers and to develop transportation infrastructure other than motor vehicles.[95]

While a federal role in promoting better infrastructure would be a positive development, local government decisions should be better scrutinized by state agencies. With the overwhelming majority of land use decisions made at the local level,[96] state legislation should require all local planning to conform with state-mandated growth management principles, provide local governments with informational resources and financial incentives for growth management planning, and expressly limit the ability of local governments to amend or create exceptions to state-mandated growth management and anti-sprawl plans.[97]

This does not mean that there is no room for improvement upon resource-by-resource driven environmental law. In fact, many of the same principles apply for improvement to occur—better federal law, a larger state role, and more sensible local practices. Thus, in the wetlands context, federal and state governments must provide a wetlands regulatory structure that permits local legislation to tailor rigorous wetlands protection to local interests and geography, coupled with rigid state oversight to ensure compliance with overall natural resource protection goals.

At the federal level, several actions need to be taken to create the foundation for better inter-governmental coordination. For example, given the Court's unwillingness to clarify *Rapanos*[98] and the unclear guidance as to which wetlands are actually subject to federal control, more action is needed. The executive branch apparently lacks the political resolve to state, through agency rule-making,[99] that a wide range of wetlands are subject to federal oversight or to adjust the balance of power between the Corps and EPA as discussed below. The legislative branch could clarify the scope of wetlands jurisdiction by passing the Clean Water Restoration Act (CWRA). Sponsored by Sen. Russ Feingold (D-Wis.), the bill would replace

---

94. *Id.* at 91.

95. *See* Buzbee, *supra* note 92; Jess M. Krannich, *A Modern Disaster: Agricultural Land, Urban Growth, and the Need for a Federally Organized Comprehensive Land Use Planning Model*, 16 CORNELL J. L. & PUB. POL'Y 57 (2006).

96. Kleppel, *supra* note 7, at 54.

97. Anthony, *supra* note 47, at 392.

98. The Court has denied certiorari to cases attempting to clarify *Rapanos*. *See. e.g.,* United States v. McWane, Inc., 129 S. Ct. 630 (2008).

99. This course of action is suggested by Justice Roberts' concurring opinion in *Rapanos*.

the statutory phrase "navigable waters" with "waters of the United States."[100] The CWRA defines "waters of the United States" as:

> all waters subject to the ebb and flow of the tide, the territorial seas, and all interstate and intrastate waters and their tributaries, including lakes, rivers, streams (including intermittent streams), mudflats, sandflats, wetlands, sloughs, prairie potholes, wet meadows, playa lakes, natural ponds, and all impoundments of the foregoing, to the fullest extent that these waters, or activities affecting these waters, are subject to the legislative power of Congress under the Constitution.[101]

The stated purpose of the CWRA is to "provide protection to the waters of the United States to the fullest extent of the legislative authority of Congress under the Constitution."[102] Perhaps in this case everyday environmentalism includes calling one's congressman.

Congressional passage of the Clean Water Restoration Act, which would expand the scope of federal authority over wetlands, would be a very good place to start. Federal law should not preempt stronger state and local regulation, promoting environmental federalism. In terms of federal enforcement, EPA must more readily exert the veto authority granted to it under the Clean Water Act. Rather than acquiesce to what can become almost routine issuance of wetlands fill permits by the Corps, EPA could more actively review the effects of permit issuance for "unacceptable adverse effects." EPA generally has been too reluctant to exert this authority. In addition, the Agency could exert more authority by defining and expanding its jurisdiction over wetlands, relative to that of the Corps.

Action is needed at the state level as well. States, if they have not done so already, must pass wetlands protection legislation and protect water resources through water quality standards, in particular looking to fill any regulatory gaps created by court decisions and current administrative guidance by the EPA and the Corps. According to the Association of State Wetlands Managers, two-thirds of the states "currently lack regulatory programs that comprehensively address wetlands and isolated wetlands [i.e., those wetlands not subject to federal jurisdiction] in particular,"[103] and states could, when allowed and appropriate, use their own authority to veto Corps permits.

Local governments can play an immensely important role in wetlands protection because, as stated earlier, most land use decisions are made at the local level. In other words, local governments are currently best positioned to reduce the amount of land devoted to suburban development. Although local governments often desire the economic and tax benefits of development, they also might tailor wetlands protection to their community's needs and their constituents' desire for more green space. In terms of "best practices" in local zoning, municipalities should

---

100. Clean Water Restoration Act of 2007, S. 1870, 110th Cong. § 5(1) (2007).

101. S. 1870, 110th Cong. § 4(3).

102. S. 1870, 110th Cong. § 2(3).

103. *See* Ass'n of State Wetlands Managers, http://aswm.org/swp/index.htm.

designate buffer zones around wetlands and other important natural resources free from development and infrastructure,[104] enact density schemes around wetlands as part of subdivision control regulations, maintain natural open space, and minimize impervious surfaces. That said, local governments might do well to revisit existing zoning laws and incorporate ecological values into a new zoning process. It has been suggested that ecologically planned land use begins with a "natural resources inventory," creating a different baseline and protecting natural assets rather than promoting development.[105] Such a baseline, for example, may make localities aware of the value of ecosystem services provided by existing wetlands and force reconsideration of wetland mitigation plans that allow development in exchange for the creation of "new" wetlands.[106] And greater state oversight of local and regional planning, coupled with greater scientific resources, could be an important factor in ensuring that the unique value and contribution of particular natural resources, like wetlands, are properly understood, measured, and valued.

Second, it follows that, in addition to better inter-governmental coordination, more comprehensive land use planning should be used that accounts for the valuation of ecosystem services threatened by sprawl, i.e., those services risked by development and provided by nature which, if lost, would require creation of man-made products that replace those services. For example, a broader and a more nuanced understanding of the value of wetlands is needed. Wetlands protection must depend not only on exercising regulatory authority but also on developing policy and incentives that account for the value of wetlands.[107] These values can then be integrated into the planning process as part of the cost-benefit analysis of planning decisions and can be factored into creating monetary incentives to maintain existing wetlands.

---

104. James M. McElfish, Jr., Rebecca L. Kihslinger & Sandra Nichols, *Setting Buffer Sizes for Wetlands,* 30 NATIONAL WETLANDS NEWSLETTER 6, 10 (Mar.-Apr. 2008); Lowell, *supra* note 2, at 258-259; JOHN NOLON, OPEN GROUND: EFFECTIVE LOCAL STRATEGIES FOR PROTECTING NATURAL RESOURCES 36 (2003).

105. Charles P. Lord, Dr. Eric Strauss & Aaron Toffler, *Natural Cities: Urban Ecology and the Restoration of Urban Ecosystems,* 21 VA. ENVTL. L. J. 317, 338 (2003).

106. In developing future legislation at any governmental level, significant limitation should be placed on when and how developers are allowed to mitigate wetland losses. Wetlands "mitigation" or "replication" is the process of restoring or creating new wetlands in exchange for permission to fill or develop wetlands. Jonathan Douglas Witten, *Carrying Capacity and the Comprehensive Plan: Establishing and Defending Limits to Growth,* 28 B.C. ENVTL. AFF. L. REV. 583, 592 (2001). And wetlands mitigation banking should be cause for concern, as it creates a market where entities could potentially purchase mitigated wetlands from a commercial entity. While creation of new wetlands in exchange for the destruction of old may fly in the face of a conservation ethic and despite arguments that wetlands loss is actually exacerbated by the lack of jurisdictions requiring mitigation, the real ecological concern is that these mitigated wetlands fail to provide the same level of ecosystem services. Mitigation projects may be of little use if they are isolated from other water bodies or habitats where they could filter runoff or provide homes for wildlife. Jerry L. Anderson, *The Environmental Revolution at Twenty-Five,* 26 RUTGERS L.J. 395 (1995).

107. Millennium Ecosystem Assessment, *Ecosystems and Human Well-Being: Wetlands and Water* 12 ("Economic valuation can provide a powerful tool for placing wetlands on the agendas of conservation and development decision-makers.").

Valuing ecosystem services remains difficult, especially valuing nonmarket goods like pollution filtration or flood prevention as opposed to a market good such as drinking water. Unfortunately, limited empirical data exist on nonmarket values of freshwater ecosystem services.[108] Data suggest that wetlands increase nearby home values, save millions of dollars by treating stormwater and managing floods, and support billion-dollar industries such as fishing and hunting.[109]

Better tools to evaluate the true costs of suburbanization are equally important. Suburbanization is both inefficient and destructive. Low density suburbanization destroys the natural environment at a brisk pace, encourages increased automobile use, and requires expensive infrastructure like roads, sewers, and water lines over a great distance. "For example, a Rutgers University study found that prohibiting sprawl would have an economic impact of $357 million upon a limited number of landowner/developers over twenty years, whereas permitting sprawl would cost state residents $8 billion for otherwise unnecessary infrastructure."[110] Thus, unless local planning commissioners can effectively measure both benefits and *costs* of development, while also accounting for the financial benefits of wetlands, wetlands will continue to lack adequate protection under a land planning process that enables individual private land interests to trump common public goods.[111]

Third, new legislation can develop financial incentives or disincentives to protect wetlands. Jurisdictions could reduce taxes in exchange for wetlands preservation or can create an environmental tax on wetlands destruction.[112] States with few wetlands perhaps can exempt wetlands from property taxation without risking a large budget shortfall. States with numerous wetlands could assess an environmental tax on wetlands destruction based on the value of ecosystem services.

However, traditional resource-by-resource legislation is likely to still play an essential role as wetlands demand public and expansive regulation. Wetlands benefit a large number of individuals, but individual disaggregated interests are small and short-term economic interests remain powerful. Thus, a fully market-based approach using taxes and incentives for wetlands, absent better valuation of ecosystem services, would encourage development.[113] Instead, such market mechanisms

---

108. M.A. Wilson & S.R. Carpenter, *Economic Valuation of Freshwater Ecosystem Services in the United States: 1971-1997*, 9 ECOLOGICAL APPLICATIONS 772, 772 (1999).

109. Wilson & Carpenter, *supra* note 108, at tbl. 3 & 4; Lowell, *supra* note 2, at 250; Christine A. Klein, *The New Nuisance: An Antidote to Wetlands Loss, Sprawl, and Global Warming,* 48 B.C. L. REV. 1155, 1200-01 (2007) (citing EPA, FUNCTIONS AND VALUES OF WETLANDS (2001), *available at* http://www.epa.gov/owow/wetlands/pdf/fun_val.pdf).

110. Klein, *supra* note 109, at 1213 (citing Henry R. Richmond, *Sprawl and Its Enemies: Why the Enemies Are Losing,* 34 CONN. L. REV. 539, 572-73 (2001); ROBERT W. BURCHELL ET AL., IMPACT ASSESSMENT OF THE NEW JERSEY INTERIM STATE DEVELOPMENT AND REDEVELOPMENT PLAN (1992)).

111. Seventy-five percent of wetlands are privately owned. EPA, THREATS TO WETLANDS (2001), *available at* http://www.epa.gov/owow/wetlands/pdf/threats.pdf.

112. *See* Ryan M. Seidemann & Catherine D. Susman, *Wetlands Conservation in Louisiana: Voluntary Incentives and Other Alternatives,* 17 J. ENVTL. L. & LITIG. 441 (2002) (see Appendix A for listing of wetlands tax treatment in various jurisdictions).

113. John D. Echeverria, *Regulating Versus Paying To Achieve Conservation Purposes,* SJ053. A.L.I.-A.B.A. 1141 (2004).

must be incorporated into a more protective regulatory regime that evaluates and protects as a default rule those wetlands empirically proven to provide the most significant ecosystem services.

Fourth, and finally, local land use planning should adopt a high-density development and sustainable agenda through practical initiatives. The question remains how best to convert a general goal, such as reducing sprawl's ills, into tangible programs with discrete and achievable goals.[114] What particular practical tools should be considered if a jurisdiction decides to initiate anti-sprawl efforts?

Efforts to counter sprawl began as early as the 1980s, with the "slow growth" movement quickly turning into the "smart growth" movement[115] and leading to "new urbanism" and lesser known approaches[116] that attempt to install more sensible land use practices. Smart growth and new urbanism stand for basic development principles that seek to avoid and limit sprawl through an infinite number of design and regulatory ideas. These initiatives generally advocate channeling growth to already developed areas, promoting compact building design, protecting open space and critical environment areas, and creating walkable neighborhoods.[117]

In the case of wetlands protection, and to lessen stormwater runoff and pollution, land use planners can, in designing suburbs, reduce the amount of pavement and other impervious surfaces by limiting car habitat (e.g., narrowing roadways, reducing parking lot sizes) and create more clustered and dense development. Perhaps the most thorough discussion and analysis for wetlands protection through community planning can be found in the EPA's publication *Protecting Water Resources with Smart Growth*, which addresses everything from development planning to education.[118]

It is easy to support many of the most practical ideas to limit sprawl like neighborhood playgrounds, narrow streets, more street life, bike friendly neighborhoods, and street parking. While the ideas behind smart growth and new urbanism are admirable, skeptics suggest these movements cannot succeed because they are architecturally driven (often funded by design savvy firms) and do not ultimately change behavior, leading to a more compact form of suburbanization that remains car dependent.[119] In other words, new urbanism and many efforts to curb sprawl

---

114. Buzbee, *supra* note 92, at 125.

115. Hayden, *supra* note 1, at 194.

116. Pickett et al., *Urban Ecological Systems: Linking Terrestrial Ecological, Physical and Socioeconomic Components of Metropolitan Areas*, 32 ANNUAL REVIEW OF ECOLOGY AND SYSTEMATICS 127 (2001).

117. Oliver A. Pollard, III, *Smart Growth: The Promise, Politics, and Potential Pitfalls of Emerging Growth Management Strategies,* 19 VA. ENVTL. L.J. 247 (2000); Smart Growth Online, *Smart Growth Network*, http://www.smartgrowth.org/sgn/default.asp (last visited Dec. 21, 2010); Congress for New Urbanism, http://www.cnu.org/ (last visited Dec. 21, 2010); Timothy Beatley, *Americanizing Sustainability: Place-Based Approaches to the Global Challenge*, 27 WM & MARY ENVTL. L. & POL'Y REV. 193, 197 (2002).

118. EPA, PROTECTING WATER RESOURCES WITH SMART GROWTH (2004), *available at* http://www.epa.gov/dced/pdf/waterresources_with_sg.pdf.

119. Beatley, *supra* note 117, at 197.

are not deep visions.[120] They modify but do not stop sprawl. From the perspective of everyday environmentalism, the related concern is whether the focus on these design models unnecessarily limits existing policy discourse[121] and forecloses efforts to activate changes in individual behavior.

Changing Individual Behavior to Reduce Sprawl

To date, relatively few ideas have been put forward that would directly change consumer preferences and either make the choice to live in sprawl less desirable or the choice to live in dense communities more desirable. Consumers need to have information about the environmental costs of sprawl, but little information has been made available. It is also unclear how best to deliver information about these ecological costs. Economic incentives should be established to encourage people to live in communities that lack the negative ecological footprint of sprawl. However, existing law and public policy have very few programs to drive changes in individual behavior, though some are discussed below. The bottom line is that it is time for people to think about the environment before they decide where to live.[122]

In terms of everyday environmentalism, the fundamental question is what socio-ecological approaches might address land use consequences, drive individual responsibility, and change preferences about where to live and how to develop? The answers remain unclear, but three potential themes can be identified to start.

First, local land use planning should account for the activities of citizens within that community. At least one locality may understand that land use planning must modify the impacts of daily life. Marin County, California, is developing a land use planning model with an eye towards the impacts of automobile usage, with sustainability as an underlying theme.[123] While Marin County's land use plan considers many well-known anti-sprawl ideas such as locating housing near activity centers and focusing intensive development at transportation nodes, it attempts to do so with an eye toward reducing greenhouse gas emissions and traffic congestion. The County's plan even calculates the ecological footprint of the average resident. Thus, the state and county have embarked on an experiment to mitigate greenhouse gas emissions by linking development patterns and individual driving patterns. Writes Professor Dan Tarlock, "[T]he question of how to modify individual resource consumption is now critical, and California is trying to push localities to adopt land-use patterns that force individuals to modify their driving habits and the consumption of gasoline."[124]

---

120. Meredith, *supra* note 90, at 491-92.

121. *Cf.* Beatley, *supra* note 117, at 199.

122. Author Peter Annin states, "[I]t's time for people to think about water before they decide where to live." Peter Annin, The Great Lakes Water Wars 249 (2006).

123. This description of the Marin County program is taken from *Addressing Climate Change at the State and Local Level: From Litigation to Land-Use Initiatives to Reduce Automobile Emissions* by Rachel Medina and A. Dan Tarlock, Sustainability (forthcoming).

124. *Id.*

Second, knowledge about the future environmental benefits of dense development should become more widespread. Professor John R. Nolon calculates that doubling the density of future development, as 100 million more Americans join the population in the next three decades, will decrease carbon dioxide emissions by 1.2 gigatons per year, compared with housing them at current densities.[125] He goes on to argue that a 25% shift of the nation's next 100 million residents from single-family dwellings on quarter-acre lots to transit-oriented and high-density developments would prevent 876,951 acres of impervious surfaces and reduce annual stormwater runoff by 477 billion gallons.[126] Information on the benefits of dense development and costs of sprawl must also be developed for particular regions with due consideration to local concerns, and the communication of that information must be provided in a consumer friendly format that will make sense to residents and have the potential to influence behavior.

Third, finally, and surely the most untapped strategy to limit sprawl, public policy must figure out how to put forward initiatives to limit sprawl that would directly change consumer preferences. The cutting-edge future of environmental law will focus on informational mechanisms, economic and market incentives, and empirical inquiry into the effectiveness of programs that target the individual. However, the varied concerns of land use make it difficult to determine how to implement these new tools on individuals to mitigate sprawl.

Much debate centers on whether sprawl and suburban development are a product of true consumer preference. Some studies show that people want dense development.

> When people are shown slides of traditional pre-war grid-patterned urban neighborhoods—sidewalks lined with front porches, fairly close spacing between houses, active shopping streets—they generally prefer that layout to the typical post-war suburban cul-de-sac arrangement.[127]

These studies support the view that these true preferences are thwarted and that "massive suburban development was no simple market response to consumer demand; it was federal government policy subsidized in many ways."[128] But, even if high-density living actually is not a true consumer preference (for it may not be and many may like the suburbs),[129] it does not matter. Initiatives targeting

---

125. John R. Nolon, *The Land Use Stabilization Wedge Strategy: Shifting Ground to Mitigate Climate Change*, 34 WILLIAM & MARY ENVTL. L. & POL'Y REV. 1 (2009). A gigaton is one billion tons.

126. *Id.*

127. UNDERSTANDING SPRAWL: A CITIZEN'S GUIDE 7, http://www.davidsuzuki.org/publications/downloads/2003/Understanding_Sprawl.pdf.

128. Katharine B. Silbaugh, *Women's Place: Urban Planning, Housing Design, and Work-Family Balance*, 76 FORDHAM L. REV. 1797, 1834 (2007).

129. *See* Michael Lewyn, *Sprawl in Europe and America*, 46 SAN DIEGO L. REV. 85, 88 (2009) (internal citations omitted) ("[D]efenders of the status quo assert that sprawl is an inevitable result of consumer preferences in an affluent, open society."); Michael Lewyn, *You Can Have it All: Less Sprawl and Property Rights Too*, 80 TEMPLE L. REV. 1093, 1094 at n.7 and accompanying text (2007); ROBERT BRUEGMANN, SPRAWL: A COMPACT HISTORY (2005).

individual behavior either need to reinforce existing eco-friendly preferences or to change market preferences, especially where suburban preferences are weak. These initiatives should include providing information, targeting environmental ethics, and appealing to financial interests. These efforts can help overcome the trends of sprawl resulting from government policy and subsidized infrastructure.

Again, likely due to the many factors leading to land use decisions and the variety of environmental consequences, very few plans have been put forward to directly change individual behavior to limit sprawl. Books like this and other news sources can help consumers gain information about the environmental costs of sprawl, but it is unclear how best to deliver information about its ecological costs at important decision points.

For example, imagine if when deciding to sell a newly built house or condominium, the developer was required to provide an environmental impact assessment for the buyer's review or if all homes came with an eco-label (see a discussion of eco-labels in Chapters Three and Four) that not only discussed energy efficiency, as required by some municipalities, but also contained information about the distance from commercial districts, anticipated driving miles, and land use disturbances as a result of development. Would this lower market demand for sprawl and nudge developers and politicians to develop denser communities and associated mass transit infrastructure?

Financial and economic incentives, unlike informational mechanisms, have begun to play the earliest role in encouraging people to live in denser communities and limit the negative ecological footprint of sprawl. Potential financial instruments to invoke include subsidies to live closer to work and incentives to buy in urban areas.

As a start, states are developing smart growth programs that provide grants to individuals buying homes near their work. The state of Maryland's Live Near Your Work Program, a part of its smart growth management legislation, provides low-interest mortgages in targeted revitalization urban neighborhoods and provides monetary incentives for state employees to purchase homes near their workplaces.[130] New Jersey maintains a similar home mortgage incentive program that provides low-interest mortgage loans to homebuyers purchasing homes in towns where they are employed.[131] The idea is to encourage people to live closer to their jobs, which will reduce the need for cars and increase the use of alternative transportation such as walking, biking, and public transit. Recently, the U.S. Department of Housing and Urban Development has begun to support initiatives

---

130. Tom Daniels, *Smart Growth: A New American Approach to Regional Planning*, 16 PLANNING & RESEARCH 271 (2001); Parris N. Glendening, *Maryland's Smart Growth Initiative: The Next Step*, 29 FORDHAM URB. L. J. 1493, 1504 (2002).

131. State of New Jersey, Housing and Mortgage Agency, *Live Near Your Work*, online at http://www.state.nj.us/dca/hmfa/consu/buyers/close/live.html.

that support transit-oriented development, recognizing both the financial cost savings and environmental benefits associated with living near transit hubs.[132]

Unlike home energy efficiency, transportation options, and food choices, the development of policies and programs to activate individual behavior to lessen sprawl is in its infancy. Ways to influence individual behavior through information and economics need to be developed, and then empirical evidence must be generated and evaluated to determine what programs are effective in changing consumer choice and preferences.

132. U.S. Department of Housing and Urban Development, News Release, *HUD and DOT Announce Interagency Partnership To Promote Sustainable Communities*, online at http://www.hud.gov/news/release.cfm?content=pr09-023.cfm; written statement of Secretary Shaun Donovan, U.S. Department of Housing and Urban Development, Hearing before the Subcommittee on Transportation, Housing and Urban Development, and Related Agencies, Committee on Appropriations, U.S. House of Representatives, *Livable Communities, Transit Oriented Development, and Incorporating Green Building Practices into Federal Housing and Transportation Policy*, Mar. 18, 2009, online at http://portal.hud.gov/portal/page/portal/HUD/press/testimonies/2009-03-18.

CHAPTER SIX

The Unforeseen Costs of Everyday Life: The Destruction of Small Organisms

> Like any livestock, healthy bees require good pasture. And that's what fewer and fewer bees can find. You might say that, like us, they're suffering from "suburban disease": more roads, big-box stores, and developments, fewer wildflowers.
>
> ROWAN JACOBSEN, FRUITLESS FALL 151 (2008)

Whether the focus is on the household carbon footprint, food choices, or residential developments, individual choices, at least in the aggregate, substantially affect ecological processes, often with disastrous consequences. At some level, many people know they should be more energy efficient, know that something is slightly amiss with pesticides or buying produce from across the globe, and know that the drive from home to work is too long. Yet, as discussed throughout this book, people are not always sure why or how individual choice relates to environmental concerns. An even greater challenge, then, is presented by the need to educate the public and decision-makers alike about a largely unseen environmental impact of everyday life: the destruction of small organisms.[1]

The costs of destruction of small organisms remain underappreciated and ignored by public policy as well as the public. However, their important ecological fate is tied, in part, to everyday environmentalism, especially since the concept, in part, means gaining information about the relationship between human development and nature. These tiny life forms, without which the planet and humanity could not survive, are all victims of the energy, food, and lifestyle choices discussed in Chapters Three through Five. While this chapter does not argue that individual behavior like driving a lot or eating food sprayed with pesticides leads directly to the destruction of small organisms, this chapter does demonstrate how individual actions that in the aggregate significantly contribute to increased fossil-fuel use and land degradation are, in turn, factors that contribute to pollinator and soil biota loss.

---

1. As used in this chapter, the term "small organisms" refers to organisms other than large megafauna or even small animals including mammals and reptiles, and instead references microscopic organisms in land and air, small insects, and small soil biota. For example, soil biodiversity can be described as including microfauna, mesofauna, macrofauna, and megafauna even though all organisms are under 25mm in body width. *See* PETER H. RAVEN, NATURE AND HUMAN SOCIETY: THE QUEST FOR A SUSTAINABLE WORLD 231 fig. 1 (2007).

When it comes to endangered species, the average Americans usually hear the call of Dorothy in *The Wizard of Oz*, "Lions and tigers and bears, oh my!"[2] People grow distraught over the loss of lions, tigers, and bears, and other large animals common to the modern human era (also known as "characteristic megafauna"). Polar bear habitat loss and the climate crisis are becoming more widely known problems, but the destruction of small organisms, such as bees, butterflies, ants, and worms, remains an underappreciated concern with potentially huge consequences. Energy use, food choices, and residential geography not only affect carbon emissions, wetlands, and public health, but also harm pollinators and soil biota.

Smaller organisms are under great pressure due to the pollination demands of industrial agriculture, increased chemical residues on agricultural products, and sprawl-induced habitat fragmentation. Individual choices have unanticipated consequences and can work in concert. Sprawl is related to transit choices and home energy usage. Food options are often dictated by residential geography. All work in concert to create the climate crisis, water and air pollution, and the destruction of small organisms. Public policy, with only some exceptions, sheds few tears for small organism population loss, a result one might call vertebrate chauvinism. These losses, however, will certainly hurt since small organisms ensure food security, sustain healthy ecosystems, and support economic markets by pollinating crops and other plants and enriching the soil.

Part A of this chapter discusses the ecological importance of pollinators, bugs, and soil biota, including their role as a "canary in the coal mine," also known as an indicator species, warning when other environmental problems may be on the horizon. Part B describes the law's limited protection of small organisms and raises the concern that the government obsession with protecting large animals will ultimately result in the demise of more important, but smaller in size, creatures. Part C identifies the decision-making tools of (1) information dissemination and (2) financial valuation of ecosystem services as essential factors in developing strategies to protect small organisms. Interrelated consumer choices like suburban residency and purchasing non-organic foods can have unanticipated impacts like destroying small organisms. Accordingly, public policy initiatives must determine how to: (1) make individuals aware of these inter-relationships and the importance of small organisms and other natural resources to fully functioning ecosystems; (2) increase and fund scientific research so better information is available; and (3) encourage decision-making processes that, similar to the discussion of wetlands in Chapter Five, properly value the foundational role of small organisms when making policy choices.

---

2. WIZARD OF OZ (MGM 1939).

A. The Need for Bees (and Other Small Invertebrates)

Pollinators and soil biota provide foundational ecosystem services, including seed reproduction, flood and drought mitigation, and agricultural pest control. These small organisms are significantly underappreciated given the value of their role in nature, as well as the direct economic value of pollinators as key assets in million dollar agricultural industries. Yet, populations of many of these small organisms are in decline. The causes of their decline are complex, but the various impacts of modern development and consumer choice undoubtedly are contributing factors.

Pollinators and Bugs

Among the underappreciated and underprotected organisms are pollinators, which are necessary for the reproduction of seed plants. The importance of pollinators cannot be overstated. More than three-quarters of flowering plants, and most fruits and vegetables, need animals for pollination. "Even the production of milk and cheese . . . starts with pollination of alfalfa, a staple in the diet of dairy cows."[3]

Understanding the population dynamics of pollinators, including suspected and documented population losses, is no easy task, in part because of the organisms' small size and transience.[4] At a minimum, though, the survival of some pollinator populations is in doubt. Declines are evident in several vertebrate population species such as bats and hummingbirds and in smaller species, including bees, butterflies, and wasps.[5] Other pollinator populations, such as flies and beetles, may be declining rapidly, but insufficient data are available. The causes for pollinator decline include competition with non-native pollinators, habitat loss and fragmentation, and range and migration changes caused by global warming.

Bees are certainly the most well-known and well-protected pollinator, making up the cornerstone of the pollinator industry and creating major economic gains for the agricultural industry.[6] Two-thirds of the 2.4 million domesticated bee colonies in the United States travel around the country each year pollinating crops. According to the U.S. Department of Agriculture, bee pollination adds $15 billion in value to American crops. Without bees, the nation would lose not only billions of dollars in agricultural production, but also entire portions of its agricultural

3. Don Behm, *Bees Flee Hives: National Collapse of Honeybee Colonies Felt in Wisconsin*, MIL-WAUKEE J. SENTINEL, May 12, 2007.

4. For comprehensive discussions of pollinator activities and population dynamics, see COMM. ON THE STATUS OF POLLINATORS IN NORTH AMERICA, NATIONAL RESEARCH COUNCIL, STATUS OF POLLINATORS IN NORTH AMERICA, STATUS OF POLLINATORS 201-02 (2007) [hereinafter STATUS OF POLLINATORS], *available at* http://www.nap.edu/catalog.php?record_id=11761.

5. *Id.* at 73 tbl. 2-6.

6. The following sources provided data regarding the relationship between bee pollination and the economy: American Beekeeping Federation, *available at* http://www.abfnet.org/node/27; David Stipp, *As Bees Go Missing, a $9.3B Crisis Lurks*, FORTUNE, Aug. 28. 2007, *available at* http://money.cnn.com/galleries/2007/fortune/0708/gallery.bees_crops.fortune/; U.S. Department of Agriculture, Agricultural Research Service, online at http://www.ars.usda.gov/News/docs.htm?docid=15572; RENEE JOHNSON, CONGRESSIONAL RESEARCH SERVICE REPORT FOR CONGRESS: RECENT HONEY BEE COLONY DECLINES (2007), *available at* http://www.nationalaglawcenter.org/assets/crs/RL33938.pdf.

output. Honeybees pollinate more than 90% of the U.S. production of blueberries, carrots, broccoli, onions, and apples. Ironically, the pollinator population finds itself stressed due to such demands, suggesting a need for a different food production model.

The most amazing (and troublesome) bee pollination story is that of the California almond crop. Each spring more than 1.3 million bee colonies, about one half of all the honeybees in the United States, are trucked to California almond orchards. One hundred percent of the $2.2 billion U.S. almond industry depends on honeybee pollination. This is an expensive proposition. As pollination fees have risen, from $35 per colony in the late 1990s to $75 in 2005 to around $150 in 2007, almond growers spend potentially $200 million yearly on honeybee rentals.

One reason for increased pollination fees is that fewer bees are available for pollination because of a drop in colonies both domestically and abroad. The number of bee colonies nationwide is down from 5 million in the 1940s to 2.4 million today. In one year alone (2006), beekeepers reported losses of up to 90% of their hives, with some populations facing extinction. Understandably, concerns exist that, with continued population decline, beekeepers will not meet demand for their services.[7]

Why has this bee population decline occurred? A number of explanations have coalesced. Infection from parasitic mites, first reported in the United States in the late 1980s, poses an imminent threat to American bee colonies. Also, managed bees used in greenhouse pollination potentially carry high pathogen loads, infecting native species when they escape from greenhouses.

Pesticides, especially insecticides, destroy or weaken honeybee colonies, often through accidents or careless application. For example, a mosquito-control program in Manitoba resulted in bee colony losses of $850,000 in 1983, and insecticides killed more than one million colonies in California between 1966 and 1979.[8]

Colony Collapse Disorder (CCD) is a condition in which the honeybee colony, still filled with honey and bee pollen left undisturbed by the usual pests, lies empty of adult bees.[9] Adverse conditions may fuse together in causing CCD. Scientists do not know the direct cause of CCD, though they have no shortage of opinions: diseases and pests such as American foulbrood (the most common and destructive bacterial bee disease), nosema (a spore-forming protozoan that invades bee digestive tracts), and varroa mites (a parasite and the king of honeybee killers); lack of genetic diversity in the colony population; poor bee management, including use and inappropriate use of chemicals in the colonies; immunity disorders; environmental toxins; chronic stress from hives being shipped across the country; poor nutrition

---

    7. For further information on honeybee population and colony decline, see the following sources: U.S. DEPT. OF AGRICULTURE, AGRICULTURE RESEARCH SERV., COLONY COLLAPSE DISORDER ACTION PLAN 1 (2007), online at http://www.ars.usda.gov/is/br/ccd/ccd_actionplan.pdf; J.C. Biesmeijer et al., *Parallel Declines in Pollinators and Insect-Pollinated Plants in Britain and the Netherlands*, 313 SCIENCE 351 (2006), *available at* http://www.sciencemag.org/cgi/reprint/313/5785/351.pdf.
    8. *Id.* at 79-80.
    9. For further information on Colony Collapse Disorder, see Jamie Ellis, *Colony Collapse Disorder (CCD) in Honey Bees*, http://edis.ifas.ufl.edu/IN720; ROWAN JACOBSEN, FRUITLESS FALL (2008).

from being fed high fructose corn syrup; and genetically modified crops grown from seeds dipped in insecticides.

Beyond bees, the pollinating world also encompasses beetles, butterflies, moths, and flies, though these species contribute in other ways besides pollination. While truly accurate population estimation proves burdensome if not impossible, evidence suggests that these bugs, for the same reasons as bees, are in decline. However, unlike bees, their numbers play a less direct and less obvious role in the natural ecosystem and American agricultural economics.

Butterflies and moths are a food source for birds and bats and pollinate cacti, orchids, and trees.[10] Some species developed such specialized relationships with particular plants that only they can physically reach some flowers' nectar. These insects offer economic benefits even in their larval state as demonstrated by *Bombyx mori* larvae (silkworms), which fuel an entire silk industry. In addition, adult butterflies and moths carry an aesthetic value.

Policy and science must pay particular attention to pollinators like butterflies that foreshadow population and range declines of other species. An "indicator species," butterflies sense and quickly respond to habitat and climate changes, serving as an indicator for the future health of other wildlife species.

Flies help soil ecosystems, pollinate fruit and vegetable crops, and provide a food source for other animals. Fly larvae decompose dung and break down animal carcasses, helping to incorporate nutrients into soil. In addition, flies pollinate cocoa plants, and fly larval populations in aquatic ecosystems can account for up to 80% of a fish's food. In fact, the viability of the nation's fishing economy is influenced by changes in insect populations.

Winged species find themselves aboard a descending flight. Take the state of the butterfly and the moth in Great Britain: 59 butterfly species have become extinct since 1800, with population decline in three-quarters of the 54 remaining species. Two-thirds of the 337 moth species show decreasing population trends over the last 35 years, with 62 species becoming extinct during the 20th century. Similarly, experts have documented shifts and declines for several flower fly species in the United Kingdom and the Netherlands.

What accounts for the loss of key small organisms? Human activity certainly plays a role. Humans inundate the air with greenhouse gases, spray pesticides on fields, and develop the lands of natural species. Greenhouse gas emissions lead to increased carbon dioxide and lower nitrogen concentrations in plants, making plants less nutritious for the larvae that feed on them. Increased temperatures could

---

10. In addition to STATUS OF POLLINATORS, *supra* note 4, sources relied on for additional information on butterflies, moths, and flies include: Butterfly Conservation, http://www.butterfly-conservation.org/; R. FOX ET AL., THE STATE OF BRITAIN'S BUTTERFLIES (2007), http://www.butterfly-conservation.org/uploads/sobb2007summary.pdf; KARI HELIÖVAARA & RAUNO VÄISÄNEN, INSECTS AND POLLUTION (1993); MICHAEL J. SAMWAYS, INSECT DIVERSITY CONSERVATION (2005); NAT'L RESEARCH COUNCIL OF THE NATIONAL ACADEMIES, STATUS OF POLLINATORS IN NORTH AMERICA (2007).

cause the extinction of some insect species, though admittedly climate change will create both winners and losers as some species will adapt better than others.

The suffix "cide" is used to indicate the act of killing. Billions of pounds of pesticides are used each year in the United States to kill "pests."[11] Unfortunately, these chemicals, especially through increased pesticide applications, kill natural predators of those organisms that hamper agricultural plants, leading to increased pests in the future.

Finally, development, agricultural fragmentation, deforestation, urbanization, and suburbanization have created huge habitat loss for insects. While insects are mobile and can migrate, roads and highways have created barriers to movement and increased insect mortality. Even the most mobile insects have an increasingly difficult time adapting to resource losses and habitat shifts caused by human development. For example, plant extinctions in Hawaii have resulted in the loss of five species of moths, undermining specialized pollination relationships. The loss of insect biodiversity can have grave consequences for an ecosystem. The extinction of a single niche species can lead to catastrophic shifts in the food web, resulting in secondary extinctions and a loss of biodiversity.

Great synergies exist between an organism's function and habitat. Small organisms fight human intervention on two fronts. Both their bodies and their habitats are threatened directly by pesticides and indirectly by climate change and human development. These factors are, in turn, driven in part by individual behavior.

Soil Biodiversity

Soil consists of more than its chemical components. Soil biota are often ignored, intentionally or unintentionally,[12] despite their importance to ecosystems and economies across the world. Imagine a world with only dry arid dust as soil. Soil acts as a living organism. Its biodiversity and dense biology have no peer, though soil varies from one system to the next (compare, for example, forests with farmlands).[13] Just one cubic meter of land can contain 10 million roundworms, 45,000 earthworms, and 48,000 mites and wingless insects. A single gram of soil can contain millions of individual organisms, including thousands of bacterial species. According to the Convention on Biological Diversity:

---

11. TIMOTHY KIELY, DAVID DONALDSON & ARTHUR GRUBE, PESTICIDES INDUSTRY SALES AND USAGE, 2000 AND 2001 MARKET ESTIMATES 10 (2004).

12. J. R. MCNEILL, SOMETHING NEW UNDER THE SUN: AN ENVIRONMENTAL HISTORY OF THE TWENTIETH CENTURY WORLD 21 (2000) ("Here I will entirely neglect our impact on the fungi, bacteria, rodents, and worms that inhabit the soil …").

13. For information on soil biota and biodiversity, see the following: Food and Agricultural Organization of the United Nations, Land and Water Development Division, Soil Biodiversity Portal, *available at* http://www.fao.org/ag/AGL/agll/soilbiod/default.stm; Diana H. Wall & Ross A. Virginia, *The World Beneath Our Feet: Soil Biodiversity and Ecosystem Functioning* in NATURE AND HUMAN SOCIETY: THE QUEST FOR A SUSTAINABLE WORLD 225 (Peter H. Raven ed., 1997) [hereinafter NATURE AND HUMAN SOCIETY].

Soil organisms contribute to a wide range of essential services to the sustainable function of all ecosystems, by acting as the primary driving agents of nutrient cycling, regulating the dynamics of soil organic matter, soil carbon sequestration and greenhouse gas emission; modifying soil physical structure and water regimes, enhancing the amount and efficiency of nutrient acquisition by the vegetation, and enhancing plant health. These services are not only essential to the functioning of natural ecosystems but constitute an important resource for the sustainable management of agricultural systems.[14]

Soil biota also help mitigate floods and droughts and control agricultural pests. These ecological reasons for preserving biodiversity are amplified by economic ones. The value of these ecosystem services may exceed $1.5 trillion U.S. dollars, as seen in Table 5.

Table 5: Total estimated economic benefits of biodiversity, with special attention to the services that soil biota activities provide worldwide (modified from Pimentel et al., 1997)

Activity	World economic benefits of biodiversity (x 10^9 / year)
Waste recycling	760
Soil formation	25
Nitrogen fixation	90
Bioremediation of chemicals	121
Biotechnology	6
Biocontrol of pests	160
Pollination	200
Other wild food	180
Totals	1,542

Source: FOOD AND AGRICULTURAL ORGANIZATION OF THE UNITED NATIONS, LAND AND WATER DEVELOPMENT DIVISION, SOIL BIODIVERSITY PORTAL, *Why should soil biodiversity be managed and conserved?*, http://www.fao.org/ag/agl/agll/soilbiod/consetxt.stm.

In addition, half of the Earth's land is devoted to agriculture, which supplies 99% of the world's food, figures that potentially subject our food supply to a large-scale disaster in the event of a collapse of soil biotic populations in key areas.

Soil organisms have a hierarchical relationship in food webs, as seen in Figure G, whereby energy and nutrients are converted by one organism eating another, with the primary producers providing fuel for the food web through photosynthesis.

---

14. Convention on Biological Diversity, 31 I.L.M. 818 (1992), http://www.cbd.int/doc/legal/cbd-un-en.pdf.

Figure G: The Soil Food Web

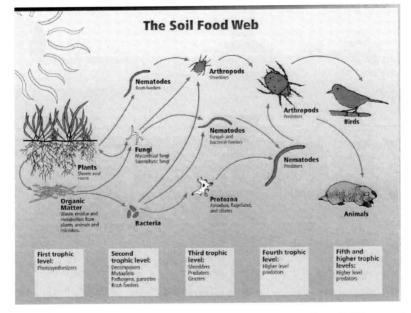

Source: USDA Natural Resources Conservation Service, http://soils.usda.gov/SQI/concepts/soil_
biology/soil_food_web.html.

Groupings of organisms based on function are less hierarchical, having broader interactive effects based on habitat modification and nutrient creation. Perhaps the best functional group team name is "ecosystem engineers," with a roster of termites, ants, and worms that burrow through sediment impacting soil structure, hydrology, and plant growth and creating habitat for other organisms. Thus, these "ecosystem engineers," which do not pollinate, also provide important ecosystem services.[15] For example, ants engineer the world's soil structures and maintain adequate levels of organic carbon and nitrogen content in soils by breaking down soil and pushing nutrient rich soil to lower soil strata. Soil engineers also increase plant and tree diversity by distributing and burying seeds and creating new pathways for water and nutrients.

A simple description of the importance of soil engineers such as worms comes from the children's story *Bob and Otto*. Bob (a caterpillar) and Otto (a worm) are best friends, yet Otto is sad after he chose to dig all day instead of joining Bob, who climbed a tree, ate heartily, and transformed into a butterfly. But Otto soon feels better when Bob says,

---

15. For information on these bugs, see DAVID C. COLEMAN, ET AL., FUNDAMENTALS OF SOIL ECOLOGY (2d Ed. 2004); ALISON LEADLEY BROWN, ECOLOGY OF SOIL ORGANISMS (1978); SAMWAYS, *supra* note 10.

"But while you were digging, you loosened the soil … so the roots could drink water, so the tree could grow tall, so the leaves would be green, so I could eat the leaves, and grow wings. I owe it all to you, Otto . . . ."[16]

Meanwhile, "litter transformers" eat dead plants, excreting highly nutritious materials benefiting soil health. Micropredators, like microscopic and transparent roundworms and single-celled animals known as protozoa, facilitate nutrient production, breaking down their prey of bacteria, fungi, and algae and turning them into usable plant nutrients. The role of roundworms as a basic building block of the Earth's terrestrial ecosystems cannot be overstated. "[I]f all the matter in the universe except the nematodes were swept away, our world would still be dimly recognizable."[17] Similarly, soil microflora (e.g., fungi, bacteria, nitrogen fixers) help facilitate nutrient cycles, provide further decomposition, and biodegrade toxins. These soil biota are essential.

Given the diversity, expansiveness, and complexity of soil, it comes as no surprise that much of its mechanics remain a mystery, continually challenging scientific research and surely confounding policy initiatives. However, soil life is known to suffer from some of the same causes of destruction as pollinators and other insects and to be susceptible to plowing, desertification, landfill, fertilizers, and chemical spills. Land- and air-based small organisms find themselves facing similar environmental challenges, evincing and leading to far greater ecosystem concerns. Soil biota face similar environmental threats as organisms above ground do and serve as indicators to reflect changes in soil structure.[18]

While measuring population changes of small organisms is a difficult task,[19] protecting small organisms is paramount because small species' health is essential to the health of larger ecosystems and even economies. Small organisms serve as the foundation nutrients for all species in the ecosystem, while also indirectly impacting markets dependent on natural resources (e.g., timber, fishing). Where this role already has been recognized, these species are commodities themselves (e.g., bees).

The essential but largely unseen role of these small organisms leaves us with a difficult but simple question: how can law and public policy protect these species when their contribution, and even existence, are not generally recognized by either decision-makers or the public?

16. ROBERT O. BRUEL, BOB AND OTTO (2007).
17. J.G. Baldwin, S.A. Nadler & D.H. Wall, *Nematodes: Pervading the Earth and Linking All Life* in NATURE AND HUMAN SOCIETY 176 (citing N.A. Cobb, *Nematodes and Their Relationships*, U.S. DEP'T OF AGRIC. YEARBOOK 457-90 (1914)).
18. Daniel A. Fiscus & Deborah A. Neher, *Distinguishing Sensitivity of Free-Living Soil Nematode Genera to Physical and Chemical Disturbances*, 12 ECOLOGICAL APPLICATIONS 565, 565 (2002).
19. *See, e.g.,* Ebbe S. Nielsen & Laurence A. Mound, *Global Diversity of Insects: The Problems of Estimating Numbers* in NATURE AND HUMAN SOCIETY, *supra* note 1, at 213.

B.   Law Overlooks Small Organisms

Humans have observed, though not always classified, around 2.5 million species. The total number of species on Earth, however, is estimated to be somewhere between 14 million and 100 million, if one counts viruses and potentially 30 million insect species.[20] Even by conservative estimates, there may be more than 150 times more invertebrate species than vertebrates. Although small organisms vastly outnumber larger species, the scope of legal protection for them pales in comparison. The United States, as exemplified by the Endangered Species Act, emphasizes protection of larger vertebrates such as panthers, manatees, and key deer, while it ignores those organisms necessary to humanity's daily ecological preservation—worms, beetles, and butterflies. The United States Fish and Wildlife Service, under the Endangered Species Act, lists as threatened or endangered 374 vertebrate species, but only 238 invertebrates.[21]

International and national law protects mostly vertebrate endangered species from hunting, illegal trade, and habitat destruction, with less attention paid to small organisms. National and state laws do protect some small organisms, like honeybees, that have clear economic importance and value, and have small programs to stop soil erosion. In any case, though, the destruction of unforeseen organisms is so far off the radar for policymakers in the United States that no framework exists that comes close to engaging the key decision-making tools for influencing individual behavior as discussed in the Introduction and in prior chapters. Instead, there is essentially cognitive severance between everyday activities and any awareness of how these activities impact these small organisms and have other unforeseen impacts.

International Initiatives

Founded in 1948, the International Union for Conservation of Nature and Natural Resources (IUCN), better known as the World Conservation Union, encourages diversity conservation and manages the IUCN Red List of Threatened Species.[22] The Red List provides information on species' conservation status and population trends "designed to determine the relative risk of extinction" and "catalogue and highlight those taxa that are facing a higher risk of global extinction."

Of the 1,642,189 described species on the Red List, 1,232,384 (75.0%) are invertebrates (of which 950,000 are insects), while only 51,259 (3.7%) are vertebrates.[23] Due to biases toward the well-known taxonomic groups and inadequate understand-

---

20. PAUL K. CONKIN, THE STATE OF THE EARTH: ENVIRONMENTAL CHALLENGES ON THE ROAD TO 2100 131 (2007); BRIAN GROOMBRIDGE & MARTIN D. JENKINS, WORLD ATLAS OF BIODIVERSITY: EARTH'S LIVING RESOURCES IN THE 21ST CENTURY 18 (2002).

21. *See* U.S. Fish & Wildlife Serv., Endangered Species Program, Species Information, http://www.fws.gov/endangered/wildlife.html#Species.

22. Find the Red List at http://www.iucnredlist.org/info/introduction, and learn more in a book written by the IUCN's survival commission—JONATHAN E.M. BAILLIE ET AL., A GLOBAL SPECIES ASSESSMENT (2004), *available at* http://www.iucnredlist.org/static/introduction.

23. 2008 IUCN Red List: tbl. 1, http://www.iucnredlist.org/documents/2008RL_stats_table_1_v1223294385.pdf.

ing of smaller species, only 4,116 invertebrates (insects, mollusks, crustaceans, corals, and others) have been evaluated for extinction risk, compared with 26,604 vertebrates (mammals, birds, reptiles, amphibians, and fishes). Unfortunately, as a percentage of species evaluated, invertebrate species (41% threatened on average) are in far greater peril than vertebrates (22% threatened on average).

Effective policy must rely on accurate information and, at minimum, support scientific research to determine what organisms are at risk and why. The Red List, while not prescriptive, is an invaluable tool that supports communication and education, guides future legislation, and informs current conservation projects, suggesting appropriate direct action on individual habitats and species.

In the area of biodiversity conservation, two major international agreements exist, the Convention on Biodiversity (CBD) and the United Nations Convention on International Trade in Endangered Species of Wild Flora and Fauna (CITES). The CBD remains an international agreement with no binding regulations but great promise. CITES is far less ambitious but does provide for specific regulation.

The CBD, which was drafted at Rio de Janeiro's Earth Summit in 1992 and reaffirmed at the 2002 World Summit on Sustainable Development, has been called an "Endangered Species Act" for the whole world.[24] Parties who ratified the convention pledged to reduce the rate of biodiversity loss by 2010. The United States Senate, however, has not ratified the agreement, despite the U.S. being a signatory.

Like most international conventions, the CBD contains no binding rules, but must be implemented by individual countries.[25] For example, the island nation of St. Lucia proposed a series of projects to stop biodiversity loss, including creating scientific inventories, establishing management programs for rare and threatened species, and promoting sustainable agriculture.[26] The United Kingdom's Biodiversity Action Plan, created in 1994 in response to the CBD, establishes criteria for identifying species and habitats of conservation concern.[27] So far the United Kingdom has developed action plans for 391 species and 45 habitats, including plans for small species such as bees, wasps, butterflies, flies, and worms.

While the CBD does not specifically mention small organisms, decisions made by parties to the CBD suggest broad policy initiatives that would protect biodiversity among the smaller species. For example, to support agricultural biological diversity, the parties have advocated governmental programs that encourage organic and no-till farming, integrated pest management, and alternatives to agricultural chemicals, as well as partnerships between researchers, policymakers, workers, and farmers to develop strategies to protect micro-organisms of agricultural interest.[28]

---

24. CONKIN, *supra* note 20, at 141.

25. For a list of national reports, see the CBD website at http://cbd.int/reports/list.shtml?type=nbsap.

26. CONVENTION ON BIOLOGICAL DIVERSITY, NATIONAL BIODIVERSITY STRATEGY AND ACTION PLAN OF ST. LUCIA: PROTECTING THE FUTURE (2000), http://www.cbd.int/reports/list.shtml?type=nbsap&alpha=S.

27. For more information on UKBAP, see www.ukbap.org.uk.

28. COP 3 Decision III/11 15(e), 15(j), 15(k), 16(c), *available at* http://www.cbd.int/decision/cop/?id=7107..

Programs developed under the CBD include the International Initiative for the Conservation and Sustainable Use of Pollinators (Pollinator Initiative) and International Initiative for the Conservation and Sustainable Use of Soil Biodiversity (Soil Biodiversity Initiative). The Pollinator Initiative seeks to promote a coordinated worldwide effort to monitor pollinator decline, address the lack of taxonomic information on pollinators and promote pollinator diversity, especially in the agricultural context.[29] Various nations have implemented their own pollinator initiatives to raise public awareness, work on conservation and restoration, engage in bee surveys and monitoring, and conduct training for best management practices.[30]

Similar to the ideals advocated by the Pollinator Initiative and the CBD itself, the Soil Biodiversity Initiative envisions building local partnerships to share knowledge, researching and developing soil bioindicators and technologies to monitor soil and ecosystem health, and creating mechanisms to evaluate farm practices and ability to implement change.[31]

CITES, which was drawn up in 1973 and entered into force in 1975 with the United States as a ratifying party, is the second major international agreement addressing species loss.[32] The World Conservation Union had long argued for controls on the trade of endangered species, and CITES now seeks to ensure that international trade in specimens of wild plants and animals does not threaten species survival. Under CITES, selected species are subjected to varying levels of controls, such as import and export permits and proper shipping methods to minimize harm. CITES protects more than 2,000 invertebrate species, but with only plant species facing controls. Unfortunately, while data focus on the trading of larger species and their assets (e.g., hides and ivory),[33] little information exists on the practice of illegally trading smaller organisms and the extent of any enforcement against such practices.

Federal Law

The Endangered Species Act (ESA) serves as the keystone of American wildlife policy and is designed to protect threatened and endangered subspecies of all types, large *and* small. In fact, the constitutionality of the ESA was upheld by the U.S. Court of Appeals in a case involving the Delhi Sands Flower-Loving Fly, a pollinator that lost nearly all of its historical habitat.[34] A species gains protection under the ESA when the U.S. Fish and Wildlife Service (FWS) or the U.S. National Marine

29. COP 5 Decision V/5 Part II; Agricultural Biodiversity Case Studies, http://www.cbd.int/agro/casestudies.shtml.

30. *See, e.g.,* Plan of Action of the African Pollinator Initiative, http://www.fao.org/ag/aGp/agps/C-CAB/Castudies/pdf/apipoa.pdf; Brazilian Pollinators Initiative, http://www.fao.org/docrep/010/a1490e/a1490e00.htm; European Pollinator Initiative, http://www.fao.org/ag/AGP/AGPS/C-CAB/Castudies/pdf/9-002.pdf and http://www.europeanpollinatorinitiative.org/.

31. For more information of the Soil Biodiversity Initiative, see http://www.fao.org/AG/agl/agll/soilbiod/initiative.stm.

32. For more information on CITES, see www.cites.org.

33. GINETTE HEMLEY, INTERNATIONAL WILDLIFE TRADE: A CITES SOURCEBOOK 29-48 (1994).

34. Nat'l Home Builders Ass'n v. Babbitt, 130 F.3d 1041 (D.C. Cir. 1997).

Fisheries Service (NMFS) determines that the species faces habitat destruction, finds itself over-utilized for whatever reason, fears attack from disease or predation, or confronts manmade threats to its continued existence.[35] The ESA makes it illegal to take, harass, harm, pursue, hunt, shoot, wound, kill, trap, capture, or collect an endangered species.[36] It also requires all federal agencies and private parties receiving federal funds or permits to consult with FWS and NMFS to ensure that their actions do not jeopardize the existence of any endangered or threatened species.[37]

While the design is for universal protection of all species, in reality, larger species garner more regulatory protection. For example, only three of the NMFS's 60 threatened or endangered marine species are invertebrates.[38] The FWS' listings also are dominated by vertebrates, though this pattern is slowly changing. Over the last decade, the FWS has listed more invertebrates than vertebrates as threatened or endangered. And unfortunately, overall species listing has significantly declined, especially during the administration of President George W. Bush.[39] Similarly, the FWS spends far more money protecting mammals (more than $122 million) than insects (just over $7 million).[40]

Various other federal statutes and regulations create direct and indirect protections for a broad set of organisms: animals cannot be taken from a national wildlife area, park or monument, or the continent of Antarctica; waterways cannot be filled without a permit; and use of agricultural pesticides is regulated.[41] Federal legislation does protect some specific small organisms, especially honeybees. The Honeybee Act attempts to protect the honeybees in the United States by regulating importation to prevent the spread of disease and parasites.[42] For example, the trade of honeybees into Hawaii is prohibited, as the island state is considered free of honeybee pests and parasites, and people can import honeybees only from Australia, Canada, and New Zealand.[43] However, very little information exists about the success of the

---

35. 16 U.S.C. § 1533, ESA § 4.

36. 16 U.S.C. §§ 1532, 1538, ESA §§ 2, 9.

37. 16 U.S.C. § 1536, ESA § 7.

38. National Marine Fisheries Serv., Endangered and Threatened Species under NMFS' Jurisdiction, http://www.nmfs.noaa.gov/pr/pdfs/species/esa_table.pdf.

39. U.S. Fish & Wildlife Serv., Federal Endangered and Threatened Species by Calendar Year, http://ecos.fws.gov/tess_public/pub/speciesCountByYear.jsp.

40. U.S. FISH & WILDLIFE SERV., FEDERAL AND STATE ENDANGERED AND THREATENED SPECIES EXPENDITURES FISCAL YEAR 2004, *available at* http://www.fws.gov/endangered/pdfs/Expenditures/2004ExpendituresReport.pdf.

41. *See, e.g.,* 16 U.S.C. §668dd (prohibiting harming or possessing an animal in a National Wildlife Refuge); 16 U.S.C. §§ 2402-03 (prohibiting any activity that will harm animals or animal habitats in Antarctica); Clean Water Act § 404, 33 U.S.C. § 1344; 36 C.F.R. §§ 7.27, 7.46, 7.73, 7.84 (regulating uses and possession of animals in Dry Tortugas National Park, Virgin Islands Coral Reef National Monument, Buck Island Reef National Monument, and Channel Islands National Park); Federal Insecticide, Fungicide and Rodenticide Act, 7 U.S.C. §§ 136 et seq.; 40 C.F.R. § 161.202 (stating that data requirements for pesticide registration help assess hazards to nontarget organisms).

42. *See, e.g.,* Honeybee Act, 7 U.S.C. §§ 281-82, 284.

43. 7 C.F.R. §§ 322.2, 322.4.

Honeybee Act. Further, despite numerous proposals, Congress has not sought a plan to reverse Colony Collapse Disorder.[44]

Only limited federal law, through legislation like the Soil Conservation and Domestic Allotment Act of 1935 and the 1977 Soil and Water Resource Conservation Act, protects soil, and it does so with a strong view of soil as a physical entity rather than a biological one, focusing efforts on soil erosion and water quality to improve agricultural productivity.[45] While some soil conservation programs do exist that facilitate some biological approaches,[46] such actions face pressures of industrial agricultural norms. Very little is known about the relative success of the Soil Conservation Act, even in dealing with the physical problems of erosion and flooding.

State & Local Policy

Like the federal government, many states have broadly worded statutes protecting threatened and endangered species, including invertebrates.[47] State governments have also acted to regulate honeybees, through both statutes and regulatory programs.[48] Nearly all the state statutes are concerned with the health of the honeybee population, specifically the concern for introduction and spread of disease. To a varying degree, these statutes and state programs regulate honeybee transportation and importation, inspection, eradication and quarantine to stop disease, and registration, as well as control pests and pesticide use.

---

44. RENEE JOHNSON, CONGRESSIONAL RESEARCH SERVICE, RECENT HONEY BEE COLONY DECLINES (2007), *available at* http://fas.org/sgp/crs/misc/RL33938.pdf; *Colony Collapse Disorder and Pollinator Decline: Hearing Before the H. Subcomm. on Horticulture and Organic Agric.*, 110th Cong. (2007) (statement of May R. Berenbaum, Professor of Entomology, University of Illinois Urbana-Champaign, Chairwoman, Comm. on the Status of Pollinators in North America), *available at* http://www7.nationalacademies.org/ocga/testimony/Colony_Collapse_Disorder_and_Pollinator_Decline.asp; *Colony Collapse in Honey Bee Colonies, Hearing Before the H. Subcomm. on Horticulture and Organic Agric.*, 110th Cong. (2007) (statement by Coevolution Institute), *executive summary available at* http://www.pollinator.org/Resources/Mar%2029%20CCD%20Comments,%20Exec%20Summary.pdf.

45. *See, e.g.,* Soil Conservation Act, 16 U.S.C. § 590; Soil and Water Resources Conservation Act, 16 U.S.C. §§ 2001 - 2009); National Resources Conservation Service, NRCS Conservation Programs, http://www.nrcs.usda.gov/programs; Farm Service Agency, Fact Sheet, Conservation Reserve Program, http://www.fsa.usda.gov/FSA/printapp?fileName=pf_20070525_consv_en_crp07.html&newsType=prfactsheet.

46. *See, e.g.,* Conservation Security Program, 16 U.S.C. § 3838a; NAT'L RES. CONSERVATION SERV., U.S. DEP'T OF AGRICULTURE, CONSERVATION SECURITY PROGRAM 1-2 (2004), *available at* http://www.nrcs.usda.gov/programs/csp/pdf_files/CSP_%20brochure.pdf; 7 U.S.C. § 5821 (Integrated Management Systems); 7 U.S.C. § 5822 (Integrated Farm Management Program Option).

47. California, Connecticut, Delaware, Florida, Georgia, Hawaii, Illinois, Iowa, Kansas, Maine, Maryland, Massachusetts, Michigan, Minnesota, Mississippi, Missouri, Nebraska, New Hampshire, New Jersey, New York, Ohio, Vermont, Virginia, Washington, and Wisconsin have laws that protect invertebrates deemed endangered or threatened.

48. Some form of state legislation exists for regulation of honeybees in Alabama, Alaska, Arizona, Arkansas, California, Colorado, Connecticut, Delaware, Florida, Georgia, Hawaii, Idaho, Illinois, Indiana, Iowa, Kentucky, Louisiana, Maine, Maryland, Massachusetts, Michigan, Mississippi, Missouri, Montana, Nebraska, Nevada, New Hampshire, New Jersey, New Mexico, New York, North Carolina, North Dakota, Ohio, Oklahoma, Oregon, Pennsylvania, Rhode Island, South Carolina, South Dakota, Tennessee, Texas, Utah, Vermont, Virginia, Washington, West Virginia, Wisconsin, and Wyoming.

Due to unique economic interests, whether alfalfa or honey, states seek to protect any number of pollinators and insects.[49] However, with most pollinator projects in their infancy, still securing funding, or relying on early data, we cannot know for certain of their success. That said, early results are promising: new population data exist, and various techniques (such as maintaining untilled soil and planting diverse flowers) are underway to attract and maintain healthy pollinator populations.[50]

States also have, to an even greater extent than their federal partners, sought to promote sustainable agricultural practices to preserve soil quality. Statutes promote agricultural research, education, and training for proper soil conservation and fertilization techniques, usually with the help of state university resources and administrative agencies.[51] But again, it remains unclear to what extent the determination of soil health remains focused on soil chemistry and physical structure as opposed to soil biology. The range of programs is varied. Some promote biologically intensive agriculture while others simply promote more reasonable and proper use of chemical inputs. In either case, the programs have promoted little discussion of the importance of soil biota as a means to attain sustainable food production.

C. Steps to Protect Small Organisms

In many ways, the endangerment of small organisms parallels the challenges posed by climate change. In both cases, the science is complex and not easily understood; the causes are diffuse; and the impacts are equally diffuse, wide-ranging, and often far-removed from the underlying behavior that policy might seek to modify. Yet, ignoring these concerns because we are not immediately impacted is not an option. Nature's web requires us to protect one species to safeguard another,[52] starting with the foundational producers within an ecosystem.

---

49. *See, e.g.,* Alfalfa and Clover Seed Industries Act, IDAHO CODE ANN. §§ 22-4201 to 22-4218; Virginia Plant Pollinator Advisory Board, VA. CODE ANN. §§ 3.1-610.23-.28; Washington Ladybugs or other Beneficial Insects, WASH. REV. CODE §§ 15.61.010-.900.

50. *See, e.g.,* New Mexico Native Pollinator Project, http://www.pollinatorparadise.com/nm.htm; The Xerces Society, California Pollinator Project, http://www.xerces.org/california-agricultural-pollinator-project/; Migratory Pollinators Project, Center for Sonoran Desert Studies, Arizona-Sonora Desert Museum, http://www.desertmuseum.org/pollination/, Chatham County Center, North Carolina Cooperative Extension Biodiversity Project: Farmscaping for Pollinators and Wildlife, http://www.ces.ncsu.edu/chatham/ag/SustAg/biodiversityproject.html; The Urban Bee Project, University of California, Berkeley, http://nature.berkeley.edu/urbanbeegardens/index_research.html.

51. *See, e.g.,* VT. STAT. ANN. tit. 6, § 4701; Sustainable Agriculture Research and Education Act of 1986, CAL. FOOD & AGRIC. CODE §§ 550-555; Fertilizer Act, 505 ILL. COMP. STAT. 80/6a; Center for Sustaining Agriculture and Natural Resources, WASH. REV. CODE §§ 15.92.005-.110; UC Sustainable Agriculture Research and Education Program, SAREP Mission and Goals, http://www.sarep.ucdavis.edu/concept.htm; Minnesota Board of Water and Soil Resources, Reinvest in Minnesota Reserve Program Fact Sheet, http://www.bwsr.state.mn.us/easements/rim/factsheet.html; Illinois Department of Agriculture Fertilizer Research and Education Council, http://frec.cropsci.uiuc.edu/; Center for Sustaining Agriculture and Natural Resources at Washington State University, http://csanr.wsu.edu/.

52. Conkin, *supra* note 20, at 135 ("In many cases, the survival of one species depends upon the survival of others. If the pollen-bearing plants that provide the only food for specialized insects die off, so do the insects. In the same sense, without pollinating insects some plants will be unable to produce.

Similarly, the agenda to protect small organisms, like the topics of earlier chapters, needs to include both traditional regulation and activating change in individual behavior through information dissemination. More specifically, and similar to the problem of sprawl, of the decision-making tools to be considered to promote everyday environmentalism (see the Introduction) policy-makers should focus on (1) revising existing government action to recognize local conditions and value the ecosystem services of small organisms and (2) information generation and dissemination in an effort to establish a broader understanding of the valuable ecosystem services provided by small organisms and the need to shift activity patterns that harm them.

First, existing law and public policy can be modified to limit introduction of pesticides, fertilizers, and other destructive forces, as well as include valuation of ecosystem services provided by small organisms when creating land use and agricultural policy. Second, interrelated individual choices like suburban residency and purchasing pesticide-intensive foods, in addition to contributing to global warming, can have unanticipated impacts like cooperating in the destruction of small organisms. Public policy initiatives must determine how to make individuals aware of these interrelationships and the importance of small organisms to fully functioning ecosystems. In addition, further resources are necessary to generate better scientific information about small organisms.

Bringing Long-Term Balance to Environmental Policy

Much of the danger to small organisms results from the introduction of pests, diseases, and practices that destroy habitat due to short-sighted environmental regulation. Due to immediate economic interests, such as pollination dependency and demand for agricultural production, many products with only short-term value enter the environment at great long-term costs.

For example, the United States recently imported honeybees from outside North America for the first time since 1922, likely increasing risks for the existing bee population.[53] To limit the introduction and proliferation of pests, parasites, and disease, national governments, especially the United States, must consider ending pollinator importation across the globe, despite the strong economic demands for importation, and enlist mitigation measures.[54]

Similarly, inorganic fertilizers, pesticides, monoculture, and tillage harm soil biota. While these practices have facilitated increased global food production, such activities ignore the benefits of soil biodiversity, causing loss of organic matter and soil biota habitat as well as lower nutrient retention. Legislation and policy should

---

Without specific birds, many species of insects will soar in numbers. The linkages are often so complex that it is almost impossible to predict the effect of any extinction. It is also almost impossible to identify critical species in an ecosystem, or those whose survival is vital to the health of the whole.").

53. STATUS OF POLLINATORS, *supra* note 4, at 199.

54. *See, e.g.,* Laurie A. Mitchell, *Attack of the Killer Bees: Will Regulation Save Us?*, 8 SAN JOAQUIN AGRIC. L. REV. 103 (1998).

promote integrated soil management and organic agriculture, which yield healthier crops and cause less ecological disturbance.[55] Organic practices such as crop rotation, limited pesticide use, organic fertilizers, and minimum tillage increase the density and diversity of soil invertebrates and maintain ecosystem services. To this end, and as discussed in Chapter Four, consumers should buy produce that is organic or from sustainable farms.

Admittedly, tradeoffs exist in developing any sensible and sustainable pollinator or soil biodiversity policy. An additional irony is that, at the time when food production experienced its greatest increases, soil degradation was at its worst. Intense fertilizer use and modern agricultural methods mask soil erosion and degradation. Today, agricultural practices that allow lesser developed countries and many farmers to feed their citizens and compete in the market also create long-term environmental damage. At the same time, only with chemical fertilizers have some nations avoided starvation. For example, despite millions facing starvation, for the last two decades the African country of Malawi has been pressured by wealthier nations to adhere to free-market policies and eliminate fertilizer subsidies, even though the United States and Europe extensively subsidize their own farmers.[56] Malawi's president has reinstated fertilizer subsidies for farmers too poor to afford fertilizers. In this way, illustrating the importance of targeting the appropriate populations, Malawi averted a hunger crisis and now even exports some food. A *New York Times* Earth Day article noted that, while an organic and fertilizer-free world sounds great, it could result in massive malnutrition in Africa and Asia.[57]

Thus, eco-policies must not lose sight of social, economic, and environmental justice concerns. While recent domestic and international policies have allowed lesser-developed countries to continue to pollute to achieve developed status, this development norm remains unsustainable, and richer nations must help poorer ones in exchange for environmental compliance until standards of living become less disparate. (This same argument applies to the climate change problem.)

Limiting destruction and mitigating existing damage is not an exact science. It does not mean we should try to return to an unrealistic past. It is far easier to limit the prospective harm and maintain the ecosystem in its current state. Policy should not, until that goal is achieved and barring immediate needs for cleanup to protect public and environmental health, invest heavily in returning resources to some past state. To do so is futile and ignores nature's dynamism. To which date

---

55. Like global warming, agricultural practices create winners and losers on soil biota. Integrated soil management (ISM), in considering the interaction between the soil environment and its organisms, recognizes this fact. ISM options include both direct (inoculation) and indirect interventions (mulching, tillage, irrigation, crop rotation) impacting soil biota. While ISM recognizes the importance of soil biota, care must be used in determining which options are most environmentally friendly. *See* Food and Agricultural Organization of the United Nations, *Integrated Soil Biological Management Practices and Enhancement of Soil Biota Function,* http://www.fao.org/ag/agl/agll/soilbiod/managtxt.stm.

56. Celia W. Dugger, *Ending Famine, Simply by Ignoring the Experts,* NY TIMES, http://www.nytimes.com/2007/12/02/world/africa/02malawi.html.

57. John Tierney, *For Earth Day, 7 New Rules to Live By,* N.Y. TIMES (Apr. 20, 1970).

would we return? Old growth forests thrived with the help of Native Americans burning the underbrush. Earthworms are not native to North American northern forests, having found their way there from ballast water dumped by European ships off the east coast.[58] More aggressive European honeybees changed North American agriculture after European settlers brought them to Jamestown in 1622 for honey, not pollination.[59]

To implement forward-looking programs such as agricultural innovation, honeybee policy, or habitat protection, perspectives toward implementation and resources must change. First, natural resource management programs must be based upon a better understanding of local conditions and local data—pesticide and fertilizer use, climate, socio-economic conditions, and participation of farmers and policymakers. Hence, as discussed above, it is important to address the need for greater research and information, recognizing that regional and local initiatives may be most effective in this regard. There is no doubt that more research and empirical data are required to understand the importance of small organisms, especially compared with large animals. Without question, existing research on small organisms can, at best, be characterized as poor,[60] and developing effective policies will be hampered by this lack of information. Second, environmental policy must be developed based on a long-term economic view, recognizing the value of a sustainable ecosystem, rather than making decisions for short-term economic gain. This is no easy task. "It is difficult to describe the need to protect a species that most people will never see and that has no obvious economic, commercial, recreational, or aesthetic value."[61] For example, is protecting a fly worth relocating a needed hospital?[62] Yet, preserving biodiversity and species populations for the long haul is critical to protecting valuable ecosystem services.

Animals provide food, medicinal ingredients, and economic value—ecosystems support farming, fishing, lumbering, manufacturing, and freshwater supplies. While these natural services may sometimes be difficult to measure and value, they are substantial and essential. Pollinators facilitate billions of dollars of agricultural growth, and the continued existence of soil biota can help ensure healthy soil for generations. Shortcuts like fertilizers, heavy tillage, pesticides, and infested imported bees only forestall long-term ecosystem and economic health. And balancing imperiled species only against short-term economic interests, losing sight of longer-term costs, is especially problematic given the precarious nature of their existence—"reasonable" accommodation may lead to annihilation or extinction.[63]

---

58. Charles C. Mann, *America, Found & Lost*, NAT'L GEOGRAPHIC, May 2007, at 34.

59. *Id.* at 50.

60. STATUS OF POLLINATORS, *supra* note 4, at 58 (describing information about population sizes of flies as "virtually nonexistent").

61. *Endangered and Threatened Wildlife and Plants; Final Rule to List the Illinois Cave Amphipod as Endangered*, 63 Fed. Reg. 46,900, 46,902 (Sept. 3, 1998).

62. John Copeland Nagle, *Biodiversity and Mom*, 30 ECOLOGY L. Q. 993 (2003).

63. Federico Cheever, *Butterflies, Cave Spiders, Milk-Vetch, Bunchgrass, Sedges, Lilies, Checker-Mallows and Why the Prohibition Against Judicial Balancing of Harm Under the Endangered Species*

Information Dissemination and Production

Small organisms are in peril due to agricultural practices that use chemicals, carbon emissions that accelerate species loss, and suburbanization that fragments habitat. The everyday choices of the average person, including household management, dietary, and dwelling decisions, in the aggregate create significant environmental impacts that ultimately result in harm to small organisms on the land, in the air, and even in the sea. Yet, these little creatures go unrecognized and unprotected. Information-focused efforts will be key to their protection. As the most under-represented natural group, small organisms demand recognition for their role in interdependent ecosystems and for the important ecosystem services they provide.

Research is needed to further evaluate the relationships among soil organisms and between pollinators and their environment to determine key species and function groups. To this end, farmers, beekeepers, consumers, and environmental policymakers can develop strategies to target species that perform the most important ecosystem services, as well as identify those species that serve as the best indicators for overall environmental health. While broader research will be expensive and difficult, the information can show how using natural and biological processes, rather than chemicals, might lead to agricultural gains and better protection of ecologically important small organisms. In addition, existing data on biodiversity must be put to better use. A strong information flow is needed among scientists, policymakers, and consumers in order to ensure that all are positioned to make environmentally conscious decisions.

Going forward, as a first step, individuals and policymakers must recognize the alignment between small organisms and individual behavior, serving as an additional rationale for greater and creative regulation targeted at consumer choice. The current food model stresses pollinators and soil biota due to pesticides and fertilizer, and bees, the subjects of carbon heavy transportation, are fed high-fructose corn syrup, a fossil-fuel-generated commodity grain (see Chapter Four). Increased greenhouse gas emissions, from which personal automobile travel is a major source (see Chapter Three), make plants less nutritious for small organisms and will fundamentally alter their biodiversity and biogeography. Sprawl results in habitat loss and fragmentation (see Chapter Five).

Second, public relations and educational campaigns can help individuals recognize and appreciate the importance of small organisms as discussed in Part A above. Pollinators are indicator species that not only have value themselves but also foreshadow dangers in the larger ecosystem. Soil is a living organism, rather than simply material in which plants grow. The concerns, however, extend beyond pollinators, soil biota, and other bugs. There are other small organisms that mandate protection but for which we have even smaller amounts of information. For example, what lies in the sea? Perhaps the most important organism on Earth: plankton, small organisms drifting through the Earth's oceans. Phytoplankton, which generate energy from photosynthesis, account for more than 95% of "oceanic primary productivity," the energy needed for the rest of the ecosystem to prosper.[64] Without these microscopic phytoplankton, oceanic ecosystems would degrade. Animal zooplankton eat their smaller plant brethren, the primary producers, and themselves are eaten by secondary consumers like fish, shellfish, and some whales. Plankton face harm from invasive exotic species and increased ultraviolet radiation due to climate change, yet the details and causes of their population dynamics remain largely unknown.

Still, it is true that honeybees have not gone unnoticed. The need to transport millions of colonies so we can eat nuts, fruits, and vegetables ensures this. Other pollinators like bats, butterflies, and flies still lack the necessary cachet unless they have obvious aesthetic value. Similarly, society notices the impacts of obvious soil erosion but has not noticed soil biota. Nonetheless, where some public awareness exists, it should be used as the platform for broader public outreach.

There is no doubt that a series of well-crafted public outreach and educational campaigns are necessary to raise awareness about the environmental concerns surrounding small organism loss. It is, similar to climate change (see Chapter Two), difficult to craft a single message or identify a single symbol for such a complex and yet seemingly elusive problem. Again, similar to climate change, it can be difficult to garner support, from both a political and public interest standpoint, to protect against a harm that is not immediately obvious. Tigers and polar bears get recognition; roundworms do not. This is simply a function of humanity: we focus most on what we can see. We buff and shine our coffee tables, but leave dust under our television set. Thus, more intentionality, in terms of both information dissemination and traditional regulation, will be required to preserve the small and unnoticed. For without tiny species, ecosystems will be in peril. As President Franklin Delano Roosevelt said, "The nation that destroys its soil destroys itself."[65]

For the purposes of protecting small organisms, one of the most unrecognized natural resources affected by ecological harm, everyday environmentalism in all the areas covered by earlier chapters will also reduce negative impacts on small organisms. Individual behaviors like driving less or eating pesticide-free foods improve small organism populations; and, in the aggregate, decreased fossil-fuel consumption and improved land use practices limit pollinator and soil biota loss. Thus, better daily decision-making in each of those areas, whether made with any consideration for small organisms or not, still may have beneficial effects.

---

64. The following source proved valuable for information on plankton: Jerry R. Schubel & Cheryl Ann Butman, *Keeping a Finger on the Pulse of Marine Biodiversity: How Healthy Is It?*, in NATURE AND HUMAN SOCIETY, *supra* note 1.

65. NATURE AND HUMAN SOCIETY, *supra* note 1, at 225 (citing Franklin D. Roosevelt (1937)).

CHAPTER SEVEN

Conclusion

> Even environmentalists, committed to the rescue of wild places, have failed to address
> the problem of human ecology in the place where we live and work.
>
> JAMES HOWARD KUNSTLER, THE GEOGRAPHY OF NOWHERE:
> THE RISE AND DECLINE OF AMERICA'S MAN-MADE LANDSCAPE 249 (1994)

Without a doubt, in American society, consumption is king, with its ascension
causing major and unforeseen ecological problems. Whether the focus is on bigger
cars, homes, backyards or meals, consumers have been driven by marketing and
permitted by policy to make this coronation in their everyday lives—but at the
unforeseen expense of natural elements in the environment. The democratization of
pollution sources, in the aggregate, comes with considerable environmental costs,
and new ideas and strategies must be created in an effort to address key environmental policy questions.[1] How can society understand the environmental costs of
daily life? What is the appropriate role for traditional environmental regulation?
And what might promote changes in cultural and social norms so that everyday
choices become more environmentally friendly?

The preceding chapters address these queries in the context of the household
carbon and waste footprint (Chapter Three), food choice (Chapter Four), residential
geography and sprawl (Chapter Five), and the unforeseen costs of destruction of
small organisms (Chapter Six). From this, two overwhelming themes emerge for
promoting everyday environmentalism, both relying on information as a driver for
change. First, and most obviously, there must be a concerted and basic effort to
raise awareness of the environmental costs of individual behavior in the aggregate
and of the potential power of changes in individual behavior. Second, to generate
change in individual behavior, policymakers should evaluate and apply specific
decision-making tools to: (1) promote focused efforts to increase public awareness
of the aggregate environmental costs of particular individual behavior, (2) determine the appropriate level of government or private action best suited to address
that category of behavior, (3) create and promote use of broader information and
labeling so individuals can evaluate the ecological costs of a service or product,
(4) create economic incentives to influence individual behavior and take account of

---

1. *See* Timothy P. Duane, *Environmental Planning and Policy in a Post-Rio World*, 7 BERKELEY
PLANNING J. 27, 31 (1992).

the value of ecosystem services, (5) use policies and approaches that target the key audience and products, and (6) support and facilitate effective community initiatives and personal efforts. Appendix A to this chapter provides examples of how these types of tools have already been used to promote everyday environmentalism in the context of the issues covered in this book.

Knowledge & Individual Behavior

The primary driver to promoting everyday environmentalism is literacy, gained through knowledge about the consumption patterns of the United States (see Chapter One) coupled with an understanding both of the aggregate environmental consequences of daily consumer choice and of how people can change their behavior to mitigate or avoid those harms (Chapters Two through Six).[2] The consequences of everyday choices often are underestimated. Individuals in the United States account for 30% to 40% of the nation's greenhouse gas emissions, or 8% of the *world's* total.[3] Unfortunately, "ignorance is bliss"; consumers may not want to know the consequences of their actions and power of consumer choice. For example, as Americans moved toward a more industrial food system, marketers argued that consumers were busy and need not be "bothered" with the additional task of knowing where their food came from.[4] Entities that profit from these consumer choices generally have little incentive or requirement to evaluate or provide information on the associated negative environmental impacts.

In addition, the consequences of human behavior often are unforeseen.[5] It has become more difficult to appreciate the ecological consequences of our daily activities as modern society becomes further removed from our sources of food and energy, and from the natural resources that serve as raw materials. "Culturally, we are just beginning to reconsider how our consumption is connected to a broader context of consequences."[6] Understanding these connections demands a desire to know and access to necessary information. Knowledge can result from incentives to know, public relations and marketing campaigns, government regulatory tools,

---

2. For a discussion of the role of information in protecting the environment, see THOMAS DIETZ & PAUL C. STERN, NEW TOOLS FOR ENVIRONMENTAL PROTECTION: EDUCATION, INFORMATION, AND VOLUNTARY MEASURES (2002); *see also* Hope M. Babcock, *Assuming Personal Responsibility for Improving the Environment: Moving Towards a New Environmental Norm*, 33 HARV. ENVTL. L. REV. 117, 118 (2009) ("The best way to change norms is through education ... but supplemental measures are necessary."). This use of the term 'literacy' is drawn from Ann Vileisis' *Kitchen Literacy*.

3. *The Forum, Creating the Carbon-neutral Citizen*, 24 ENVTL. L. FORUM 46 (2007); Michael P. Vandenbergh & Anne Steinemann, *The Carbon-Neutral Individual*, 82 NYU L. REV. 1673 (2007).

4. ANN VILEISIS, KITCHEN LITERACY: HOW WE LOST KNOWLEDGE OF WHERE FOOD COMES FROM AND WHY WE NEED TO GET IT BACK 167 (2007).

5. For example, writer Rowan Jacobsen argues that bees are dying from the dominant American suburban lifestyle and landscape. In an effort to deal with loss of habitat, monocrops, and continually decreasing population resulting in increased pollination demand, bees are fed high fructose corn syrup, transported across the country, and given antibiotics, miticides, and fungicides. ROWAN JACOBSEN, FRUITLESS FALL: THE COLLAPSE OF THE HONEY BEE AND THE COMING AGRICULTURAL CRISIS 151-153 (2008).

6. *Id.* at 238.

and peer pressure (all potentially facilitated by law and public policy), as well as ecological disasters like Hurricane Katrina or species extinction.

Once individuals gain perspective on the environmental consequences of their actions, further knowledge is needed to determine how to make better and basic choices in their daily lives. As discussed in the preceding chapters, small individual shifts in behavior can be quite significant in the aggregate. In terms of initial modifications in behavior, the low-hanging fruit include, to name a few: trying to eat organic and local foods, eating less meat and shifting away from red meat, living close to where you work and play, seeing if your household can get along with only one car (and try to make it a fuel efficient one), walking and taking public transit, composting as much as possible, stopping engine idling, buying compact fluorescent light bulbs, adjusting down the thermostat, decreasing household water temperature, keeping proper tire pressure, and working to educate yourself about the ecological *and* economic costs of your actions in the long term.[7] Engine idling, for example, accounts for a substantial portion of carbon emissions and fuel consumption, measured at 1.6% of all U.S. carbon dioxide emissions and 10.6 billion gallons of fuel per year.[8] Attempts to address idling through public education campaigns have proven successful in Canada, and similar success in the United States would prevent 7 to 26 million tons of carbon dioxide emissions each year and reduce fuel consumption by 660 million to 2.3 billion gallons each year.[9] Recall that generating public awareness is a tool always to consider when seeking change in individual decision-making.

In many instances, public law and policy have promoted infrastructure, food choices, agricultural practices, and other behaviors that harm the environment. Consequently, as part of everyday environmentalism, individuals should make themselves aware of political and legal processes that determine our transportation infrastructure, food labeling, and residential zoning and development patterns. Scientists, economists, writers, and scholars must actively seek to engage the public in the discussion and should work to reach out and explain issues, legal arguments, and policy programs to the public. Modifying individual behavior through regulation is a key emerging component of environmental policy, and its implementation depends upon a better understanding of the underlying relationship between human consumption patterns and the environment.

---

7. *See* Michael P. Vandenbergh, Jack Barkenbus & Jonathan M. Gilligan, *Individual Carbon Emissions: The Low Hanging Fruit*, 55 UCLA L. Rev. 1701 (2008); MICHAEL BROWER & WARREN LEON, THE CONSUMER'S GUIDE TO EFFECTIVE ENVIRONMENTAL CHOICES: PRACTICAL ADVICE FROM THE UNION OF CONCERNED SCIENTISTS 85 (1999).

8. Amanda R. Carrico, Paul Padgett, Michael P. Vandenbergh, Jonathan Gilligan & Kenneth A. Wallston, *Costly Myths: An analysis of idling beliefs and behavior in personal motor vehicles*, 37 ENERGY POLICY 2881 (2009).

9. *Id.* at 2887.

The Regulatory Role & Individual Behavior

Law plays a role in providing information, creating incentives for change, and shifting social and cultural norms.[10] Legal regimes and policy initiatives can instill environmentally friendly behavior in daily choices by developing successful informational labeling about environmental harm, creating regulatory tools that effectively value ecosystem services, and advancing advocacy and community programs designed to trigger eco-friendly behavior. These approaches also need to be bolstered by more traditional regulatory approaches that focus on protecting specific natural resources, such as wetlands and small organisms.

Informational labeling exists for products through programs such as Energy Star, Leadership in Energy Efficiency Design (LEED) Certified, and USDA Certified Organic. Yet, industry often has balked at the added costs of informational labeling, as evidenced by objections to new country of origin labeling requirements for food products in the United States. Some industry resistance has receded because environmental labels create value-added products that people will pay more for, including foods, sustainable residences, and a wide variety of household products. The goal is for regulatory policy and shifting consumer demand ultimately to make such environmental labels ubiquitous, resulting in new production norms, more consumer options, and lower costs.

Drawing on other initiatives, such as those in the European Union, the United Kingdom's Carbon Trust program,[11] or even the state of California's proposed carbon labeling legislation,[12] the United States federal government could mandate life-cycle eco-labeling on consumer products with carbon intense and environmentally degrading production. Sweden has recently embarked upon an ambitious carbon labeling and information program.[13] Foods in grocery stores and on restaurant menus will list the amount of carbon dioxide produced per kilogram of the product.

---

10. Both historically and currently, social norms impact environmental health. *See, e.g.,* Antonio González López & María Amérigo Cuervo-Arango, *Relationship Among Values, Beliefs, Norms and Ecological Behaviour,* 20 PSICOTHEMA 623 (2008); Johan Colding & Carl Folke, *Social Taboos: "Invisible" Systems of Local Resource Management and Biological Conservation,* 11 ECOLOGICAL APPLICATIONS 584 (2001); Bruce A. Byers et al., *Linking the Conservation of Culture and Nature: A Case Study of Sacred Forests in Zimbabwe,* 29 HUM. ECOLOGY 187 (2001); Michael P. Vandenbergh, *Order Without Social Norms: How Personal Norm Activation Can Protect the Environment,* 99 NW. U. L. REV. 1101, 1165-66 (2005).

11. The Carbon Trust (www.carbontrust.co.uk), a non-profit funded by the British government, has developed a graphic depicting the number of grams of carbon dioxide inside a human footprint.

12. Cal. A.B. 19 (2009-10). The bill, short on details, requires a state board to develop a cradle-to-gate carbon labeling program.

13. For the details on Sweden's initiative, see Elisabeth Rosenthal, *To Cut Global Warming, Swedes Study Their Plates,* N.Y. TIMES GLOBAL (Oct. 22, 2009); Sweden National Food Administration, *The National Food Administration's environmentally effective food choices* (May 15, 2009), http://www.slv.se/upload/dokument/miljo/environmentally_effective_food_choices_proposal_eu_2009.pdf; Climate Labelling for Food, *Project Description: Standards for Climate Label for Food Version, No 2009:1,* http://www.klimatmarkningen.se/wp-content/uploads/2009/02/project-description-english.pdf.

How would such an eco-labeling scheme work? Phasing in eco-labeling requirements, expert panels would determine what product groups create the most environmental harm by looking at criteria such as the carbon footprint of production (e.g., fossil-fuel consumption, food miles), environmental degradation (e.g., nature of waste disposal, use of pesticides), and sustainability and biodiversity (e.g., origin of raw materials, fishery status, land use), including impacts on organisms not usually considered (e.g., soil biota, pollinators). Products could receive a "green seal" or environmental rating, allowing consumers to compare similar products. More research is needed to determine how much carbon footprint and eco-labeling information consumers can effectively integrate into their decision-making process. Technological advances can also be used to inform consumers of their energy footprint (in dollars) through in-home and car displays and monitors. To encourage recycling and initial purchase of more environmentally friendly products, access to this information should exist at relevant times and locations, notably including point of purchase. Ideally, products (however large or small) should include information about carbon footprints, distribution miles, energy consumption, land use consequences, and waste production.

Establishing mandatory eco-labeling will not be easy. The complexity of eco-labeling criteria will challenge the collective brain power of whatever executive agency takes on this responsibility (preferably consolidated in the environmentally focused Environmental Protection Agency, rather than agencies with a more discrete focus like the Food and Drug Administration, U.S. Department of Agriculture, Housing and Urban Development or Department of Energy). Producers, whether food makers, home builders, or electronics manufacturers, have the best information on production, distribution, and disposal chains, and the government will have to mandate accurate compilation of this information to properly assess a product's environmental footprint. Government eco-labels are more effective than private ones, and it seems simple seal-of-approval logos and labels may influence consumer behavior more than the complex information-disclosure labels.[14]

Legally created financial incentive programs also can promote environmentally friendly choices and tax environmentally destructive behavior. A shift to pollution and carbon taxes is favored by many legal scholars and most economists.[15] Revenue generated from environmental taxation could then be spent on research and development for green technologies and infrastructure. Recently, the University of Vermont's Gund Institute for Ecological Economics proposed replacing Vermont's property- and income-based tax structure with new "green taxes" on things like

14. Abhijit Banerjee & Barry D. Solomon, *Eco-labeling for Energy Efficiency and Sustainability: A Meta-Evaluation of US Programs,* 31 ENERGY POLICY 109 (2003).

15. Robert Mann, *The Case for the Carbon Tax: How to Overcome Politics and Find Our Green Destiny,* 39 ENVTL. L. REP. 10118 (2009); William D. Nordhaus, *To Tax or Not to Tax: Alternative Approaches to Slowing Global Warming,* 1 REV. ENVTL. ECON. & POL'Y 26 (2007); Revven S. Avi-Yonah & David M. Uhlman, *Combating Global Climate Change: Why a Carbon Tax is a Better Response to Global Warming than Cap and Trade,* 28 STAN. ENVTL. L. J. 3 (2009); Janet Milne, *Carbon Taxes in the United States: The Context for the Future,* 10 VERMONT J. ENVTL. L. 1 (2008).

gasoline, land use, water, and waste.[16] Direct financial incentives to individuals, like the "Live Near Your Work" programs discussed in Chapter Six, can be used to encourage living near work and promote use of mass transportation. These financial instruments can limit land development, encourage habitat conservation, conserve water, and reduce reliance on fossil fuels. This would mark a fundamental shift from the historical lack of valuation of ecosystem services and domination of automobile transportation. The U.S. common law system "evolved over time to disfavor leaving land in its wild, undeveloped state, meaning owners of lands and the accompanying diversity of ecosystems have little incentive to treat them as a fund of natural capital providing valuable ecosystem services."[17]

Regulating individual behavior is a supplement to already existing forms of environmental law and natural resource protection policies. For example, while home buyers should know the consequences of sprawl and incentives should exist to encourage living in dense communities with a transit hub, some resources, like wetlands in particular, still demand expansive resource-by-resource public regulation due to barriers to modifying individual behavior. Wetlands benefit a large number of individuals, but individual disaggregated interests in many cases are small. Thus, a fully market-based approach that taxes sprawling development may meet limited success unless policymakers can design overall planning legislation that better integrates mechanisms to value ecosystem services.[18]

In terms of evaluating the effectiveness of economic incentives, policymakers need to recognize the basic desire for individual choice, as well as the legitimate concern that increasing the cost of engaging in certain behaviors through taxation may have a greater impact on price-sensitive individuals. Regardless of the tool used, long-term success in regulating individual behavior is uncertain absent steps to internalize new norms as discussed below.[19] For some products that individuals need and must consume frequently, like food, eco-labels may prove a better tool because taxation may put an undue burden on the most price-sensitive individuals. However, making available and marketing cost-effective alternative practices or products (e.g., the low-hanging fruit) is also key to internalizing new behavioral norms.

Basically, the cutting-edge challenge for law and public policy will be to change social and cultural norms to promote everyday environmentalism.[20] Individuals themselves must lower their waste and carbon footprints and make sensible food

16. Peter Hirschfeld, *UVM Institute suggests radical overhaul of Vt. Taxes*, TIMES ARGUS, Dec. 9, 2009.

17. Christopher Lant, J.B. Ruhl & Steven Kraft, *The Tragedy of Ecosystem Services*, 58 BIOSCIENCE 969, 971 (2008).

18. John D. Echeverria, *Regulating Versus Paying to Achieve Conservation Purposes*, SJ053. A.L.I.-A.B.A. 1141 (2004); James Salzman, *A Policy Maker's Guide to Designing Payments for Ecosystem Services*, http://ssrn.com/abstract=1498629.

19. Babcock, *supra* note 2, at 174.

20. *Cf.* Babcock, *supra* note 2, 33 HARV. ENVTL. L. REV. 117; Hope M. Babcock, *Global Climate Change: A Civic Republican Moment for Achieving Broader Changes in Environmental Behavior*, 26 PACE L. REV. 1 (2009).

and housing choices, even absent direct legal mandate. The informational tools and economic incentives discussed above are important components to meeting this challenge. Advocacy, public relations and education efforts, and local community initiatives also need to play a role in changing social norms, sometimes with the help and influence of direct regulation. In addition to federal and state efforts to implement eco-labels and create financial incentives, many concerns of everyday environmentalism are best addressed at the local level to bring out greater individual responsibility.[21] Local initiatives must be designed to supply environmental knowledge and instill environmental values, the two drivers for changes in ecological behavior.[22]

Local knowledge and local efforts can promote significant, positive environmental changes, but only if local level systems garner an appreciation for the links between social, economic, and ecological systems and where institutions also maintain this focus.[23] For example, in the wetlands management context, scholars have recognized that policy has failed to communicate the linkages between natural systems and social values. In other words, science must do a better job of communicating to local decision-makers by providing local content when giving expert advice, and science must account for and test how to achieve management goals through local initiatives.[24] Law then can promote these efforts. For example, environmental regulation of individual behavior, while sometimes difficult to enforce, can strengthen public education campaigns. Returning to the idling example, a series of Canadian case studies "concluded that the presence of regulation legitimized public education efforts, reduced public resistance to [anti-idling] ordinances, as well as attracted media attention to the problem."[25]

Formal regulation can also help facilitate everyday environmentalism in various ways by making eco-friendly choices easier and cheaper and providing better access to information. Think recycling stations, manufacturer take-back programs, and eco-labels. Yet, many citizens also want to take part in a communal cause and want social marketing and educational programs to appeal to individual desires to do the right thing.[26] Government funding can support these community

21. Nancy Kubasek & Alex Frondorf, *A Modest Proposal for Ameliorating Urban Sprawl*, 32 REAL ESTATE L. J. 246 (2003) ("Environmental problems addressed at the local level and neighborhood level bring out greater individual responsibility than do issues addressed at the state or national level.").

22. Florian G. Kaiser, Sybille Wölfing & Urs Fuhrer, *Environmental Attitudes and Ecological Behavior*, 19 J. ENVTL. PSYCHOLOGY 1 (1999).

23. Per Olson & Carl Folke, *Local Ecological Knowledge and Institutional Dynamics for Ecosystem Management: A Study of Lake Racken Watershed, Sweden*, 4 ECOSYSTEMS 85 (2001).

24. Bryan G. Norton, *Improving Ecological Communication: The Role of Ecologists in Environmental Policy*, 8 ECOLOGICAL APPLICATIONS 350 (1998); Edgar W. Jenkins, *Environmental Education and the Public Understanding of Science*, 1 FRONTIERS IN ECOLOGY & ENV. 437 (2003); Lowell Pritchard Jr., Carl Folke & Lance Gunderson, *Valuation of Ecosystem Services in Institutional Context*, 3 ECOSYSTEMS 36 (2000); Colding & Folke, *supra* note 10.

25. Carrico, *supra* note 8, at 2887 (citing Lura Consulting, *The Carrot, The Stick, and The Combo: A Recipe for Reducing Vehicle Idling in Canadian Communities* (2005).

26. Catherine M. Kalinowski, Gary D. Lynne, Bruce Johnson, *Recycling as a Reflection of Balanced Self-Interest*, 38 ENV. & BEHAVIOR 333 (2006).

efforts. Neighborhood associations, municipalities, schools, and libraries can host educational programs, create competitions for the most eco-friendly city, supply home energy audits, support farmers' markets, and encourage walking, biking and outdoor activities.

The key to building ecological norms for everyday life is to determine what community programs should actually look like to effectively shift norms. To know where to begin, better answers to some empirical questions are needed. Environmental science and ecology must have sufficient information to take into account current social norms. Information is needed to understand why residents live where they do, eat what they choose to eat, and make other behavior choices. In order to modify behavior, it is also important to identify key barriers to change (e.g., money, time, access). Then, based on pilot projects, community initiatives and public marketing campaigns can be evaluated to see which prove most effective. The goal is to identify which behaviors can be most effectively modified and through what methods, as well as to determine what audience or sub-groups should be targeted to gain the most significant environmental benefit.

Similarly, law and policy must endeavor to find tradeoffs that are low-cost to consumers and high-value to the environment, even when consumers balk at the most eco-friendly option. Such tradeoffs include purchasing corded electric rather than gas lawn mowers (if an old-fashioned push mower is not acceptable), eating chicken over beef (if not going vegetarian), using hybrids or mass transit (rather than biking), and only idling in extreme hot or cold weather.[27] Environmental policy-makers need to know what types of public education efforts are the most effective, how laws and regulation can best support these efforts, and which behaviors among what populations should be targeted. While the best method to change social and cultural norms is education, supplemental measures remain necessary, though the precise combination or number of approaches may vary depending on the targeted behavior and target audience.[28]

The key challenge is matching the proper tools to the behavior or norm that requires modification. Tools include informational disclosures (like eco-labels and informational schedules), economic and market-based incentives (such as subsidies and taxes), traditional regulatory measures that permit or ban behavior, and standards for pollution, energy efficiency and product performance.[29] The advantage of non-enforcement approaches, however, like information, public education, and market-based incentives, is that they offer "ex ante approaches that seek to prevent

---

27. Many consumer guides provide consumer choice information. *See* JOANNA YARROW, HOW TO REDUCE YOUR CARBON FOOTPRINT: 365 SIMPLE WAYS TO SAVE ENERGY, RESOURCES, AND MONEY (2008); BRANGIEN DAVIS & KATHARINE WROTH, WAKE UP AND SMELL THE PLANET: THE NON-POMPOUS, NON-PREACHY GRIST GUIDE TO GREENING YOUR DAY (2007); ED BEGLEY, JR., LIVING LIKE ED: A GUIDE TO THE ECO-FRIENDLY LIFE (2008); MICHAEL BROWER & WARREN LEON, THE CONSUMER'S GUIDE TO EFFECTIVE ENVIRONMENTAL CHOICES: PRACTICAL ADVICE FROM THE UNION OF CONCERNED SCIENTISTS (1999).

28. Babcock, *supra* note 2, HARV. ENVTL. L. REV. at 155.

29. *See* Jay P. Kesan & Rajiv C. Shah, *Shaping Code,* 18 HARV. J.L. & TECH 319 (2005).

noncompliance from occurring in the first place."[30] Regulatory methods designed to influence individual behavior, recognizing their advantages and disadvantages, combined with public education may be sufficient to achieve norm and behavioral change, when tailored to meet the particular harm and audience.[31]

A Greener Manifest Destiny

Answers to empirical questions about individual behavior are the type of self-reflective and introspective data points that have the potential to change the way we live. Answering them requires knowledge; and if the answers are troublesome or science indicates that they cause ecological harm, public relations, government regulation, and community efforts can work in tandem to provide the opportunities for change. However, a real opportunity for improving the environment through your daily actions depends upon not only information and regulation but also humility.

Undeniable links exist between how humans live and the health of the environment. Chemical fertilizers and pesticides used in agricultural production pollute lakes and kill beneficial insects. Beef cattle are fed commodity grain produced with pesticides to create steaks shipped miles away. The television and the car contribute to the climate crisis, which, in turn, impacts insect migration patterns and public health. The local geography of your home defines where you shop, how you get there, and your carbon footprint. Household environmentalism, food protection, residential development, and nature's living organisms, even tiny ones, are inextricably linked. Science informs us of these relationships and should inform law and policy how to protect them as well.

While scientific inquiry can then productively be driven by a desire to understand linkages between ecosystems as opposed to a desire to exercise our dominion over nature, we must appreciate that we do not fully understand these linkages.[32] Humility requires, as suggested by Socrates in Plato's *Apology*, recognizing that wisdom comes from knowing that we know nearly nothing and cannot know everything. We must be wary of continuing to consume, control, and exploit a natural environment, as well as cause ecological changes, which we do not fully understand. We cannot afford to delay action on complex issues such as climate change and the destruction of small organisms until the science is fully developed and understood. We can instead see multiple improvements and mitigating impacts by shifting

---

30. Babcock, *supra* note 2, at 165 (citing Tseming Yang, *International Treaty Enforcement as a Public Good: Institutional Deterrent Sanctions in International Environmental Agreements*, 27 MICH. J INT'L L. 1131, 1158 (2006)).

31. *Id.* at 174.

32. *Contra* JACOBSEN, supra note 5, at 174 ("But when dealing with complex ecosystems, with countless variables and feedback loops, science must throw up its hands. Look at the amount of attention paid to human nutrition, with rudimentary progress. Or our continuing inability to predict weather. Science's goal is to understand *why* something works so that it can manipulate and control the system. We have an obsession with knowing and controlling, and disdain more intuitive relationships with the world. But sometimes it isn't necessary to master a system in order to work harmoniously with it.").

norms in individual behavior. While the benefits of everyday environmentalism remain to be fully defined and quantified, the aggregate impacts of these steps are certain to help limit the otherwise potentially disastrous future cost of arrogance and ignorance. Everyday environmentalism *may* (for one cannot *know*) help our country find a greener manifest destiny.

Appendix A—Examples of How Policy Tools Can Influence the Environmental Effects of Everyday Behaviors

	Public Awareness	Government Action	Information & Labeling	Ecosystem Services & Economics	Target Audience & Products	Community & Personal Efforts
Energy Consumption & Waste (Chapter 3)	Individual Carbon Release Inventory	Better municipal building codes; Federal regulation of household appliances, including emission/energy standards and extended producer liability; Improved transportation infrastructure	Energy Star; Leadership in Energy and Environmental Design; Life-cycle analysis; EU flower logo	Carbon Tax; Technology investment; Pay-As-You-Throw Programs	Energy inefficient products; E-waste	Change social norms; Pick "low-hanging fruit"; Waste drop-off locations
Food Choices (Chapter 4)	Understanding the industrial food system; Learn about carbon and information labeling programs	Federal pesticide regulation; Federal or state eco-labeling regime for food; Provide resources to strengthen the local food market	Organic labeling; Carbon footprint labeling	Individual procurement power in purchasing value-added products	High-emissions foods in production and distribution (e.g., processed foods and meat)	Buying local and organic; Encouraging a plant-heavy diet

	Public Awareness	Government Action	Information & Labeling	Ecosystem Services & Economics	Target Audience & Products	Community & Personal Efforts
Sprawl (Chapter 5)	Understanding environmental costs of sprawl; Understanding the complexities of land use law; Knowledge about the future environmental benefits of dense development	The power of local land use control; Improving the existing land use planning system; Local land use planning should account for the activities of citizens within that community	More environmental impact information available at time of home purchase	Valuation of wetlands benefits like flood protection; Financial initiatives to limit sprawl that would directly change consumer preferences	Suburban residences and business; Transportation systems development	Consider full costs of geographic location
Unforeseen Impacts (Chapter 6)	Increase knowledge about destruction of soil biota and small organisms	Natural resource management programs must be based upon a better understanding of local conditions and local data	Increase research on small organisms	Valuation of pollination and soil biodiversity; Long-term economic view, recognizing the value of a sustainable and healthy ecosystem	High-intensity agricultural practices	Encourage public relations and information campaigns

Index